The
ZANDE
SCHEME

Winnowing grain.

NORTHWESTERN UNIVERSITY African Studies

Number Seventeen

This volume has been published with the aid of a grant from the Program of African Studies, Northwestern University.

The
ZANDE
SCHEME

An Anthropological Case Study of
Economic Development in Africa

CONRAD C. REINING

Northwestern University Press

EVANSTON, ILLINOIS

1966

CONTENTS

PREFACE   xiii

I THE SETTING   1

II CHANGES IN POLITICAL ORGANIZATION   12
   Pre-European Organization   12
   Immediate Effects of European Conquest   17
   The Chiefs as Agents of the Administration   20
   Reaction of the People to the Chiefs   27

III CHANGES IN DOMESTIC ORGANIZATION   39
   Household Organization   39
   Changes in the Position of the Head
      of the Household   44
   The Instability of Marriages   48
      Marriage Procedure   50
      The "Women's Charter"   52
      Individualization of Marriage Arrangements   56
      The Changed Significance of Marriage
         Payments   58
      Change in Age at Marriage   59
      New Marriage Regulations   61

IV CHANGES IN THE SUBSISTENCE ECONOMY   68

    Subsistence Activities   69
    Imported Commodities   81
    Commercial Development   86
    The Role of Money   90

V TERRITORIAL CHANGES   98

    Pre-European Territorial Organization   99
    Summary of the Moves   101
    Reactions to Resettlement   109
    Resettlement in the Light of Zande Requirements   121
        The Rate of Movement of Homesteads   122
        The Influence of Witchcraft on Residence   125
        The Relation of Shifting Cultivation to the
            Movement of Homesteads   126
        Residential Requirements   129
    Motives for Resettlement   131

VI THE DEVELOPMENT SCHEME   140

    The Basic Proposals for a Social Experiment   142
    Modification of the Basic Proposals   147
    Division over Policy   153
    Construction for the Scheme   159
    Sales of Manufactured Products   165
    Cotton Production and Prices   172
    Zande Attitudes Toward Rewards   179
        The Cultivators   179
        The Laborers   184
        The Worldly Wise   186
    Attitudes of Europeans Toward Rewards
      for the Azande   189
    The Lack of Effective Communication   194
    Commercial Standards   203

VII RETROSPECT   218

APPENDICES   233
    I. Prices paid to the Azande for their cotton,
       1939–55   233
    II. Summary of cotton area and yields for the
       Zande Scheme, 1947–48 to 1954–55   234
    III. Spot prices for American middling 15/16-inch
       cotton lint in the United Kingdom, 1937–55   235

BIBLIOGRAPHY   236

INDEX   243

FIGURES

1. The Zande Area   2

2. The Subdistricts of Zande District in 1953   3

3. The Chiefdoms of Zande District in 1953   21

4. The Courtyard of Makembu   41

5. The Courtyard of a Monogamous Zande Household   41

6. A Large Zande Homestead   41

7. Cash Income for Zande District, 1931 to 1951   89

8. Plan of "H plan" Village Unit   105

9. Plan of Straight-line Village Unit   105

10. Diagrammatic Map Showing "Lines" for a Portion of Zande District   110

11. Diagram Showing Part of the Central Path of an Actual Line   111

12. Comparison of Zande Cotton Prices with Those of the
    Congo, 1945–46 to 1953–54   176

PREFACE

The original object of my research was to determine the effects of a development scheme upon the people of Zande District in what was then the Anglo-Egyptian Sudan. The research, which took place during 27 months between August 1952 and August 1955, was financed by the Sudan government, with a contribution from the Social Development Fund of the Equatoria Projects Board. I visited the Azande living in the Belgian Congo and that part of French Equatorial Africa which is now the Central African Republic, and, although relatively little time was spent in these countries, some useful comparisons with the life of the Azande in the Sudan were obtained. Unless specifically stated otherwise, information in this book concerns the Azande of the Sudan. The Sudan government allowed me to pursue my study much as I pleased, with the understanding that it was for academic purposes. A copy of the resulting D. Phil. dissertation for the University of Oxford was accepted as my final report to what had become by then the Republic of the Sudan.

The approach to the investigation of the impact of the Zande Scheme upon the people was that of the field anthropologist. I went to their homes, studied their language, lived in one of their homesteads, cultivated their traditional food crops around my courtyard, and participated in as many of their activities as possible, taking notes all the time. The locale of the first year's research was near the juncture of the boundaries of the three countries, where the people had been the last to be resettled as a preliminary to agricultural development. They had been in their new homes for less than a year when I arrived and had not yet grown their first cotton crop. Here I was able to see the Azande in the first stage of the Scheme, and since I knew nothing about it, I expected to learn from them. I soon found that they had little or no knowledge of the workings of the Scheme, let alone its aims and policies. Instead of getting information from them, I was constantly questioned by them about the development scheme and what was going to happen. Because I was a white man, they felt that I should possess full information about the doings of the European administrators.

My lack of knowledge about the development scheme and the administration had one advantage: I was not able to ascribe knowledge to the Azande that they did not possess, and therefore was able to assess clearly the paucity of their information. But it was a barren experience, which showed that I must lift my sights, include more than the Azande in my studies, and go to other sources for a more complete picture. It was obvious that if I was to evaluate the impact of the Scheme upon the people, I had to know more about it. Those aspects of the administration, and its officials, that affected the life of the Azande had to be considered. Although this study is primarily about the Azande, to summarize those European attitudes and policies that impinged directly upon them is highly important. We cannot give too much weight to the importance of the attitudes and assumptions of the officials who originated the Scheme, formulated the policies, and supervised their implementation.

It also became evident that investigation could not begin with the development scheme, for many aspects of Zande society, as observed, had undergone changes that had started long before the development scheme, and much of the policy of the Scheme itself was guided by pre-Scheme policies. So it was necessary to go back in time as far as possible, in order to find out about Zande society in pre-European times, and then to trace the effects of European administration from the start.[1]

Although the Azande are among the best documented of African peoples, detailed information about the colonial period is scarce. For the history of the Scheme even the published articles were too superficial for my purposes, since they had been written either by officials for the general European public or by observers who gathered their information from officials during short visits. None of the officials in my time had been associated with the Zande Scheme for any significant period, because there had been a rapid turnover in most of the administrative positions in the nine years since the original proposals had been made for the Scheme. Furthermore the Scheme was a complex affair, calling for the services of a variety of officials and technical experts, none of whom could tell an observer about all aspects of the Scheme. Only the governor's office in Juba oversaw the entire Scheme, but at a distance that allowed only a superficial grasp of the situation. As one of his first acts after my arrival, the district commissioner had handed me a stack of thick, battered files pertaining to the Scheme. At that time it had seemed pointless for a field anthropologist to leaf through interminable pages of old government files. Later I came to see the wisdom of his gesture, for I needed to assemble background information from the contributions of the numerous officials of the previous 10 years or so.

In my first year I concentrated on acquiring information about the daily life of the Azande in a remote area. When I moved closer to the center of the district in my second year, I was able to combine my studies of the Azande in their homes, in town and country, with research in the files of various agencies,[2] mostly in Zande District but also as far distant as Juba and Khartoum. The files utilized were unclassified, and the various responsible officials were most helpful, giving permission to use material for the purposes of this study. Almost 5,000 selected pages of files were recorded on microfilm, and they form the basis of my information

1. Professor Evans-Pritchard has agreed that he and I should divide the study of the history of the Azande so that he will concentrate on the pre-European period and I upon the European period. His recent publication of numerous articles on the pre-European Zande scene is of great value to this report, in obtaining a base for comparison with the modern Azande. These articles are listed in the Bibliography.

2. They are listed in the Bibliography under "Sudan Government Files."

about the history of the Zande Scheme. Files, however, are not a complete source of information. Other documentary sources have been investigated, and in the course of my observation of the Azande verbal communication with non-Zande individuals was also useful for filling in gaps in the records.

This study is unique in the degree to which it attempts to specify the influence of non-Africans in the modern African scene. I do not undertake to study British culture as such, but merely to account for changes in Zande society that have originated with the British administrators. No society in Africa is entirely unaffected by outside powers, but the tendency among anthropologists has been to study those least affected and, further, to assume that any changes that occurred were not significant enough to be considered. Such a device was no longer possible with the Azande, for they had been influenced too much to permit the ignoring of outside influences. Moreover, since some important changes have arisen almost entirely from the culture of the European administrators, with little modification from Zande culture, the administrators had to be included in the society under study.

Until the development scheme started, very few Europeans had resided in Zande District: a district commissioner, with an assistant only in the latter years, a doctor or two, a few missionaries, and a few traders. The missionaries had been influential in the introduction of different standards of values, cultural as well as religious, for they were the educators, since there were no government schools. The traders have introduced not only goods and commerce but also some new values, mainly by the example of their way of life. But the roles of all outsiders have been circumscribed by administrative policies, so it is the relationship of the administration to the Azande that will receive major attention.

My focus is upon Zande society, but the unit of study is the society of Zande District. In my time this included, along with the Azande, representatives of about 20 non-Zande societies. At the industrial center were British, northern Sudanese, Egyptians, Greeks, Syrians, and Italians in addition to members of 15 southern Sudanese ethnic groups. Only three of these—the Azande, northern Sudanese, and British—need be considered here, with the northern Sudanese entering into prominence only in the latter part of the time covered by the study.

Since Zande society was undergoing a transition from one way of life to another, the analysis must be in terms of change. In the following chapters some of the major changes are discussed under five different aspects—political, domestic, economic, territorial, and cash cropping. I have attempted to base my analysis upon the viewpoint of social organization and to account for changes in the nature of relationships between persons and groups of persons. This approach has been useful in dealing with the Zande portion of the society of Zande District, but since the relationship between the non-Zande and the Azande was not of a relatively predictable, homogeneous nature, it did not lend itself to inspection through questions of social organization. Intercultural matters have been handled by comparing attitudes and values originating in the different cultures. The broad social and time base utilized in the study has created considerable complexity, and I have often envied those persons who are responsible only for the analysis of single, stable societies.

At the beginning of my field research I was already aware that the anthropological study of change had been relatively unproductive of a body of theory;[3] hence I would have preferred to avoid focusing on changes. In the 10 years since then, little further progress has been made toward improving theoretical control over analysis of change. Therefore I have been forced, as have hundreds before me, to develop my own schema. I relied upon questions about changes in Zande social organization and about the nature of contact between Zande and non-Zande elements. But the inclusion of non-Zande elements in my frame of reference left me in even more of a theoretical desert. For although there has been general agreement that the European influence in a contact situation should be considered in any study of change resulting from contact between Europeans and tribal peoples,[4] most studies of culture contact have included little specific investigation of this influence. Shortly after the beginning of my field research, a salient summary of the study of acculturation produced by the Social Science Research Council stated that the "donor" culture usually had been taken as an "independent variable" in most acculturation studies.[5] This statement again pointed up the difficulties

3. Beals, 1953, pp. 621 and 638.
4. An early statement is found in Schapera, 1935, pp. 317–18.
5. Social Science Research Council, 1953.

inherent in my approach, but I decided to persevere because of the demands of the human scene I observed. Even after the completion of my field research, the first president of the African Studies Association alluded to the neglect of study of Europeans in Africa.[6] Because no prototypes existed, I have attempted to pioneer in that area.

This report covers the entire period of colonial administration of Zande District and therefore chronicles the impact of that rule upon the Azande of the Sudan. I feel, however, that it has a value beyond that of a historical analysis of a brief but important period, for the spirit of economic development, which began late in the colonial period, has become stronger with independence. The African administrator in independent African countries is prone to believe that he can cope with the complexities of African life better than did his European predecessors. But the African elite, having taken many of their ideas and assumptions from the European cultures in which they were trained, often have as little understanding of the rural peoples of their ethnically complex countries as the Europeans. Communication and understanding between rural populations and their national capitals or district headquarters are not necessarily better after independence than before. Few significant changes have occurred to make communication more effective within African countries since independence, aside from the organization within some of the political parties. The region of this study affords an example—admittedly an extreme case—in which greater antipathy existed toward the administration after independence than during the colonial period. The experiences of colonial development projects are still pertinent, and the lessons to be learned from them should not be ignored. A British writer has observed that "if the Groundnuts Scheme had been conceived and executed by natives, everyone would point to it as incontrovertible evidence that they were unfit to manage their own affairs."[7] African administrators should beware of the double-edged nature of this thrust and should try to avoid the mistakes made in previous attempts at economic and social development.

6. Herskovits, 1958, pp. 7–8.

7. Waugh, Evelyn, quoted in the *Observer*, September 2, 1962.

Though the present tense is often used in anthropological writings, it is not used in this book for the period under observation. The unstable conditions prevalent at the time of the study indicated a temporary situation and the need for denoting relative time. Since then, upheavals in the countries where most of the Azande live have changed the situation drastically. The uprising in the southern Sudan that brought the study to a close, together with the chaos in the Congo since independence, have made the region virtually inaccessible and have undoubtedly altered social and economic practice. Hence it might be misleading to employ the present tense for a situation that no longer exists. Also, because the study is concerned with changes, it seemed advisable to go to the additional effort of specifying the various periods in Zande life, particularly to distinguish between precolonial and observed behavior. The present tense has been employed for facts of nature that are deemed to be relatively immutable. (Termites, for example, probably still swarm at the same seasons.) But social facts about the Azande which can be predicted with equal sureness or about which current information is available are rare.

This book is a sincere attempt to examine in scholarly fashion the colonial situation of the Azande and is in no way intended as an exposé. Admiration is the chief feeling I have for most of the British colonial administrators I have known. The two men who administered Zande District so ably for almost 40 years were not known to me personally, and their names are not used in the text. They are referred to as the first and second district commissioners. While their names cannot be hidden, this device symbolizes my belief that, while their personalities were of undoubted significance in Zande history, their identities are not important in this analysis.

I wish to acknowledge my indebtedness to many of the British and northern Sudanese who were so kind to me and my family during our stay in Zande District, where one could not move or live without calling on someone's hospitality at every turn. Among them, I thank particularly Mr. and Mrs. Pierre de Schlippe, Mr. and Mrs. Robert Wood, Mr. Jeremy Grantham-Hill, Dr. Henry Farrell, Mr. Brian Kendall, and Mr. Harry Lyon. While Zande benefactors are too numerous to list, I should mention the universal Zande patience, good humor, and hospitality without which I could not have survived the difficulties of field work in a confused and frustrating situation. My language teacher and assistant, Tito Barabara, has my gratitude, as has his successor, Yarda Dakpa.

Among scholars, the foremost in my indebtedness is Professor E. E. Evans-Pritchard, who arranged for me to do this research and who has been the most important source of information about the life of the Azande prior to the time of my investigation. His writings, even aside from the pertinence of their contents, have been a guide and inspiration. One of my main regrets has been that his genius has not been more transmissible. Dr. Paul J. Bohannan has been helpful in many ways and at many times in the process of bringing this book into reality. My wife, Priscilla Copeland Reining, also enters into this category. In addition to being my companion in part of this field research, she has, as a fellow anthropologist, given inestimable support and advice at all stages of this work. I also acknowledge the benefits derived from the semiannual conferences of the East African Institute of Social Research, which I was permitted to attend although I was not formally associated with the Institute. These meetings with other social scientists in a metropolitan university setting proved to be stimulating and revitalizing experiences.

This book would not have been possible without the grant from the National Science Foundation that enabled me to devote full time for six months to the preparation of the material presented here. I thank the Library of Congress for permitting me to take leave from my duties there for that period, and also Howard University for administering the grant.

Some parts of the book have appeared in the *American Anthropologist*, the *Proceedings of the Minnesota Academy of Science*, and *Markets in Africa* (edited by Paul J. Bohannan and George Dalton). Permission to use the previously published material is gratefully acknowledged.

Relatively few studies go as deeply into both sides of the situation in development schemes in Africa as does this one.[8] A recent bibliography of agricultural development in sub-Saharan Africa[9] reveals that most of the numerous publications in the field have

---

8. A notable exception is Baldwin, 1957, a source of encouragement for this work.
9. Library of Congress, 1963.

been relatively brief and written from the point of view of the administration. More deep studies should be made, and I have attempted to show how anthropologists can be of important service without losing scholarly status. Anthropology has changed greatly since the day when it was interested primarily in the strange doings of savage peoples. It is entering a new phase in which some of the past debate about applied versus pure anthropology will, I feel, be resolved in order to put some of its special techniques to work for desperately needed African agricultural development. A great obstacle in making a good study of any society is the time required. The delay in publication of this research is only one example of the many years needed to assemble, digest, and present anthropological data. While some time could have been saved in this case if there had been no academic requirements and no necessity to earn a living, I have real doubts that a published anthropological product can be well balanced without years of conscious and unconscious sifting and ordering. I enthusiastically recommend anthropological devices to the planners and administrators of development schemes, but with the realization that the ideal will be difficult to achieve.

I

THE SETTING

The Azande[1] occupy a large area in the center of Africa, along the Nile-Congo divide, which served as a convenient marker for the partition of the territory among outside powers. The Azande had come under the administration of three countries: the Belgian Congo; French Equatorial Africa, in what is now the Central African Republic; and the Anglo-Egyptian Sudan. Figure 1 shows the approximate territory of the Azande in these countries and Figure 2 shows some of the features of Zande District in the Sudan. At the time of this study, about 400,000 Azande were reported to be living in the Congo, about 30,000 in French Equatorial Africa, and about 170,000 in the Sudan. Zande District in the Sudan occupied about 21,000 square miles; the area of the Azande in French territory was somewhat less; and in the Congo it was about 30,000 square miles. The Azande were unevenly distributed throughout their territory, being concentrated along the divide and leaving vast areas uninhabited.

The Azande are a predominantly agricultural people cultivating a variety of crops under what is usually described as shifting cultivation, a common procedure in tropical forest country. Their

---

1. The usual practice of using the plural form *Azande* and the singular *Zande* will be followed.

1

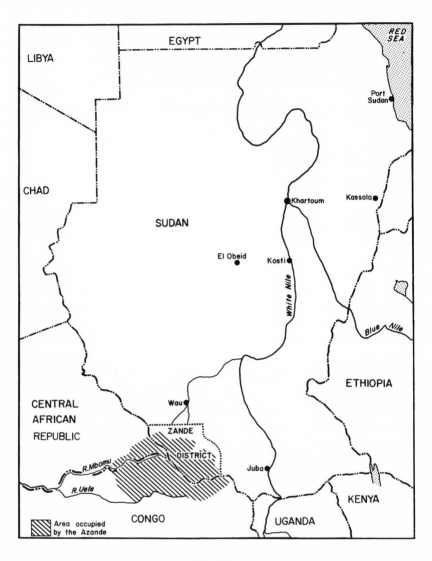

FIGURE 1
THE ZANDE AREA

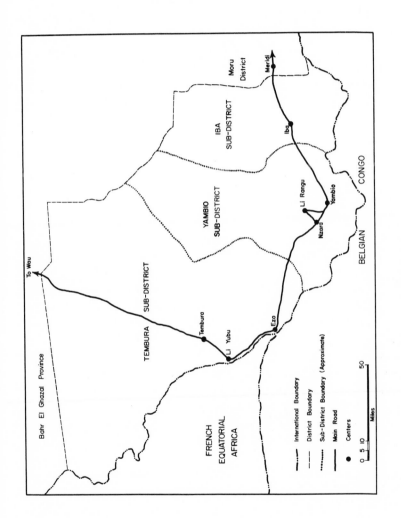

FIGURE 2

THE SUBDISTRICTS OF ZANDE DISTRICT IN 1953

main crops are cassava, eleusine, maize, peanuts, sweet potatoes, and bananas. They have no pastoral traditions, and they keep as domesticated animals only dogs and chickens. Since they depend upon wild animals for their meat supply, they are keen hunters. They also exploit forest and field for many other products of importance in daily life.

Although the area of the Azande contains a watershed of the continent, there is no particularly high ground, and except for occasional granitic hills the territory tends to lack distinguishing features, being relatively uniform and monotonous, with few vistas. With no knowledge of the direction of flow of the streams, one can cross over the actual divide without recognizing it. The entire region lies between 1,800 and 3,000 feet of altitude.

The region is well watered, receiving 40 to 60 inches of rainfall per year and containing numerous springs, particularly along the divide, which give rise to a multitude of streams. These cut the countryside into its most characteristic pattern, that of gently rolling terrain, rising slightly between streams. Zande conceptual use of streams shows their importance among the natural features. The Azande indicate distances by the number of streams between points. They count the streams crossed during a journey to measure its length and will designate streams when pressed for an exact location, such as the birthplace of a person. Many streams have usable water for most of the year, though the volume drops during the dry season. Most of the water necessary for countless activities in everyday life must be carried to the homesteads, though certain activities are performed at the streams. In either case, the distance between stream and household should be as short as possible. One of the most important changes in the life of the Azande has been their removal from the streams along which they lived before European administration.

Zande country lies very close to the equator, between four and five degrees 30 minutes north latitude, and the average altitude is only about 2,100 feet; yet the climate is surprisingly clement. Various reasons have been suggested for this mild climate near the equator in the center of a large continent, far from the tempering influences of the oceans. The most likely explanation is that there is a fortunate combination of prevailing air currents from the equatorial rain forests to the south and from the masses of swampy land in the Nile regions to the northeast, both of which could act like large bodies of water in moderating the temperature of the air. Whatever the explanation, the pleasant fact remains that this area is relatively cool. The maximum shade temperatures rarely exceed 90 degrees Fahrenheit, while the minimum for an entire year is usually above 60 degrees, This mild temperature combines with a generous rainfall to make Zandeland a green and pleasant place, particularly in contrast to the hotter and drier savannah and steppe regions to the north and east.

The year is divided into two distinct portions, the rainy season and the dry season. The rains begin in March or April and end in October or November. The season varies somewhat each year, being shorter in duration with less rain in the northern parts of Zande country than in the southern parts. The rainy season is the summer of the year, when the natural flora becomes green and grows, and it is then that the Azande engage in their agricultural work. They have some tremendous climatic advantages, mainly the complete absence of frost and the very long growing season. These, however, are counteracted by such disadvantages as the poverty of tropical soils and the multitude of pests. During the rainy season the terrain seems to close in. Visibility is particularly poor when all the trees are in full leaf and most spaces between them are filled with tall grass. Paths and even roads become narrow canyons through grass often twice the height of a man. It is possible to travel through 100 miles of Zande country at this time of year without seeing more than a few feet in any direction, except for an occasional opening where a stream traverses the path or road. The cessation of the rains brings higher temperatures and lower humidities. The grasses mature and dry up; the trees, with some exceptions, lose their leaves; and the countryside again becomes open, particularly when the dry grasses burn over large areas. The grain and other crops remaining on the Zande cultivations also mature in the hot, dry weather, and the first months of the dry season are harvesttime.

The greater part of the country is covered by scrub forest. Some large trees interspersed among shrubs and small trees make up the "bush," with tall grass occupying all spaces that are not dominated by trees or rocks. The very few natural open spaces occur mostly where the lateritic rock or ironstone, which predominates in the geological formation of the region, is exposed in sheets with little or no soil on it. Only tufts of short grasses, if anything, will grow on these formations, and here some visibility is possible even in the rainy season. Gallery or fringing forest occurs along many of the streams and in depressions where the water table is relatively close to the surface. The types of flora growing along the streams are different from those in the areas between streams, where the rigors of the dry season and bush fires have favored certain hardy trees, shrubs, and grasses. The gallery and depression forests—reminiscent of the equatorial rain forests to the south of Zande country with their giant trees and intertwined lianas—support a rich fauna, some of which is different from that in the country between the streams. The Azande exploit the variety of plant and animal life afforded by both kinds of forests.

Along with the variety of flora and fauna comes a variety of insect life, some of which is of vital significance in the life and history of the Azande. One of the most important is the tsetse fly, the carrier of sleeping sickness; both the animal and human types of the disease are found in the region. The threat of an epidemic of human sleeping sickness in the period between 1915 and 1925 first caused European administrations to take an active interest in this region, because it was feared that the illness might spread to neighboring areas. In an effort to control the disease the Azande were moved away from the streams and onto the roads, away from the dense vegetation which is the habitat of the local type of tsetse fly, so that existing cases of sleeping sickness might be more easily detected. The roads are generally built on high ground, in drier and better drained areas not frequented by the fly. Many other biting flies and various biting gnats and midges infect their human victims with filaria of various types. Mosquitoes, although not present in swarms in most of Zandeland, are common and infect most of the inhabitants with malaria.

Microfauna and microflora are represented in full variety, and the ailments they cause present an almost complete medical catalogue. It is far easier to list the diseases that do not afflict the Azande than to enumerate those that do. Of the common tropical African ailments, the only ones from which the Azande appear to be free are guinea worm, found immediately to the north of their country, and yaws. The Azande are without doubt deprived of full vigor by the ailments they collect, since as many as eight diagnosable parasites and diseases can afflict one individual at one time, but they manage to carry on their work unless they are stricken by a major illness. Some diseases that are regarded as minor in Europe, such as colds and measles, cause epidemics among the Azande from time to time.

The history of the area has been one of centuries-long invasions and warfare.[2] Much of the present territory of the Azande was occupied relatively recently in the course of a great conquest and assimilation campaign, which was stopped only by European conquest. Prior to that time the Azande were divided into a number of independent chiefdoms, separated by broad belts of uninhabited bush. The chiefdoms made war upon each other as well as upon non-Zande peoples.[3] The Azande in this study were an amalgam of many tribes. Of these, many had undergone a remarkably complete process of assimilation to the Zande way of life, although some, particularly on the periphery of the territory, had been only partially assimilated at the time of European entry.[4]

In the latter half of the nineteenth century, a number of European travelers and explorers traversed Zande country, and by 1886 French and Belgian expeditions from the west and south penetrated what is now Zande District in the Sudan. The British were primarily concerned with the northern Sudan after the reconquest in 1898, and not until 1902 was a British post established at Wau. By then there were a number of French and Belgian posts on the northeastern slopes of the Nile-Congo divide. In 1904 a British military outpost was established in Tembura, and by 1907 the last of the Belgian outposts in what is now Zande District had been withdrawn.[5] The Nile-Congo divide was accepted as the boundary of the Sudan, and, although not demarcated for a number of years, Zande District came under British influence. The administration of the Sudan was officially

2. Baxter and Butt, 1953, pp. 20–24, gives a summary.
3. See Evans-Pritchard, 1957 (a) and 1957 (b), for a discussion of Zande raids and warfare.
4. Baxter and Butt, 1953, pp. 20–23 and 26–29, and Evans-Pritchard, 1953, summarize information available on the pre-European history of this area and classify the Zande peoples.
5. *Bahr el Ghazal Handbook*, 1911, p. 4.

a condominium of Great Britain and Egypt until independence in 1956. In actuality few Egyptians held high posts other than in the postal service, and the administration was essentially British. The Sudan Civil Service, however, was distinct from the British Colonial Service, being associated instead with the British Foreign Office.

From 1905 to 1911 there was only military administration in the Zande area of the Sudan. The northern Sudanese garrisons were replaced by units of the locally recruited Equatoria Corps in 1913,[6] although British officers continued in command until the garrisons were disbanded in 1922. The first civil administrator was posted to Tembura in 1911 and was transferred to Yambio in 1918.[7] Tembura had been on the route of approach in the early days but became the remote station after 1918, when the route to the east was developed. Yambio, about equidistant from Wau and Juba, is more accessible from the direction of Juba because there is river traffic all the year on the main Nile, whereas the River Jur to Wau is navigable only for a few weeks of each year when the stream is in flood.

Zande country in the Sudan was divided into two districts until 1931. Yambio District had continuous administration, but Tembura District was often without a civil administrator of its own. The first civil administrator remained until retirement in 1932; he was succeeded by the second district commissioner, who remained in an official capacity in Zande District until 1949. The extraordinary continuity provided by the fact that only two men occupied the top administrative post for almost 40 years had a considerable influence on the affairs of Zande District, as we shall see.

Members of the Verona Fathers Mission arrived in Tembura District in 1908 and first established a mission at Mupoi, a few miles east of Tembura. The Church Mission Society established its station at Yambio in 1912. Until 1930, by administrative order, Tembura District was the exclusive "sphere" of the Catholics, while Yambio District was allotted to the Protestant missionaries. The Verona Fathers Mission has had the larger operation of the

6. Zande District Handbook, 1936, p. 5.
7. Larkin, 1955, p. 61.

two missions, because of the considerably larger numbers of missionaries available to the Catholic organization.

The educational system was slow to develop, primarily because of the shortage of funds and trained personnel. The missions at Mupoi and Yambio established schools almost immediately and, between 1916 and 1919, started a system of "bush schools," or "out schools," where rudimentary education was carried on, primarily religious instruction with some reading, writing, and arithmetic. All educational facilities were financed and managed by missions until 1927, when the government first established a resident inspector of education in the province and granted about £150 a year to each mission for "elementary vernacular schools."[8] These were located at the main mission stations and had courses for four years, from which boys could go on to intermediate school or trade school or become teachers in bush schools or clerks for a governmental agency. In 1930 a normal school was started at Mupoi. The government gave no financial assistance to the lowest level of teaching in the outlying schools until the early 1940's, when they were reorganized as "approved village schools." Most educational facilities in Zande District before the Second World War were financed from mission funds or personal contributions. The schools and churches were generally built with the aid of the chief of the area. The pay of teachers has been extremely low, even by Zande standards.

No educational facilities above the elementary vernacular level existed in Zande District; those students going on to intermediate school or trade school had to leave the district. The few who went on from intermediate school were usually sent to Uganda for their higher education. There was no special training for girls, and only a few attended even the most elementary classes. Teaching was in the vernacular, though English was taught as a subject.[9]

The scene, then, is the center of Africa. Zande country at the time of this study consisted of the remotest parts of three colonial territories, each oriented to its capital and seaports. As a result, communications were poor, transport was slow and costly, and

8. Egyptian currency was official in the Sudan throughout the Anglo-Egyptian condominium. One pound Egyptian equaled about $5.00 until the devaluation of sterling, after which it was worth about $2.87; 100 piastres equal one pound.

9. Zande District file No. 2.B.3/1, pp. 102–5 and 63–68.

little communication was possible among the three territories. Goods had to come at least 1,600 miles overland to Zande District of the Sudan, by a combination of railroad, river steamer, and road transport, either from Alexandria or Port Sudan. The two post offices in Zande District had been established only recently in preparation for the development scheme. The mail was carried by a truck that traversed the district once a week in each direction. The nearest airport was at Juba, 330 miles from the district head-quarters; Juba was also the southernmost port on the Nile. There were no railroads and no surfaced roads in the southern Sudan. Communication in the other two countries was similarly difficult. For example, in French Equatorial Africa the only regular mail service for a distance of some 500 kilometers from Bangassou to Obo, the easternmost French station in Zande country, was by bicycle. The cost of transport made imported goods expensive and tended to reduce the income received for produce and labor in the region. Goods were delivered as much as 18 months after the order had been placed. Such delays increased costs and decreased the efficiency of commercial or governmental enterprise.

Formerly the primary mode of transport had been by human porters, there being no beasts of burden in Zande country, but human porters quickly disappeared with the advent of motor transport in the early 1920's. Some 1,500 miles of earth or gravel roads had been constructed in Zande District by 1934, and trans-port was almost entirely by motor vehicles. The roads within each of the three territories had been developed as part of that country's larger road system. Those in Zande country at the time of this study were of basic importance to the Azande as well as to outsiders. The Azande tended to live along the roads, and they traveled almost exclusively by road—by motor vehicle, if possible, or by bicycle or on foot.

The remoteness of the region, combined with its lack of valu-able natural resources, has kept it in a relatively undeveloped economic state. The main concern of the European administra-tions for years was the maintenance of law and order, although there was some minor commercial activity based on the sale of forest produce, such as pepper, honey, and beeswax. In the early 1920's the Belgians began to introduce cotton as a cash crop among the Azande and other tribes in the northern Congo. The other two countries did not follow this example immediately. The three southern provinces of the Sudan, those occupied by Negro peoples, were kept isolated, even from the northern Arabic provinces. The general policy was to restrict commercialization of the southern provinces in order to avoid hardships among the population. In the 1930's cotton was tentatively introduced on a small scale into some parts of the southern Sudan, including the easternmost part of Zande District, but with little success. A change in "the Southern Policy" in the 1940's brought forth plans for the general development of the southern Sudan. The Second World War brought a temporary spurt of activity and some improvement of roads in this region. After the war Zande District was chosen as the site of an experiment in social and economic development, based on the peasant cultivation of cotton. That development scheme, which was put into operation in 1946, is of primary interest to this report.

II

CHANGES IN
POLITICAL ORGANIZATION

Confusion, irregularity of day-to-day behavior, and lack of organization characterized the modern Zande scene at the time of my study. Because of the transitory nature of the Zande way of life, no one was sure of his social role. No Zande, whether chief or commoner, felt that he had control over the behavior of those who influenced him politically, and no one could predict what would happen next. The effects of such uncertainty will appear many times in the course of this report. My purpose here is not to present an intensive analysis of the political organization but to survey the nature of changes in the larger organization of Zande society, as a prelude to the investigation of the changes in the smaller units.

PRE-EUROPEAN ORGANIZATION[1]

As has been noted, the Azande in pre-European times were divided into a number of independent chiefdoms of varying size

1. The information in this section has been drawn from a variety of sources, the primary ones being Baxter and Butt, 1953, pp. 20–24 and 26–29, and Evans-Pritchard, 1958. The latter author, in his Huxley Memorial Lecture of 1963 (which was read after this section was completed), offers the best summary of indigenous Zande political organization and also presents and evaluates the major sources of pre-European Zande history.

and importance. All chiefs belonged to the ruling clan, the *Avungara*, whose members had special social distinction whether they were chiefs or not. Membership did not, however, provide any larger political unity, nor did it prevent intrigue and warfare among the members. There seems to have been a continual state of hostility among the chiefdoms,[2] which were separated by broad belts of uninhabited bush and forest.

A chief ruled by sending out governors, often relatives and usually *Avungara*, to administer portions of his territory, and those provinces were divided up among powerful commoners who served as deputies. The chief organized both the defense of his territory and the military expeditions to other Zande chiefdoms or foreign tribes. When other people were conquered, they were taken into the realm of the chief, under one of his governors. The chiefdom had little identity or permanency beyond the person of the chief. When he died, his territory was divided among his heirs, some of whom might already be ruling provinces in his territory, with subsequent adjustment and perhaps acquisition of new territory by some of the heirs. The various territories were designated by the names of the chiefs ruling them, and place names changed with the chiefs. Europeans continued this practice, and localities were most often known by the name of the current chiefs, but there was a tendency to retain some names permanently. The administrative centers at Yambio, Ezo, and Tembura, for example, have officially retained the names of the former chiefs whose homes had been at these places at the time of European conquest.

The chiefs combined in their offices all political and administrative functions as well as many economic ones. They were the military and political leaders and the wealthiest men. The wealth was expressed in the provision of food and beer for clients and retainers. The food was produced in cultivations at the chief's home by the young men who served as warriors during military campaigns and by subjects sent in from the province. Gifts from clients also augmented the stores of the chiefs. However, since most of the goods collected were perishable, they could only be given away again.

---

2. See Evans-Pritchard, 1957 (a) and 1957 (b), for descriptions of Zande warfare and border raids.

The independent chiefs were at the apex of the political organization of the Azande; their homesteads were the centers of social,
political, military, legal, and commercial activity. In the old days
these establishments were the largest concentrations of population, containing many wives, retainers, and warriors. Statements
about their actual size have not been found, but a guess based on
estimates of the size of military units[3] and on my information
about the homestead of Renzi of Tembura would be that the
larger ones housed between 500 and 1,000 persons. Renzi's homestead was considered by Azande to be the last one resembling the
pre-European chiefs' homes, and they estimated that he had had
more than 200 wives at one time, a number of years prior to his
death in 1953. The rapid and effective "Zande-ization" of conquered peoples, which has often been commented upon, was probably accomplished largely through the device of bringing young
men to the chiefs' homes as courtiers and warriors and then, after
a period of training and inculcation, returning them to their districts to spread the language and way of life they had learned.

The impression gained by European observers that Zande
chiefs did not have any material objects which distinguished them
or their homes from other Azande may lead to the mistaken assumption that the chiefs were not distinct from the commoners.
The focal nature, plus the sheer size, of the chief's establishment
gave him special importance, regardless of the uniformity of its
material components. Judging from the modern situation, when
the same general lack of qualitative distinction between chiefs'
and commoners' homes still prevailed, the *Avungara* of the old days
undoubtedly must have formed a distinct class and must have
been outstanding as individuals. Their superior demeanor has
often been commented upon by observers.[4] Another distinction
also prevailed, in that the chiefs did not live the same sort of life as
the commoners. They did not perform manual labor but specialized in the art of administration and adjudication, even in modern
times. The scope of their operations was much greater than that of
the commoners.

The pre-European chiefs held courts in which they had great
power. Much litigation seems to have concerned adultery and

3. *Ibid.*, 1957 (a), pp. 240–41.
4. Evans-Pritchard in 1957 (c) has compiled from the literature most observations on
the nature of Zande chiefs.

sorcery, which could be punished by death or mutilation, although compensations in the form of spears or women were sometimes paid in lieu of punishment. It is difficult to reconcile the Zande sense of justice with the extreme and seemingly arbitrary sentences imposed by the chiefs, as described by early visitors and administrators. We should not assume, however, that the chiefs' positions at the time of European entry were the same as they had always been. There had been disturbing changes for some years before the European administrations were established. The ivory trade, in which the chiefs acted as middlemen and received firearms and other goods, had given them great advantages. Their added wealth and military power meant that they could acquire still more wives, warriors, and followers, which tended to make them even wealthier. The checks on this spiral were evidently not working as well as previously, and some of the more important chiefs tended to become rather despotic. As more wives were acquired, control over them became more difficult and more stringent punishments were needed for violations of domestic discipline. What seemed to be brutalities to Europeans, and what must have seemed extreme punishments to the victims and their kin, were probably regarded by the wealthy men as necessary deterrents.

It must also be kept in mind that the entire Zande area in the Sudan, as well as other parts of the Zande empire, had been conquered only recently. In some of these newly conquered areas there seem to have been degrees of despotism that would not have been possible in the more stabilized parts of the Zande empire.

Kin relationships played only a minor part in the indigenous Zande political organization, while a patron-client type of relationship was important. Even in pre-European days, when there was a greater need for mutual protection of kin than in colonial times, no definite organizing principle for households seems to have existed. One gets the distinct impression from written accounts and from modern Azande, speaking of the old days, that each householder sought the company of kinsmen and that the resulting cluster of households sought alliance with a powerful patron. It is not clear, however, how often householders decided to affiliate directly with a patron rather than in company with related householders, since the Azande have an ideal that each householder is free to choose the locale of his homestead.

A vital aspect of the patron-client relationship is that it is voluntary on both sides. Among the Azande the initiative in establishing a new relationship seems always to have been on the part of the client. The possibility that a household or a group of households could move to the area of another patron, if dissatisfied with the treatment from the current patron, was a strongly tempering influence on the behavior of the rulers. As will be seen shortly, this factor has been altered by the conditions resulting from European administration. There is no indication that chiefs ever refused to accept clients who came to them from other chiefs. They seem to have been in competition in almost all ways, and since even related chiefs intrigued and made war against each other, they would have been in competition for followers.

The Zande patron-client relationship was based upon unspecified mutual reciprocity. Formerly political and military support was given by the client in exchange for protection; he rendered services and goods in expectation of full return at a later time. The patron was expected to protect, to adjudicate, and to provide food and drink at visits of the client and in times of stress. Being generous with food and beer was still the primary manner in which prestige was attained among the Azande at the time of my study, from 1952 to 1955. An important man, when I commented on the unusual size of his grain store, observed that if a Zande has beer to give away, people will come "to hear his good advice." The generosity of the patron played a big part in the patron-client relationship, for the Zande chose and evaluated his patron by his open hand and for his wisdom. The material aspects of the relationships were largely unspecified, but, to judge by observation, each party probably always attempted to gain from the other person. While the client was respectful and helpful, his ultimate allegiance to his patron was tempered by his estimate of what advantages would accrue to him from the relationship.

At the pinnacle of the precolonial political structure was the chief of an independent chiefdom, who had no patron and who had relations only with clients and with peers who were other chiefs, often close kin. This chief had little direct contact with his people, ruling through intermediaries. These deputies would go to the chief to confer with him, but rarely, if ever, would the chief go to see a deputy.

IMMEDIATE EFFECTS OF EUROPEAN CONQUEST

The position of the chiefs was drastically altered by European conquest and the events following. British administration of Zande District in the Sudan was consolidated in 1905. After the withdrawal of the Belgian outposts the number of British stations in the district was reduced to two, at Yambio and Tembura, which have remained the main centers to this day. Administration for a number of years was in the hands of the British officers in charge of the garrisons. Law and order along British lines was demanded, brutal punishments were forbidden, the chiefs' warrior groups were disbanded, their firearms were collected, and the manufacture and carrying of shields was prohibited, although there were no restrictions on weapons other than firearms.[5]

The first civil administrator arrived in 1911 to find that there had been little active administration or apparent change outside the two military stations and that the chiefs were in charge of their territories. The official policy at that time was for the British administrator to retain the right of final decision and appeal but to interfere with the affairs of the chiefs only in cases of murder, mutilation, abduction, and slavery.[6] The impression of the first inspector was that the chiefs still retained a great deal of authority over the people and that fear of the government troops would not have been sufficient to prevent revolt, if the chiefs had been able to coordinate their efforts. He has commented on the fortunate circumstance that the different branches of the chief clan were all rivals.[7]

Although we can now see that conquest and the simple restrictions mentioned above were enough to kill the military organization and spirit of the Azande, throughout the early years of British administration it was feared that there might be an uprising of these people, who had been conquering and assimilating other tribes in all directions before the advent of European forces and some of whom had been used by Europeans in their conquest of the territory. The first period of British administration is poorly recorded, and we do not know how the governmental policies were enforced. We know only that the military and civil administrators

5. Wyld, 1949, p. 51.
6. Zande District Handbook, 1936, p. 6.
7. Larkin, 1955, p. 5.

kept an eye on the chiefs, punishing them for excesses by imprisonment and removing them from office when they were considered
unsuitable. We have hints that the new administration found itself
competing with the chiefs. Instances occurred in which the administration attempted to raise itself in the eyes of the people by
undermining the chiefs, as when the first civil administrator made
the chiefs walk around the newly designated boundaries of their
territories and presented them with maps. Not only were the
chiefs required in this way to leave their headquarters in an unusual manner and make public spectacles of themselves accompanying the British administrator, but the administrator was also
anxious for the people to see that the new administration had
power to allot land to the chiefs or to deprive them of it at will. In
one case a chief was described as needing "taking down a peg."
We cannot assess the effectiveness of the governmental restrictions
on the powers of the chiefs, since even at the time the administrators had difficulty in ascertaining the incidence of "abuses of
power" by the chiefs.[8]

The total effect of the first 20 years of British administration
must have been one of great confusion and uncertainty for both
people and chiefs. In their uncertainty the chiefs seem to have
withdrawn from public life. Most of them were afraid to show
signs of their authority for fear of being punished by the new administration. The British administration, military and civil, appears to have conducted most of its business by direct contact with
the populace, largely ignoring the chiefs in construction work on
roads, bridges, rest houses, and other public buildings.

The governmental policy was to allow the chiefs to hold courts
but to restrain their excesses. In practice the British administrators also heard cases themselves, while keeping an eye on the
workings of the chiefs. Some of the senior chiefs refused to hear
cases because they did not know the government rules and were
not sure of the validity of their own under the new system. The
people have been described as "hawking" their petty grievances
from one chief to another, and the result was said to have been
that any British official who showed the slightest interest was in-
undated by requests for legal pronouncements.[9] As a result there

8. *Ibid.*, p. 17 and pp. 42–43.
9. Phillips, pp. 7–8.

seems to have been a drift away from the official policy of indirect rule toward the dispensing of justice by the British administrators. By 1922 they were heavily burdened by court cases at their headquarters.[10]

The administration was made aware of the seriousness of the confusion when, in 1922, the population of Tembura District was ordered to resettle along the roads so as to prevent the spread of sleeping sickness. A chaotic situation ensued. The chiefs who tried to carry out the orders were deserted by many of their followers, and many senior chiefs claimed ignorance of the orders. Attendance at medical inspections fell to half the previous number, and the reason given was always that the people had run away.[11] The resettlement plan failed because the orders affected many more people than could be directly supervised by administrative agencies.

The medical department then threatened to withdraw its whole staff unless it could be given more administrative support, and a conference of medical and administrative authorities was called. This conference made the following recommendations: (1) The people should be settled in groups along the roads. (2) They should be placed around their headmen and be forbidden to change from one headman to another without the permission of both the district commissioner and the senior medical officer. (3) The authority of the chiefs should be supported by carrying out as much as possible of the sleeping sickness procedure through them. (4) The chiefs should be made responsible for the clearing of watering places and the building and maintenance of roads, bridges, and rest houses in their respective areas.[12]

The officials were still apprehensive lest the chiefs organize uprisings against the administration and lest their "atrocities" again increase if they were given recognition by the government. The opposing argument was put forward that the system of medical inspections would lead to easy detection of abuses of power by the chiefs. Evidently it was decided to risk the chance of revolt, for the recommendations were all put into force.[13] The "restoration" of power to the chiefs was credited with the success of the resettle-

10. Zande District Handbook, 1936, p. 4.
11. Maurice, 1930, pp. 226–27.
12. Ibid., p. 227.
13. Maurice, no date.

ment plan, and a new kind of political organization began to operate among the Azande—one in which the chiefs were given more
clearly defined positions as agents of the administration.

THE CHIEFS AS AGENTS OF THE ADMINISTRATION

The Tembura conference recommendations established a
general pattern for the relationship between administration and
chiefs that prevailed, with minor variations, throughout the remainder of the colonial administration. The chiefs had little part
in the formulation of policy and were relegated to the position of
administrative officials. The functions of paramount chiefs were
largely taken over by the administration, the chiefdoms were
"frozen" because of the imposed peace, and when the chiefs died
the larger chiefdoms were most often divided up among the heirs.
The five large chiefdoms in the Zande District of the Sudan at the
time of the European conquest had been divided by 1953 into the
28 chiefdoms shown in Figure 3. Few large chiefdoms survived, and
none of the chiefs deserved the once-used titles of king, or paramount chief.

When the chiefs were "reinstated," they had not regained all
the powers they had held before the European conquest. The important role of middleman in trade was denied them as the result
of a combination of factors. The main feature of pre-European
trade had been in ivory, which was exchanged for firearms, cloth,
and other goods. The monopoly of the chiefs in this trade was
shattered by the advent of the colonial administration and foreign
traders. Game conservation regulations reduced the volume of the
trade, and although the chiefs retained certain privileges regarding ivory obtained in their countries, the benefits were minimal in
comparison with what they must have derived from their former
monopoly of the brisk ivory trade. They did not, of course, have
their military powers restored to them. Furthermore, the end of
warfare and the breaking up of the military organization had a
number of indirect effects. Important among these was the reduction of the agricultural potential of a chief's household by the removal of the warriors, who were also cultivators. Because the
chief could not provide food and drink in his former generous
manner, his prestige suffered and with it his ability to attract

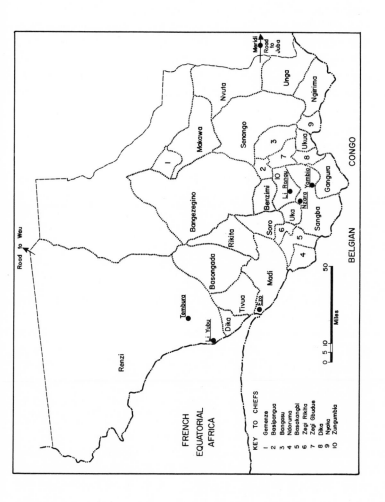

FIGURE 3

THE CHIEFDOMS OF ZANDE DISTRICT IN 1953

followers. Then, too, the cessation of warfare removed the constant threat of enemy raiding parties. This not only meant that the people were freer to travel and to move their homes, but it also eliminated much of the need for commoners to ally themselves to a powerful patron for protection. The legislation to improve the status of women, to be discussed in detail in Chapter III, also affected the potential wealth and prestige of the chiefs. One reason for the new regulations was to eliminate the practice of giving women as compensation for damages; hence the chiefs no longer had the women so transferred to marry or to give to their followers. The new regulations had another purpose: to distribute the wives more evenly among the men by reducing the ability of the wealthy "women-collectors" to acquire more wives. Since the chiefs had the largest numbers of wives, they were adversely affected by this drive against women-collectors. Yet while they undoubtedly had fewer wives and therefore lost some of their agricultural potential, the chiefs nonetheless managed to keep relatively large numbers of wives. As a matter of fact, not many Azande, other than the chiefs and subchiefs, had been able to assemble more than, say, six wives at the time of my observation. The only large collections of wives were those of the more important chiefs. Agricultural produce was still the primary source of wealth and prestige, and the chiefs were still the wealthiest of the Azande, despite reductions in their establishments.

The policies restricting the powers of the chiefs to adjudicate and to punish were not altered at the time of their "reinstatement." However, in order to relieve the British officials of the burden of court cases, a hierarchy of government courts was established in the mid-1920's, presided over by chiefs sitting on rotating panels.[14] Presumably this official system was the only one under which cases could be heard and punishments and fines levied, but the official courts could not meet the needs of the populace, so chiefs and subchiefs also continued to hold court unofficially in their homes. These informal courts were condoned because the administration realized that the authorized courts could not handle the immense volume of minor cases arising among the Azande. It was assumed that the chiefs' private courts were held merely to give advice, not impose fines or punishment. The extent to which

14. Larkin, 1955, p. 55.

this assumption was true could not be determined, for the chiefs learned how to keep their questionable activities well under cover. A knowledge of the workings of chiefs and their courts was obviously of highest importance to an understanding of the Azande, but these activities were discouragingly difficult to observe at first-hand. When a white man, such as the American anthropologist writing this report, entered the court of a chief, all activity ceased and the assembled persons concentrated on determining the status of the intruder and his business. Everyone was respectful and attentive, but there was little hope of seeing the activity that one knew went on normally. Not until near the end of my stay did I succeed in getting some of the younger chiefs to understand my position and needs, so that I was allowed to see some of the procedures of their informal courts.

The distinction between the two systems of court was not clear to the people, and some cases were brought to the chiefs that should have been heard by the village chiefs' courts. In most cases the chiefs sent serious or difficult cases on to the official courts, thus acting as a valuable screening agency. But procedural confusions abounded, as evidenced by the appeals to the district commissioner from the unofficial decisions of chiefs. In one such case that I witnessed, the district commissioner could only tell the man who had appealed that the chief's personal opinion was not the concern of the court and that the matter would have to be brought, as a new case, to the local official village court. The district commissioner then had to clarify the matter to the clerk of the court who had accepted and entered the appeal.

In later years the administration relied heavily upon the system of appeals to prevent injustice and abuses, and it worked quite well within the official courts for those people who understood the procedures. The right to appeal was freely used, and access to the district commissioner was highly appreciated by many people. It must be remembered, however, that this means of preventing injustice also had the feature of undercutting the authority of the chiefs.

As time went on, the chiefs were allowed a certain number of their own policemen, who were given uniforms and insignia, were paid by the administration, and assisted the chiefs in the execution of governmental duties. They were augmented in most cases by unpaid courtiers and messengers.

The chiefs also were given the duties of collecting taxes and selecting laborers for governmental work. During the 1920's these duties tended to be combined, since the majority of taxpayers worked on the roads in lieu of paying taxes. With the beginning of the trade in peppers, more taxes were paid in cash, and therefore more laborers had to be conscripted for work on the roads and other projects. The labor was paid for at a low rate and no food was provided—often a considerable hardship, especially for those who had to travel far from home to do the labor. No man was supposed to be liable for more than one month's conscripted labor, but there was no effective means of checking into this restriction. The authority to select laborers gave the chiefs and their assistants considerable power over the people, who spoke of reprisals being carried out upon unfavored individuals in the selection of government labor.

The amount of taxes due from each chief was based on the district commissioner's estimate of the number of taxpayers living in the chief's area. The mode of collection was left to the chief, who received a small percentage of the total collected. Cases of individual hardship occurred even in the years while I was there, when each chief had special tax clerks and when the records had improved considerably over the old days. The position of tax collector led to the extortion of irregular sums of money by some chiefs or their assistants. Few of the victims were foolish enough to make official complaints, so it was impossible to assess the extent to which money or goods were extorted.

In the way of direct compensation the chiefs were allowed ten days' free labor from each taxpayer, certain privileges in regard to firearms licenses and game permits, and a monthly salary, which ranged, in 1945, from $2.50 to $35.00 per month, with a median figure of about $10.00.

The chiefs derived other important but unstated benefits from their new positions. One way in which the government enhanced their power was by restricting the movement of people from one chief to another. Already in 1922, when the first roadside settlements were formed, persons were forbidden to move without the express permission of both the district commissioner and the medical inspector. The difficulties of obtaining such permission must have been enormous, when viewed by the Zande dissatisfied with his chief. Some sort of registers must have been made at the time of the earliest settlements on the roads, but indications are that the rosters of subchiefs and chiefs were quite confused.

One of the main concerns during the more recent resettlement of the late 1940's, in connection with the development scheme, was to get effective "village registers." The assignment of house-holders to regular plots of land, with clerks posted to the work of keeping the registers in order, meant that the chiefs had a better knowledge of the whereabouts of their people than ever before. A man had to obtain his chief's permission in order to move from his assigned plot, which put the individual Zande in a tight spot. In pre-European days the risks in moving from the area of an unsatis-factory chief must have been considerable, but a client was free to attempt such a move. Potential mobility was one of the main sanc-tions a client had against possible abuse by his chief. The possi-bility always existed that an unpopular chief might find himself with a dwindling population. Such instances occurred even in recent years, despite the attempts of the administration to stabi-lize the population on the land. The Azande were very much aware of the advantages of this mobility, and many persons com-plained to me that the chiefs kept them from making moves, either directly or by extremely effective delaying tactics. No chief wanted his people to leave him.

The position of the chiefs was enhanced as the idiom of in-direct rule took effect. They gained power in that they represented the government in the eyes of the people. They were never entirely certain of the nature of their new power, but complete under-standing was not required in order to appreciate the advantages of lying athwart the channels of communication between the people and the administration. The extent to which the abuses of the chiefs, as representatives of the administration, are detected and punished is of course a fundamental problem of all colonial administrations. The first approach to this problem in Zande District was through personal inspections by the district commis-sioner, who spent most of his time traveling about the district. Indications are that, despite diligent efforts on his part, abuses occurred.[15] The situation deteriorated for the commoner, as the chiefs became more and more practiced in the art of concealing ir-

15. *Ibid.*, p. 42.

regular activities. The instances in which the district commissioner "taught" the chiefs "lessons" when they committed abuses may have produced the desired effect in some cases, but in others the chiefs were probably taught to keep their activities well under cover.

A primary duty of the chiefs was unwritten, in that they were the keepers of the tribal discipline. The general tendency from the start of colonial administration was to assign them the task of keeping peace and quiet in their territories, while law and order in the whole district was maintained by the district commissioner with the aid of a police force based in Yambio. The assumption that the chiefs could and should impose discipline can be detected from the beginning of civil administration in Zande District. The first district commissioner relates that in the early days a police-man who had been found abusing his position was turned over to the chief of the area to "teach him manners."[16] Another instance occurred when the first district commissioner came to Yambio. He disbanded a group of "de-tribalized" young men who had been collected as a government pool for carriers and laborers, because they were exploiting the people in the guise of government serv-ants, and returned them to "tribal discipline."[17] He did not am-plify upon the mechanisms of tribal discipline, which he was at the same time eager to rid of its abuses.

The chief continued as disciplinarian until the time of my study, as could be observed in the illicit practice of some British officials of sending their employees to the local subchief to be given "ten on the bottom." About 1948, the first manager at the industrial center specifically forbade this practice when he dis-covered that British employees were getting the subchief to ad-minister beatings to messengers and other junior staff members.

At all cotton markets the local subchief or chief had the func-tion of keeping order, assisted by his own police. In June 1954 some of the cultivators remonstrated against the amount of their cotton bonus payment and returned the money to a British inspec-tor of agriculture to show their dissatisfaction. The immediate reason for the troubles, explained the inspector, was the weakness of the subchief presiding at the payment meetings. The inspector

16. *Ibid.*, p. 47.
17. *Ibid.*, p. 54.

demanded that the chief of the area himself be present at the remainder of the bonus payments. The chief's presence effectively prevented further disturbances.

REACTION OF THE PEOPLE TO THE CHIEFS

As disciplinarian the chief performed a one-sided role in that he restricted and punished but had little to offer in return. Particularly in resettlement and cash-cropping activities did this one-sided role contribute strongly to the hostility of the people to their chiefs during the period under observation.

The Zande reaction to the chiefs in that period contrasted oddly with the administration's interpretation of the nature of the relationship between chief and commoner. Throughout the British administration, as with the Azande in the Belgian and French territories, the power of the chiefs had been firmly upheld. This policy was strengthened by the administration's impression that the Zande chiefs were obeyed because they commanded their people's admiration and respect. The civil administrator in 1911 had said that the administration made itself feared by the presence of troops, but for several years its authority "was as nothing in Zande eyes, compared with their revered chiefs."[18] More than 40 years later this sort of statement was still common: "The policy is to maintain tribal structure, and to use as much as possible the authority vested in the tribal leaders, who command great respect and complete allegiance from their subjects."[19] The second district commissioner summarized this viewpoint when he reviewed the development scheme in 1948, saying that the people for the most part bore cheerful and willing allegiance to their chiefs and that maximum results were to be obtained by keeping the confidence and cooperation of these tribal heads, while at the same time "instilling in them the precepts of duty and responsibility towards their subjects."[20]

From the start of my observations there had been ground for suspicion that the obedience of the Zande to his chief might be inspired more by fear than by respect and that his servile behavior in the presence of the chief might not be sincere. This suspicion

18. *Ibid.*, p. 5.
19. Ferguson, 1954, p. 9.
20. Zande District file No. 1.C.8, p. 23.

was based on the outright accusations of those who had removed themselves from the position of ordinary cultivators. It was obvious that these ordinary cultivators were not inclined to discuss their chiefs with me and that they did not have a grasp of the administrative techniques of the European administration. The people still regarded the chiefs as powerful persons to be feared and respected, one reason being that they were the officials through which the administration acted. Other sources of information were available to me, however, because two classes of Azande were ready to talk about their chiefs: the educated persons and the laborers in the stations. Quite spontaneously laborers in the hospital station at Li Yubu told me that they had volunteered to work for the government to get out from under the thumbs of their chiefs. One condition of government service—that the obligations to the chief were no longer required of the laborer—turned out to be a primary incentive for volunteering for permanent work for the government or some other agency. The laborers, in their chiefless state, were generally bitter about the practices of chiefs, mainly complaining about the demands for labor, extortions, and delays in the execution of routine matters. Each chief was entitled to a maximum of ten days' free labor each year from each taxpayer, but I was told that this rule was often abused. Demands for conscript labor for the many governmental agencies were also handled through the chiefs. The pay for such labor was only nominal, according to the Azande, who regarded it as a great hindrance to their own work. A man was not supposed to be conscripted for more than one month's government labor a year, but my informants stated that chiefs often chose those whom they did not favor to work for a longer period.

The effort to get out from under the influence of the chiefs was not new in my time, for the first district commissioner recalled that in about 1920 an urge to be free and independent could already be noted. Young men showed a tendency to leave the district for Wau and even Khartoum, only partly owing to the desire to earn money. The chiefs called these emigrants "people of rebellion," according to the notion that once a person had been a soldier, he was independent for the rest of his life.[21] Shortly after this time came the restrictions on movement in and out of the dis-

21. Larkin, 1955, pp. 6–7.

trict, for the purpose of controlling sleeping sickness. When the restrictions were finally relaxed in 1940, there was a great movement of personnel out of the district, for the wartime work at Juba and for military service. In previous years the only alternative to life as a cultivator under a chief had been to take up service with the government within the district. It may be noted, however, that the desire to get away from the influence of the chiefs was not a sufficiently strong incentive, along with other inducements, to provide enough permanent laborers for all needed public work. Only at the industrial center of the development scheme was there ever sufficient volunteer labor to eliminate the need for periodic conscription of labor.

The resentment of the educated Azande toward the chiefs was universal. They stated their complaints somewhat differently than did the laborers. The educated persons felt that the chiefs were out to keep all powers and benefits for themselves, that they did not care about the people's welfare and did not represent the people. This reaction had all the qualities of the classical competition between the newly educated classes and the traditional rulers. Clerks and other educated Azande chafed because they felt they were being ignored in the administration of the district. They had been taught that they would become the leaders of their people, but only in the early 1950's, with the introduction of general elections and of local governmental agencies, had the educated Azande begun to find a designated place in the political scene. The first election for members of parliament, which took place in 1954, brought these educated persons into greater unity than ever before. That they were clearly in competition with the chiefs was most evident in the parliamentary elections in Zande West, where one of the candidates was the son of Renzi, the most important chief in Zande District, and the other was a commoner. Both candidates were literate and quite equally matched as to personal characteristics. The main theme of the commoner's campaign was opposition to the ruling clan. The chief's son lost heavily, getting less than one fifth of the votes, despite heavy pressure put by the chiefs upon the people to vote for him.

The general policy of the British administration in the Sudan had been to support the traditional leaders against the younger, educated element, in order to protect the population against drastic changes that might be fostered by young radicals. In 1948 the second district commissioner urged all fieldworkers in the development scheme to work through the chiefs and not through "paid employees" and to make sure that the latter performed their specific duties with respect for, and deference to, tribal authority.[22] The resettlement of the population in the late 1940's had been carried out through the chiefs, in conformity with this administrative policy. The chiefs benefited somewhat from a small cotton bonus, and their positions were strengthened by the assignment of their subjects to specified plots of land and by the improvement of the population registers. But the great work and inconvenience of resettlement and cash cropping had led to general disappointment, and the arbitrary fixing of the population had led to restiveness, which will be discussed in later chapters. Much of the hostility of the population was directed toward the chiefs, as being immediately responsible for the difficulties in the new situation.

Particularly awkward for the chiefs was the unbalanced set of functions they were forced to perform in supervising the cultivation of cash crops. This was the result of a deviation from the established organizational principles, the significance of which was not fully recognized at the time by the administration. The management of cash crops was the function of the agricultural section of the Equatoria Projects Board, the governing organization of the Zande Scheme. At the head of that section were four British employees of the Board: a senior inspector of agriculture and three inspectors of agriculture, one for each subdistrict. Below them were a number of literate southern Sudanese junior agriculturists, designed to provide liaison between inspectors and chiefs and assigned, in theory, one to each chief. At the bottom of the hierarchy were the Zande demonstrators who had had a few weeks' training in the rudiments of cotton cultivation, each of whom supervised cash-crop cultivation in three to five lines. Instructions in all matters pertaining to the cultivation of cash crops were passed down the agricultural hierarchy from the senior inspector to the cultivators. Cotton was purchased under the direct supervision of the British inspectors who headed itinerant buying teams that toured designated buying points.

22. Zande District file No. 1.C.8, p. 23.

At the start of the Scheme cotton cultivation was interpreted by the administration to be a form of public service. In order to introduce the crop effectively into the subsistence agriculture, compulsion was considered necessary for a few years. Persons who failed to sow the cash crop or cultivate it properly were punished by being required to do some public service, usually a month's labor on the roads or other public works. Since compulsion was not a function of the Board, the list of cotton defaulters was compiled by the agricultural staff and turned over to the district commissioner, who in turn empowered the chiefs to try the offenders and to punish them. During the first years there seems to have been little necessity for compulsion, as the Azande enthusiastically produced large crops of cotton. With the decline of the yield, however, punishment of individuals became more frequent. Yet the practice seems to have been variously interpreted throughout the district and, judging from the statements of chiefs and people, there was a great deal of uncertainty about the governmental policy on compulsion. The district administration, always careful to protect the people from any form of exploitation, faced a dilemma after the first few years of the Scheme. On the one hand, it desired to cease compelling people to grow cotton; on the other, the administrators realized that, owing to the unpopularity of the crop, the success of the Scheme was dependent upon continued compulsion. Finally, in 1952, the district office informed the Equatoria Projects Board that punishment of cotton defaulters could no longer be approved.

The degree to which this change in policy was promulgated among the people was difficult to ascertain. Widely varying interpretations appear to have been placed upon it, and in effect the matter seems to have been left up to each chief. The resulting variations in practice added to the confusion of the people. The cotton crops became poorer than ever, culminating in the disastrous one of 1954. Once again the need for "persuasion" of a direct nature seems to have been recognized. Clearly heightened pressure was applied in at least some of the chiefdoms in 1955 to ensure more attention to cotton cultivation, but the stated reasons for this increased pressure lacked consistency. One important chief said that he had ordered more surveillance by his headmen on his own authority, simply because he was aware that the administration's evaluation of him depended on the amount of cotton his area produced. His statement did not agree with those of others who stated that they had been told by the agricultural staff to punish all "lazy people" who were not growing cotton properly. This indicated that the agricultural staff was violating the 1952 prohibition on punishment for cotton-growing irregularities. It was not possible to determine the source of reputed orders from European officials to the chiefs to resume direct compulsion of cotton cultivation. No clarification was available from the agricultural office, only an acknowledgment that practices for the enforcement of cotton cultivation varied widely. Some chiefs, a British inspector stated, were known to have had cotton defaulters beaten right in their fields. Others required additional public service labor from those cultivators judged to be remiss, while others did little or nothing. One chief was discovered to be offering immediate release upon payment of 15 piastres to cotton defaulters who were brought to him for trial. Most of the cultivators stated that they were growing cotton simply because they were afraid of being lashed or required to work at the chief's house. They seemed to have little knowledge of the administration's orders to stop punishment for faulty cotton cultivation. Each chief was left to implement the instructions of the agricultural department in his own way. The result was confusion and resentment, mingled with resignation in many cases.

In the agricultural organization of the Zande Scheme, as fitted into the administrative organization of Zande District, the function of the chiefs in regard to the cash crop was unbalanced and confused. In the view of the cultivators, the chiefs were the compellers of an unpopular activity, concerned only with their own perquisites and contributing little to the welfare of the people. My observations at meetings of British administrative and agricultural officials with Zande chiefs and people illustrated the dilemma of the chiefs and resentment of the people toward them. In an important chiefs' meeting held at Tembura in April 1953, a number of changes in the cotton-growing program were to be announced. The advance information that cotton growing was to be stopped in much of the country around Tembura, because of poor yields, had been received with great relief by the cultivators, who had seen cotton only as a burden. At the meeting, however, it was announced that three subchiefs were ordered to grow cotton again. The news of this exception came as a surprise, and because I knew the temper of the cultivators in these subchiefships I expected objections to the official plans. Quite to the contrary, the chief himself accepted the proposition for his people. His subchiefs said nothing and afterward explained to me that they could do nothing after their chief had spoken. Furthermore, other chiefs, whose areas had been withdrawn from those where cotton was cultivated, remonstrated and asked that they be allowed to grow cotton. The explanation given by the commoners for this behavior was that the chiefs didn't care at all about the "people's feelings" and were concerned only with getting some bonus money. If the amount was small, continued my informants, it was better than nothing, from the point of view of the chiefs who disregarded the troubles brought by the crop to their people.

At another meeting the headman of a line dared to protest to the inspector of agriculture and the district commissioner about the poor prices for cotton. This man was silenced by the British inspector, then flatly contradicted by his subchief. The headman, he said to the officials, did not express the attitude of his own people, who were happy to grow cotton and to sell it at the prices being given. The watching crowd permitted itself to groan at this placatory action. Various Azande surmised afterward that the headman would suffer for his outspokenness, probably by losing his position. Yet he had voiced the unanimous sentiments of my informants.

During the time of my observations, more and more complaints against the chiefs were raised by the people. National political events brought additional aggravations. Preparations for independence of the Sudan were being made, and there was talk of the withdrawal of British officials in favor of northern Sudanese. By 1953 it was noted officially that some chiefs were having difficulty asserting their authority,[23] and by the middle of 1954 they were experiencing increased difficulty in obtaining labor for the roads and in maintaining their right to labor for their own homesteads. Sudden claims by various chiefs for extensions of their borders were interpreted in the Zande District Annual Report as attempts to bolster their waning prestige and as a reflection of un-

23. Zande District Annual Report, 1952–53, p. 2.

certainty in the national political future. Chiefs complained to me about the disrespect of their people and about the lack of spontaneous service. Most chiefs did not understand the policies behind the introduction of local governmental agencies, but they realized that some of their power was passing into hands of the educated Azande.

The general signs of unrest and of the people's dissatisfaction with their chiefs came to a head when the chiefs were called together by the northern Sudanese district commissioner in June 1955 and asked to pledge their support of the northern Sudanese officials who had replaced the British administrative, military, and police officers more rapidly than anyone had envisaged. All but four chiefs signed a document assuring their support of the current administration and disclaiming the findings of the southern political party. This apparent acceptance of the new administration proved conclusively to the people the chiefs' lack of concern for them. For the first time the chiefs were denounced openly, and some of them, including several of the most important, had to seek the protection of the district commissioner in Yambio when their lives were threatened. An attempt was made on one chief's life after he returned home, even though he had district police protection.

When the document signed by the chiefs was produced at a mass protest meeting in Yambio, the administrators were told to leave the country and to take the chiefs with them. The situation deteriorated rapidly with the arrest of some of the chiefs who had not signed the document and of the member of parliament for Zande East, for his political activities. These arrests served to intensify hostile feelings against the northerners, which erupted in a riot in the industrial center at Nzara late in July 1955. The repression of this riot with firearms helped to bring on the mutiny of the southern troops and the tragic general uprising throughout Equatoria Province in August 1955.

The dissatisfaction of the Azande with their chiefs was only one of many factors leading to the disturbances in the district, and these in turn were only a part of the cause of the final uprising. The point of this brief history is to show the decay of relationships between the chiefs and their people. That decay had begun before the development scheme but was accelerated by activities connected with it and by changes in the national political scene.

The people's overt resentment toward the chiefs seemed to indicate that the common colonial problem of how to reduce the power of the chiefs and yet retain their effectiveness as administrative officials had not been worked out satisfactorily in Zande District. A contributing factor, paradoxically, appears to have been the humanitarian interest of the administration, which caused the authority of the Zande District chiefs to be undermined to a greater extent than among the Azande in the Belgian Congo. There the chiefs were allowed final judgment in most cases other than criminal ones, which were tried by the European administrators. The lack of appeal to the administration from the chiefs' decisions undoubtedly caused many cases of individual hardship in the Congo. However, this observer's impression was one of greater certainty in relationships between people and chiefs and between chiefs and administrators in the Congo than in the Sudan. Because the chiefs in the Congo had more autonomy, their roles and purposes seem to have been clearer; the general effect was of greater solidarity among the population than in the Sudan. While the Congo chiefs had more authority, they also appear to have had an easy, bantering relationship with the people in their courts—an impression verified by my Zande informants. Although the stronger concern to prevent injustice in the Sudan was unquestionably commendable, the constant undermining of the chiefs' authority contributed to the greater confusion and uncertainty there.

The ambiguous position of the Sudan chiefs had resulted from the assumption that they could be used as part of the administrative hierarchy and still maintain their traditional relationship with their people. Actually the role of the chiefs had been altered beyond comparison by the imposition of European administration upon them. The attempt in early days to utilize them as part of the government machinery while withdrawing some of their powers had resulted in a chaotic situation. The administration had then partially revived the power of the chiefs and thereafter had assumed that their roles were now comparable to their original ones. But the position of the chief had changed from that of ruler to agent of a foreign administration. His role as a patron, in a series of reciprocal relationships to his clients, had been transformed by the removal of many of his functions and by the impairment of his ability to accumulate stores of food for his followers. On the other hand, his new position as agent for the administration, ill comprehended as it was, gave him a vantage point from which he could improvise new ways of accumulating wealth and power, while clinging to as many of the old ways as possible.

In all their grumblings about the chiefs, the Azande rarely expressed a desire for a change in the nature of their political organization, but only for the replacement of the personnel occupying positions of authority. They saw no need for changes in what remained of the traditional organization, and they still thought in terms of that organization, although it had been altered significantly. The old system had been weakened because alternatives existed for allegiance to a chief—by travel and work outside the district, by permanent service in a government station, or by acquiring an education—whereas in the old system the only alternative to allegiance to one chief was allegiance to another.

The chiefs thus appeared to have served as a barrier between the people and the administration rather than as a channel of effective communication, for they depended on the people's ignorance of administrative regulations and always did their utmost to prevent direct communication between individuals and the administration. Their power lay mostly in the restrictive aspects of their positions, and quite naturally they did as much as they could to prevent changes. Changes that spelled progress to the administration could look like retrograde steps to the chiefs. The chiefs had salvaged as much of the old life as they could, and much of their actual power was dependent upon the workings of a modified form of the old system of patronage. They had suspicions aplenty that any improvement of the standard of living of the people would result in a harder life for themselves. They had already seen the devastation wrought on their prestige by the introduction of money; the payment of money for services has been expressed by one of them as "spoiling" the people. The patron-client system, based as it was upon long-term, unspecified mutual reciprocity, tended to be disrupted by the competition of a money system involving impersonalized, regular, and predictable payment for specified services. More will be said on this matter in Chapter IV.

In my time a chief accepted gifts of money in much the same spirit as he formerly accepted the services and goods that were part of the reciprocal relationship in which he had provided protection from enemies and hospitality. Because almost all Azande were doing something illegal much of the time, such as smuggling, distilling spirits, or growing hashish, almost everyone was vulnerable. Even if an individual did not have something specific on his conscience, he usually was not sure enough of governmental regulations to risk the disfavor of his chief. Since the chief could get almost anyone into serious trouble, there was real point in not offending him and in propitiating him with gifts. What seemed to be bribes to the European were regarded as justifiable gifts by the chiefs and as wise precautions by their followers. Protection against enemies was partially replaced by protection against the administration, but since the chief was also the agent of the administration, he seemed at times to be less an independent patron than a policeman demanding protection money. Some chiefs probably were corruptible policemen by the standards of the administrators. But it cannot be assumed that such values had been accepted or even perceived by the Azande.

One primary aim of the restrictions placed on the chiefs' powers to judge and punish was to alleviate brutalities. The crux of the problem lies in differing concepts of brutality. Obviously the Zande chief did not have the same evaluation of brutality as did the British administrator. The right to punish with death and mutilation was forbidden, but this restriction did not mean a change in the chiefs' attitude toward those whom they considered offenders. In other words, the prohibition of brutal practices and punishment for breaches of this prohibition did not affect the basic concepts. The chiefs learned that certain things could no longer be done with impunity, but they did not necessarily understand the reasons behind the new regulations, let alone the standards of values that supported those reasons. From their point of view offenders were getting off without due punishment by utilizing the governmental system of courts. The administrators were not unaware of the motivations of individual chiefs but hoped that they could be educated to the ways of the administration by example, by restriction, and by monitoring. These methods did not, however, provide adequate guides or sufficient incentives for the chiefs to change their standards of values. In 1954 a subchief and his brother were tried for the murder of a man whom they had suspected of adultery with one of the subchief's wives and whom they had killed by tearing off his testicles. This extreme instance is evidence of the persistence of the old values; the situation had changed but the standards of values had not. Only the younger, more educated chiefs had acquired any degree of insight into the principles of the administrators. The process of educating the chiefs to the administration's standards had been slow in this area because of its poverty and the governmental policy of protecting the people against changes.

The Azande faced a dilemma when they expressed preferences for the successor of a deceased chief. Some argued in favor of an educated man because he would be able to communicate with the administration and with the outside world. Others wanted a man who had not left the way of life of the Azande, because he would be able to understand the everyday problems of the people better than an educated man would. No one ever thought of the possibility that someone might be available who combined these qualities. And in view of the rarity with which chiefs in Africa or elsewhere had been able to solve to anyone's satisfaction the problem of working under two different sets of standards, probably no Zande existed who could have done more than cope somehow with a fundamentally confusing situation.

III

CHANGES IN
DOMESTIC ORGANIZATION

This chapter deals with changes in the domestic organization of the Azande in the Sudan under colonial administration, examining particularly the position of the head of the household and the stability of marriages. Both these problems were suggested by the people involved in the modern scene of Zande District, for the Azande often indicated that the position of head of the household was being undermined, while both Azande and Europeans were sorely concerned with the instability of marriages.

The household of a man, with his wives, children, and other dependents, is the basic unit in Zande domestic and economic organization. When a man marries, he establishes his own separate homestead. Since multiple households are not formed, the establishments of two related men, even if they live close together, are as distinctly separate as those of unrelated neighbors. The independence of households, a crucial feature of Zande social organization, will be examined further in Chapter V. Here we are concerned with the internal organization of the household.

HOUSEHOLD ORGANIZATION

First, an explanation of the terms used: The term "homestead" refers to the physical establishment and everything associated with it—cleared space, buildings, equipment, and cultivations—corresponding to the Zande term *kporo*. In reference to the people living in the homestead the Azande use the term *aboro kporo*, "the people of the homestead," which is the sense in which I use the term "household." No Zande term exists which can be translated as "family"; *gume* is used to designate a relative and the plural *agume* is a general term for related persons. The English term "family," as used here, corresponds to *agume* and can include collateral relatives, some of whom may be members of other households. The term "family" should be used interchangeably with "household" only when there is no doubt that the reference is to the occupants of one homestead. The Azande designate the main living area, the actual site of the buildings, as the center of the homestead, *vuru kporo*, which is translated here as "courtyard."

The Zande courtyard is arranged according to the people living within it, and the main variations in its pattern can be directly linked to variations in the composition of the household. Each woman ideally has her own house and store, so that in households containing more than one adult woman there will be a number of houses and store buildings. The head of the household sleeps in the houses of his wives in turn and eats food prepared by them in turn. If the head of the household has a house for himself, it is usually regarded as the guest house, and if he has a grain store, the contents are usually reserved for special occasions. Buildings very often serve two or more functions. For example, the space under the floor of a raised store may be used as a kitchen or as a reception shelter.

Figure 4 is a diagram of the courtyard of Makembu, the headman of the line in which I first lived. His was a typical polygynous courtyard that had been established only for slightly more than a year, since it had been resettled along with the entire subchiefship. In this case the courtyard was about 100 feet long and 60 feet wide—largely bare, hard earth. The diagram shows that Makembu had three wives. Each wife had her own house, and two had grain stores. This situation was not normal, for each wife should have had her own grain store. The third wife's grain was still kept in her grain store in their previous courtyard, now abandoned, awaiting construction of one in the new homestead.

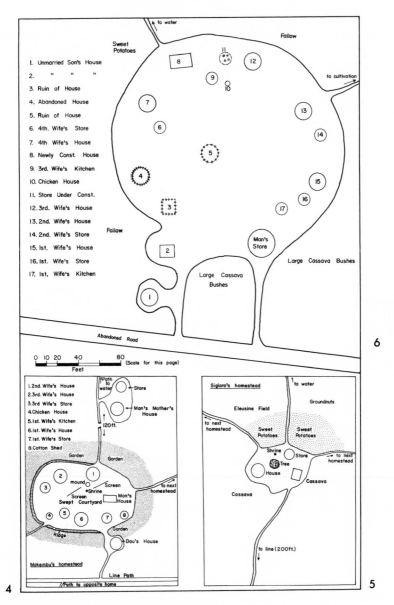

FIGURE 4
THE COURTYARD OF MAKEMBU

FIGURE 5
THE COURTYARD OF A MONOGAMOUS ZANDE HOUSEHOLD

FIGURE 6
A LARGE ZANDE HOMESTEAD

The buildings of each person tend to be grouped together. The courtyard is, in practice, considered to be roughly divided into regions, each being one person's province. Each wife has her own area of the courtyard, which is usually not demarcated unless there are screens, as there were in this case for the purpose of cutting off the view of the senior wife's and head of the household's portion of the courtyard from the parts occupied by the other two wives. A good deal of variation is found in the partitioning of a courtyard among its members—for example, when two wives who get along well together share a kitchen. Each wife nonetheless retains a tacit monopoly over a certain portion of the courtyard.

Figure 5 is a sketch of the courtyard of a monogamous household. Since most Zande men now have only one wife, this diagram represents the most common type of Zande household. It was a new homestead when I first saw it, only 18 months after resettlement, with a small courtyard, about 65 feet at the greatest diameter, well swept and well defined from the surrounding vegetation. It contained only three buildings—the house of the wife, which was used also by the man; the grain store, under which was the kitchen; and a flimsy grass shelter for keeping cotton, which was also the sitting-out space for the man. He and his wife were the only residents in this homestead.

In contrast, one of the largest Zande homesteads I knew, aside from those of the chiefs, is represented in Figure 6. It was one of the very few in the Sudan that had not been moved during the resettlement program. The head, who had four wives, was an industrious man and a good manager, as was shown by his courtyard. It was an impressive sight, almost 200 feet in diameter, neat and well developed. It contrasted greatly with all other homesteads in the vicinity because they had been started afresh in the past one or two years. The dominant feature of the courtyard was the enormous grain store of the head of the household. The walls were about the size of those of a house, supported on eight posts rather than the usual four, and the large roof was of extra-thick thatch about 38 feet in diameter, sheltering the man's lounge and reception space. It was partially walled with grass on the side of the prevailing winds. The other houses, those of his wives and a dependent female relative of his mother, were arranged around the edge of the courtyard, leaving the center clear.

In the first example, Makembu's homestead (Figure 4), there was a main courtyard with two subsidiary courtyards. One of these was an appendage to the main courtyard and was just large enough to contain one house, that of an adult daughter who had married a man from French Equatorial Africa. Evidently she and her husband, or at times she alone, spent a good deal of time in her father's homestead, so her father and husband had constructed the house for her. It could easily have been included in the main courtyard by clearing away a bit of garden on each side of the connecting path, but this had not been done and some cassava bushes had been planted to screen the house more effectively from the main courtyard. A separate house, close to the main courtyard but not included in it, seemed to be the most common arrangement for adult sons and daughters.

The other auxiliary courtyard in Makembu's homestead contained the house and grain store of the widowed mother of the head of the household. It was a complete unit, containing all the equipment required by a Zande woman for maintaining herself. Her courtyard was completely separate from the main household and out of sight, about 120 feet down the path leading from the main courtyard to the stream that served as water supply. Although considerable variation in practice was seen, the general tendency seemed to be to separate the courtyards of older adult dependents from the main courtyard.

The division of labor in Zande society requires both man's and woman's work to make a completely functioning homestead. The long-range work—that is, the construction and repair of buildings—is usually done by men, whereas the daily care of the courtyard is largely the work of the women. The well-being of the members of a household and their relationships can often be gauged as soon as one enters a courtyard. If, for example, the open space is well swept, household equipment is not lying about, and the stacks of drying grain or other food are neat and even, one knows that there is an industrious wife or, in the case of a polygynous family, probably a senior wife who is a good manager. If the buildings are in good repair and all the roofs are sound, one can assume that the head of the household is competent. In some cases the woman's work may be good and the man's work bad, or vice versa, but in most cases the homestead will either be a credit to both sides of the household or show an obvious lack of efficiency—generally traceable to some trouble in the family, such as illness, or to a lack of harmony within the household. The functioning household is ideally the result of a successful marriage, but if the head of the household is not married or if his wife has died or left him, he may try to get a female relative to live with him in order to maintain at least part of the normal daily procedure of a homestead. The considerable numbers of homesteads without wives and some even without women were probably a new feature of Zande life and without question a disturbing one.

One principle that emerges from the division of labor is that the Zande woman was more nearly independent economically than was the man. She had virtually all necessary tools at her disposal; she had the widest range of activities; and, furthermore, she did the majority of the work connected with everyday life. She could live alone more comfortably than a man could, for relatively few, albeit major, kinds of work fell outside her province. If she had a house and store, she could get along by looking for fields that did not require heavy clearing for her cultivation. On the contrary a man was continually discommoded if he had to live alone, since he could not arrange for the proper execution of his daily needs, particularly in the preparation of food. This comparison does not mean that women did in fact live alone very often or that they considered a solitary life to be agreeable. Azande of both sexes consistently referred to the ideal smoothly functioning homestead as a result of cooperation between a man and his wife or wives.

CHANGES IN THE POSITION OF THE HEAD OF THE HOUSEHOLD

In appearance the Zande homesteads observed were remarkably unchanged from those of pre-European days. Also their domestic organization seemed at first to have changed very little in its major aspects. This impression was supported by my finding that kinship terms and usages were identical with those recorded 25 and more years before.[1] Yet numerous Azande expressed anxiety about the deterioration of family relationships. My informants

1. See Seligman, 1932, pp. 507–8, for a full list.

focused on the effects that colonial administration had had upon the heads of households. Their concern underlined the significance of this position, which is the key one within the household. Just as the position of chief dominates the political organization, so does that of the male head of the household dominate all domestic organization.

Azande generally said that the authority of the head of the household had been undermined in recent years. Observation indicated the contrary—that great respect was still paid to him and that his word appeared to be law. He rarely fetched anything; even water to drink was brought to him when he called for it. He was served his meals by his women and ate before they did, often with a better choice of food. It was considered improper for women or children to be in his presence when he was eating. All this deference was given to him not simply because he was a male but because he was respected and served as head of the household by the rest of the members, male and female. His authority was symbolized by the term *ba*, used by the members of the household when addressing him. In this context the word usually would be translated as "father," but it is a term of address for any man to whom respect is shown; the Zande equivalent for "Yes, sir" is "*A ba.*"[2] *Ba* is also a generic prefix denoting largeness, importance, and masculinity.

The authority of the head of a household was further demonstrated by the fact that descent and inheritance were through him, his children being members of his clan and his family. The homestead was identified with him; when he died the homestead also died. The buildings and land were then abandoned, and the members of his household were dispersed among their relatives. When a woman died, on the other hand, her house and grain store and her cultivations were abandoned, but whether the rest of the homestead was abandoned depended on the discretion of the head of the household and his oracles. His authority was further reinforced by the fact that he represented the household to the supernatural world. He made the offerings at the household shrine, to appeal to the spirits of his ancestors. After he died, his spirit was

2. It should be noted that there is another word indicating even greater social superiority—*gbia*, meaning "master" or "chief." This term is reserved for chiefs, Europeans, and other persons of undoubted power.

the principal supernatural factor in the homesteads of his sons. His curse was of the greatest gravity to his children.

The head also represented his household in legal matters, in consulting the oracles, and in all matters external to the household. He still had considerable control over the marriage of his children, being the preferred intermediary to speak to the fathers of the girls his sons wanted to marry and the negotiator with the representatives of his daughters' suitors. It was he who dealt with outsiders entering the homestead. If he was not present when a visitor arrived, the members of his family would send for him or deliver a message to him upon his return, but they would not act in his stead, even in trivial matters. However, the head of a household might designate his eldest son or someone else to act for him, especially if he expected to be away from home for some time.

The administration had made him the taxpayer and the person responsible for the various public services to be rendered to the government and for the growing of cotton under the development scheme. He had derived from these responsibilities some additional control over his family's activities and its cash income.

With all this observable evidence to the contrary, what was the basis for the statements that the head of the household did not have the authority of former times? Although the head of a household was still powerful in his realm, a number of factors had combined to change the significance of his position in the time of European administration. Some disturbing influences suggested by Zande comments and my observations were (1) the shift from group to individual responsibility for marriage, (2) the payment of wages in money, and (3) increased freedom of movement.

Evidence was available to reveal a shift from group to individual responsibility, similar to the individualization reported in other situations of social change following contact with Western European civilization. Sons were encouraged to set up independent homes, by a combination of factors that emphasized individual responsibility rather than that of the kin group. The goal of a Zande youth in my time there was to marry and establish a homestead. Until he did so, he was dependent upon the services of female relatives for the provision of food, which generally meant that he was tied to his father. For even if he got a job he would be expected to give his family a large part of his wages while he was still a dependent member of the household. So a young man usually started making arrangements to build a homestead and get married shortly after he was judged by his chief to be capable of working and therefore liable to the annual tax.

The introduction of money wages made a youth able to arrange for marriage without the assistance of his father. A father was still under obligation to help his sons in obtaining money for marriage and in the negotiations, but such help was not absolutely necessary. His role as controller of the marriage payment had lost its significance with the substitution of money for spears and with the opportunities for earning money on an individual basis. Each young taxpayer in the early 1950's had to obtain 50 to 60 piastres a year for his taxes. It was not too difficult, except in the remote regions, to earn another 50 piastres or a pound as a payment for a marriage. The ability of a youth to earn money and the pressure to get away from the demands of his family added to the desirability of becoming the head of his own homestead. Moreover, these tendencies were reinforced by the administration's assumption that all men capable of working were the equivalent of the heads of households. Often in recent years youths were required to take a plot of land and grow cotton before they were married. The agricultural supervisors found that bachelors performed very poorly as cotton growers and generally disregarded the regulations providing punishments for cotton defaulters who were not married. But the official policy strengthened even more the growing tendency of youths under 20 years of age to earn money and establish homesteads independent of their parents. The modern Zande man undoubtedly was in the marriage market at an earlier age than had been possible for his father or grandfather.

Formerly all marriage payments were made in the form of spears and, although money had been substituted universally, were still expressed in terms of spears. In pre-European times little or no opportunity existed to earn spears by labor or other means.[3] Evidently there had been a scarcity of spears, for the primary sources available to men were marriage payments for their sisters. The father, when he received spears for his daughters' marriages, was supposed to use them for the marriages of his sons.

3. Seligman, 1932, p. 513.

Thus in the old days the head of a household could exercise a good deal of control over his sons by withholding, or threatening to withhold, the spears for their marriages.[4]

In modern times marriage payments had become part of the general money economy, and the father was bypassed in a process that he had once controlled. His power over sons had been weakened markedly because of the fact that, despite wages among the lowest in the world, for many years young men had been able to earn the money they needed for marriage.

A third factor affecting family relationships was simply the greater ease and range of travel in modern Zande country, compared with the old days when large belts of uninhabited territory surrounded each chief's area and when there was constant danger of hostilities. So while the authority of the head had not been essentially altered in the immediate context, the members of his household were capable of withdrawing more readily from the sphere of that authority. Although all members of a household had to do as he said while living in his homestead, they could leave the homestead with much greater ease than in precolonial days. Wives could travel with only a child or another woman, or even alone, whereas in the old days it was possible for a woman to travel only when escorted by an armed man. The greater mobility of sons enhanced their freedom as individuals. Daughters, in contrast, were still strongly tied to the father at the time of my study, for girls considered the homesteads of their fathers to be their permanent homes and places of refuge in the event of trouble, even after marriage.

THE INSTABILITY OF MARRIAGES

Another indication that changes had occurred in Zande domestic organization was the universal concern about the stability of marriages. The relative instability of marriages does not lend itself easily to measurement and must be largely a matter of impression, particularly since no comparative material exists from the days before European administration.

The incidence of adultery was often associated by the administration with unstable marriages. Everyone said that a great deal of

4. *Ibid.*

adultery went on, but its relative incidence, in comparison with that in other times and places, is a highly debatable matter. The only figures available were those of the chiefs' courts of Zande District. Between 1942 and 1953 the number of adultery cases heard by the 17 courts varied between 159 and 209 a year. These figures would seem to be quite constant, indicating a certain stability, either in the incidence of adultery among the Azande or, more likely, in the court system. The administration did not share this view, however, for in 1951 an official statement was made that "the increase by nearly 50 per cent of sexual offenses in the previous year indicated the need for even more severe punishments."[5]

Only a small fraction of the actual instances of adultery were represented in these figures. If instances of adultery are to become adultery cases they must be detected, but the act is, naturally, one of the most difficult of misdemeanors to detect. Furthermore, only if the matter was not capable of solution within the Zande family or by an unofficial court would it be brought to the attention of the official chiefs' courts that furnished the above figures. Domestic cases comprised the major portion of Zande litigation, but by no means all were conducted at the official courts. The Azande appealed to anyone of higher authority to hear their cases, so headmen of the lines, subchiefs, and chiefs all had their own courts in spite of a ruling that chiefs were not to hold court privately. The administration condoned these private courts because it knew that the official courts could not have carried the actual load of cases.

The only other figures available that can be used to examine the instability of marriages are the numbers of divorce cases heard by the chiefs' courts. Between 1942 and 1953 the number of cases heard each year varied between 628 and 835; as with the adultery figures, there would seem to be a general uniformity in the numbers of divorce cases over this period of time. Again, perhaps this uniformity was imposed by the court system. However, these figures probably represented a much larger fraction of the actual instances of divorce than the adultery case figures represented instances of adultery. The chiefs' courts probably handled many of the difficult cases of divorce, involving separations and the return of bride wealth.

5. Zande District Annual Report, 1950–51, p. 15.

Even if nothing definite can be said about the divorce rate, the universal anxiety about the instability of marriages remains an important social fact. Moreover, my observations indicated a good deal of fluidity in marriages. There were numerous cases in which men's wives had left them, and many of my friends and informants had gone through a number of marriages. Six or eight successive marriages were not uncommon among the men canvassed. The reader should know that most of my informants for the subject matter of this chapter were married men. I could not readily discuss such matters with women, and the unmarried men did not feel free to talk with me in this realm. Since it is possible that the comments of the men might have unduly influenced me, the observations of Mrs. G. M. Culwick are important because they assess the situation in the late 1940's from the point of view of the women and in the light of her other African experiences. She found, in the course of a year's study of nutrition in Zande households, that the women largely went their own way "under an outward submissiveness which deceives no one in tribal society." She states that it was common for a young woman to make a series of temporary marriages, and even when "a full marriage is entered into, there does not seem to be any real difficulty in getting out of it except when a dispute arises over return of bride wealth and somebody turns cantankerous, invoking the letter of the old tribal law against her."[6]

Clearly, some of the factors cited above as affecting the authority of the head of the household, particularly the individualization of marriage arrangements and freedom of travel, had also affected the stability of marriages, as had certain administrative regulations, the change in the significance of marriage payments, and the change in age at marriage. Before these points are discussed further, however, an outline of modern marriage procedure, as observed, may be helpful.

Marriage Procedure

When a man found a girl he liked, he sent an intermediary to speak with her father. If the father was interested, he consulted his brothers and sisters, and if they agreed that the man was a

6. Culwick, 1950, p. 16.

desirable husband for the girl, they asked her opinion. If she too was agreeable, the money offered by the suitor through his intermediary was accepted by the father. A few days later the suitor would visit the parents of the girl, bringing them gifts and treating them with the greatest respect. After about a month the girl would be sent to the home of her husband-to-be, to keep house for him for a period of 15 days to a month. She then would return home to make her final decision about the marriage. The suitor would consult the oracles during this period, in the presence of the girl's father and favorite brother, to find out whether the marriage would be a fortunate one. If all augured well and everybody agreed, the bride's family would gather at the groom's house for the marriage. This took place after a period of three or four months, during which time the bride might continue to visit her new home. When the girl's parents came to the groom's house, they brought food, beer, and household equipment for the new homestead. Relatives of the groom also gathered, and all ate and drank together. After the ceremony of the installation of the three hearthstones for the cooking fire of the bride, she stayed with her husband.

Zande marriage was not a definite, single act but a continuing process over an indefinite period, and the payment of the bride wealth was also generally protracted. A small part of the officially agreed-upon amount would legitimize the marriage, and the new husband was constantly in debt to his wife's family—a condition that continued even after he paid the full amount. He was obligated to help his wife's parents in their work, particularly with burial in the event of a death in her family. His behavior toward his wife's parents must always be that of formalized respect.

The amount of bride wealth paid was not a crucial factor; the attitude of the husband counted most. If he was kind to his wife and helpful to her parents, his marriage payments could remain in arrears for years. Indeed this seemed to be a desirable arrangement to some parents because it gave them a hold over the husband. They could put pressure upon him at any time by calling the wife back to their home and negotiating with her husband for her return. The emphasis, then, was on the relationship between the husband and his wife's parents rather than between man and wife. His treatment of her was important but was considered as a factor influencing the attitude of her parents toward him. The Azande explained the marriage of a man to the sister of his wife on the grounds that he got along well with his in-laws and therefore wanted to marry another of their daughters.

When questioned, the Azande said that the current marriage procedure was just as it always had been. Further probing revealed, however, that a number of administrative regulations were involved and that the procedure was a blend of traditional practices and administrative innovations. It was difficult to realize, for example, that previously infant betrothal had been practically universal and that girls had lived in their future husbands' homes for periods of one or two months over a number of years prior to marriage, which took place shortly after puberty.[7]

The "Women's Charter"

A number of changes in the Zande marriage and divorce customs, mostly in the form of prohibitions, were instituted by the Sudan government at the beginning of its administration in this region, in order to raise the status of women. Various early European travelers had commented upon the seemingly servile behavior of Zande women, as contrasted with that of women in neighboring tribes.[8] Early in his career as civil administrator among the Azande, the first district commissioner found women to be badly treated. This is how he described the fate of a Zande wife in a hypothetical case in which she had left her husband after a quarrel:

> Her husband will not care whether or no she is agreeable to return to him, nothing can induce him to believe that he will be better off if he sends her back to her family, and with the repaid spears marries another girl. He would feel that she had gained a moral victory over him should she regain her freedom at her own wish, and so, though she be sulky, disobedient, unfaithful even, and worry him to death with her escapades, he will keep her if he can. In the old days he would have resorted to force, tying her up in a hut, putting her leg in a pierced log, a sort of portable stocks, or beating her cruelly. He might have gone so far as to scarify her with knives, or kill her outright. In any case he would soon

7. See Seligman, 1932, pp. 511–15, for an account of former marriage customs.
8. An example is found in Schweinfurth, 1878, Vol. I, pp. 223–24.

have broken her spirit, and she would have become one of those hardly human incarnations of misery that were to be seen in the southern Bahr-el-Ghazal in the old days.[9]

As he learned to speak Zande, women came to him with their grievances. He decided that a number of marriage practices were repugnant to them and that they were only abused "chattels." He was determined to take steps that would lead eventually to their "emancipation" and instituted what he called the "Women's Charter." He hoped to reduce "the appalling amount of adultery that went on" by improving the lot of women and making them happier in married life.[10]

The "Women's Charter," which went into effect about 1915, included the following restrictions: (1) "Child marriage" was abolished. (2) Girls not yet married were not to be forced to "live with" their betrothed. (3) Widows were to be returned to their families instead of becoming wives of heirs of the deceased husbands. (4) The temporary exchange of wives was forbidden. (5) Marriage by exchange of women rather than by payment of spears was forbidden. (6) Marriage within the ruling clan was prohibited. And (7) women could no longer be used to pay damages. About the same time a procedure was introduced whereby women who disliked their husbands enough to go to prison to get away from them were granted divorces after being imprisoned a month or two, the reasoning being that such women would be unlikely ever to settle down and make satisfactory wives. The district commissioner hoped that the threat of prison would prevent the women from taking advantage of the fact that the government had "tied the hands of their husbands somewhat."[11]

Two other early administrative restrictions should be mentioned in this connection. The administration forbade men to punish their wives or children by the more extreme means that had been used before. Although the Azande in my time could not cite any definite rules or regulations, everyone knew that a man could get into trouble with the administration if he beat or otherwise physically punished a wife or child. They said that if a man so much as raised a hand against his child, the child would threat-

9. Larkin, 1926, pp. 15–16.
10. Larkin, 1955, p. 48.
11. Larkin, 1930, pp. 112–13.

en to go to the government court to make a case against him. The administration had also taken away the power of punishment from the chiefs, being particularly concerned to stop the extreme punishments formerly meted out. One effect was a change in the nature of punishment for adultery, in that prison terms or fines were substituted for mutilation or death. The cases were taken out of the hands of the chiefs and tried by the district commissioner himself in the early days and later by government-regulated chiefs' courts, consisting of rotating panels of chiefs.

The restriction concerning the inheritance of widows was lifted after about ten years because of the complaints of the people. It was found to be wise to return to the old system, with the reservation that if the widow and her husband's heir had an old grievance she did not have to go to him. As it worked in my time, the widow was asked by her relatives what she wished to do at the end of the one-year period of mourning. If she had a son who was the head of a homestead, she would probably go to live there; otherwise she would generally go to live as wife with her former husband's brother or other heir. In the few cases in which she chose to return to her father or brother, a settlement was made by her family with the man who had inherited her. The Azande told me that widows had always been able to do as they pleased. In view of the women's lack of objection to this system of inheritance, it seems possible that the original administrative restriction was based on a misunderstanding of the nature of the practice.

The other administrative changes remained in force and were part of the marriage and divorce procedure as observed. Some restrictions were assimilated only with difficulty, as we shall see, while others caused little disturbance. The prohibitions on the practices of wife exchange and the exchange of female relatives in lieu of bride wealth seem to have been accepted with little difficulty. The Azande rarely thought of these customs and said that they had never been of any importance. The payment of women as damages seems to have been effectively stopped by administrative ruling. This practice and the giving of women by the chiefs as wives to favored subjects may have accounted for some of the abuses to which women had been subjected, since such women might have been deprived of the normal protection of their kin. The ordinary Azande were little concerned that this practice had passed, but its cessation undoubtedly had been more important to the chiefs, whose power and wealth were diminished by losing control of the women who had been turned over to them as payments.

The device whereby a woman could obtain a divorce by going to prison was not used by the chiefs' courts. They assimilated instead the more basic idea that women were to be heard and their grievances respected. That they did not completely understand the principles involved, however, is shown by the first district commissioner's comments that the courts often released women for insufficient reason because the Azande were always eager to take over the ideas of the Europeans.[12] These changes and others were taken over by the Azande without full understanding, but with full faith. It is doubtful that they understood the changes in the marriage laws even at the time of my study. In 1954, for example, the district commissioner had to warn the chiefs of the Yambio chiefs' court, during appeal trials, that they must not accept a woman's statements without further evidence. In one case he found that the court had fined a man because of a woman's statement that she had been raped by him. When the district commissioner asked the chiefs why they had acted on her word alone, the reply was uncertain, to the effect that they had been instructed to respect the word of women. He reversed the decision because of lack of evidence and reminded the chiefs of cases in which women had invented rape and adultery stories in order to spite their enemies and that women often were known to name an innocent man in adultery cases in order to shield their lovers. The chiefs seemed to regard the presence of women in court as a special concern of the administration and not as a part of the normal procedure of litigation. Women seemed to have a favored legal position in present Zande society, in contrast to their former lot.

The Azande constantly expressed dissatisfaction with administrative restrictions imposed upon the domestic scene. At the time of my observations they were still having difficulty assimilating the prohibitions on infant betrothal and the restrictions on disciplinary powers. It is not reasonable, however, to assume, as did many Azande, that the administrative regulations and resulting changes in the status of women were alone responsible for the

12. *Ibid.*, p. 114.

confusion in the marriage situation. Other factors had combined with the direct restrictions. Consider, as an illustration, what contributed to the individualization of marriage arrangements.

Individualization of Marriage Arrangements

The ability of youths to make arrangements for marriage individually, which has already been discussed, was enhanced by the prohibition of early betrothal of girls and their resulting freedom to select their husbands. The Azande of my time realized that a youth and a girl often knew each other quite well before the youth sent an intermediary to ask her father for her hand. The flirtations of former years[13] had become occasions for courtship. The girl's family was still involved in the negotiations for marriage and they remained her protectors, but the marriage was much more a union of two individuals than an alliance of two groups, as it used to be. Therefore, said the Azande, the wife's family was not nearly so concerned as in former days with keeping her marriage stable.

When infant betrothal had been the rule, the girls' parents had had full responsibility for arranging the marriages of their daughters. Suitors asked for the hand of a girl in marriage as soon as she was born, clearly a bid for an alliance with her family. Payments of spears began when the girl was about six, and when a certain number had been paid, the girl was sent to her future husband's home to be cared for and trained by his mother or by his older wives. Only after puberty was she actually married, but she had little choice in this matter, for the marriage was a union of her family with that of the husband. It has been said that Zande marriage was never based on mutual consent, nor was it arranged with regard to age or compatibility of temperament.[14]

An abrupt change occurred with the forbidding of what the administration considered "child marriage" and with the introduction, by government regulation, of the girl's opportunity to choose her husband. Azande insisted that in the old days girls had been allowed to express their opinions about their future marriages and that their parents and brothers had been careful to pro-

13. Evans-Pritchard, 1928, pp. 457–58, and Seligman, 1932, pp. 516–17.
14. Seligman, 1932, p. 514.

tect them from abuse. But, they continued, when girls had been largely brought up on the homes of their future husbands and had become accustomed to life there, they usually did not raise objections. On the other hand, girls who grew up in the homes of their parents were not betrothed and could be courted by anyone. When they were mature, they could marry whom they wished. The Azande said that they didn't know what they wanted, that they demanded clothing and other gifts from their husbands and tended to go from marriage to marriage without settling down.

The Zande wife had always been in an ambivalent position, drawn both to her parents' home and that of her husband. The individualization of marriage arrangements and the changes resulting from administrative regulations had unbalanced the two attractions. Since the affection of the wife for her parents had changed relatively little, she could leave her husband and return to her parents on any pretext. Numerous households were observed in which the wives were "temporarily" absent. Usually they were said to be visiting their parents, but often the visits became embarrassingly protracted for the husbands. The attitudes and actions of the wife's family determined to a large extent the difficulties she would endure with her husband. In times of trouble the families of the husband and wife intervened to keep them together, but, said the Azande, the parents did not feel the same responsibility for maintaining marriages now as when they themselves had initiated the marriages.

The Azande also maintained that the intervention of the government to prevent the beating of children and wives had added to this lack of responsibility, because young girls could not be chastised for flirting before marriage and wives could not be punished for laziness. Even when parents did not agree with a wife's reasons for leaving her husband, they could not punish her, nor could they send her to live with a man she did not like. My informants contrasted the situation in the Sudan with that in the Belgian Congo and French Equatorial Africa. There, they claimed, a woman was much more content to stay with one man and did not incessantly demand gifts from him. This greater stability was attributed to the fact that girls and women could be punished for leaving their husbands. A young girl in the Belgian Congo, for example, considered herself too young and pretty to be married to an old man. As a punishment she was disfigured by having stones pushed against her face. In the Sudan such a thing would not happen, according to the Azande, because of fear of being punished by the government. While these comparisons may or may not have been accurate, the expressions of confusion and anxiety conveyed in them are important.

The Changed Significance of Marriage Payments

The change in the significance of the marriage payments, mentioned as affecting the head of the household, may also have contributed to the instability of marriages. The marriage payment had had more than just a monetary value; it was the tangible expression of the responsibility of the husband to his wife's family. When spears formerly were the accepted form of this payment, they became a symbol for the relating of two groups by marriage. When other things were substituted for spears, early in European administration, the women were concerned about the legality of the marriage transactions. Some complained to the district commissioner that they had been improperly married because articles other than spears or money had been used as payment in their marriages.[15]

The relative scarcity of spears, together with their special significance, gave rise to the use of the same spears in a series of marriages. As the disruption of a marriage could mean the return of spears that had been already used or were proposed to be used for other marriages, a family could be inconvenienced by the necessity to return the spears when a daughter wanted to leave her husband. Evidently the spears were supposed to be returned all at once, in contrast to the driblets in which they had been received. While the actual economic hardship involved could not have been very great, the inconvenience gave the wife's family a strong argument for persuading her to stay with her husband.[16] Also, when the spears received from a daughter's marriage were used for another marriage in the family, they symbolized an interlinking of the family's marriages. With the substitution of money

15. Larkin, 1955, p. 13.

16. Professor Evans-Pritchard (1934a, p. 173) has shown that the economic aspects of bride wealth among the Azande traditionally merely represented the moral standards involved and could not alone stabilize marriages.

for spears, this symbolism ceased, especially when it became possible for anyone to earn some money readily. A father still received the marriage payment for a daughter, but it made little difference whether or not he contributed to a son's marriage payments. If, in modern times, the marriage payment for a girl had to be returned, there was no possibility that her brothers' current or future marriages would be affected—as might have been the case formerly.

Change in Age at Marriage

Another factor associated with the instability of marriages is the change in marriage age. The 1953 census of Zande District in the Sudan gives the total number of men as 61,770, of women as 61,697, and of children as 48,089, and there is no reason to believe that this even proportion of men and women has not always existed. Numerous polygynous households are possible only by creating more married women than married men. This was accomplished in the old days by the marriage of girls at a very early age, while men did not get married until they were 30 or 35[17] unless they performed a special feat in hunting or in war. Even such men (according to estimate, for Azande do not keep track of age) were over 25 at the time of their first marriage.[18] At the time of my observations men tended to want to get married as soon as they were judged capable of working, which seemed to be at about 17 or 18 years of age. Girls were probably getting married slightly later than formerly—at, say, 15 or 16. The proportion of married women to men had therefore decreased markedly.

The evidence appeared to indicate that the number of polygynous households had decreased, particularly those with very large numbers of wives. It was most unusual to find a commoner with more than three or four wives at the time of my study. The largest household found in a survey of more than 1,500 commoner households contained seven wives. Only the more important chiefs maintained very large households, and some chiefs had less than 10 wives. In one subchiefship in which I lived, census records showed that out of a total of 310 households 174 were monogamous, 47 polygynous, and 89 contained no wives. Of the 47

17. Seligman, 1932, p. 516.
18. Lagae, 1926, p. 196.

polygynous households one contained six wives and one seven wives; nine had three wives; three had four; and the 32 remaining had two wives each. In this example 79 per cent of the households with wives were monogamous and 21 per cent polygynous. A check revealed that the proportion of monogamous households was probably even higher, because a number of the households listed as being wifeless were only temporarily so, since the wives had gone visiting at the time of the census.

It is impossible, however, to make meaningful comparisons between modern times and the pre-European period or the early period of European administration, because the relative proportion of monogamous to polygynous households in former times is not known. Although the impression gained from accounts about the women-collectors and the hordes of young men without wives[19] is that most households were polygynous, the possibility remains that the observers were not speaking of the typical household, which may have been small. Professor Evans-Pritchard is of the impression that the large majority of households were already monogamous during the period of his study, from 1926 to 1929.[20]

One thing is certain: The various factors discussed had combined to change the expectations of young Zande men in regard to marriage. Furthermore, the changes in ages when marriage was possible had altered the proportion of marriageable men to marriageable women, thereby increasing the demand for wives. This probably had contributed to the instability of marriages, and to the anxiety about it.

The demand for wives was further enhanced by the establishment of many bachelor homesteads in the course of the resettlement and the development of cash cropping. From what has been said, it can be understood that a household without a wife was an anomaly. Yet in the examples cited above a large number of households were reported to be without wives. As has been pointed out, some of the wives were away on visits, but in other households the wives had left their husbands, who were either attempting to manage somehow by themselves or had been able to get a female relative to help them. In other cases the heads were

19. Examples are found in Larkin, 1930 and 1955.
20. Verbal communication.

in reality members of other households with which they ate and spent much of their time, though they had been assigned plots of land and had built courtyards, of some sort, of their own. Such bachelor homesteaders were mostly youths who were looking for marriage partners and who particularly were cited by Azande as contributing to the mobility of women in and out of marriage. Various reasons for the desire of a man to be the head of a household have been mentioned in discussing the changes in the role of the head of a household. Once a man had established a household, it was very difficult for him to become a part of someone else's household again, for such reversion meant that he must again assume the role of a dependent. The misery caused by the instability of marriages was brought to my attention numerous times in observing the effects of separations on monogamous households. Polygyny can be seen as a stabilizing influence in a subsistence economy, such as that of the Azande, where ideally each household is very nearly self-sufficient. If one wife in a polygynous household is ill or away on a visit, her work can be shared by the other wives. If one wife leaves the household permanently, that household will continue to function. But if the wife of a monogamous household is indisposed temporarily or leaves permanently, the household will either operate under difficulty or cease to exist. Although the majority of households were monogamous, the polygynous establishment was still a Zande ideal, and concern about the instability of marriages added to the general apprehensiveness of the man with only one wife.

NEW MARRIAGE REGULATIONS

The balanced system of marriage described by Professor Evans-Pritchard[21] had been upset for various reasons, such as increasingly individualized arrangements for marriage, money wages, the change in the significance of the marriage payment, the change in age at marriage, and administrative changes in marriage practices.

The administrative regulations on marriage and divorce, which were designed to raise the status of women, can be regarded in retrospect as an experiment in altering some aspects of a culture without providing for changes in values. The experiment has shown that broader areas of the life of the people were affected

21. Evans-Pritchard, 1934, 1934a, pp. 172–73.

than had been planned, but this experiment was not needed to illustrate the unpredictability of arbitrary cultural changes. Studies of culture contact and change have produced more than ample evidence from many places in the world that one aspect of a culture cannot be changed without the likelihood of far-reaching changes in other aspects. Among the all too few generalizations that can be made from the large volume of such studies we are quite safe in putting forth one: that serious difficulties will ensue from arbitrary changes in the domestic organization of a people, especially if the changes are based on the values of another culture.

That the Azande had not significantly changed their basic ideas about marriage was borne out during a chiefs' meeting in 1951, when the new regulations on marriage and divorce were announced by the district commissioner. Several chiefs pointed out that an increase in the marriage payment would not decrease promiscuity, because the control of promiscuity was a matter of controlling the women and young girls. When the chiefs were asked what could be done, they made three suggestions: (1) that the old practice of infant betrothal be revived, because the fathers-in-law, the mothers-in-law, and the husbands-to-be would be much more careful of the welfare and behavior of young girls than would the fathers and mothers; (2) that physical disciplining of girls be permitted; and (3) that fathers should choose husbands for their daughters. The meeting was informed that the government could not recognize such measures, that the remedy lay largely in the hands of the people and that "all must coordinate to improve parental control and self-restraint in their sexual relations."[22] Here was a clear indication that the Azande had not yet formulated moral standards to fit the changes in marriage and divorce and that they wanted to return to the pre-European system to remedy the troublesome conditions.

Another important matter in which there has been a difference of interpretation was the position of women. The Azande of my day did not agree with the administrative view that the position of women had been unduly servile in former days. It was also difficult for this observer to see how the position of women could have changed so radically in a few years, if the marital situation had really been as disadvantageous for them as described by the first

22. Zande District files, Annual Chiefs' Meeting, 1951, Iba Subdistrict, pp. 8–9.

district commissioner. Women played a vital role in the homesteads, and a man who had committed himself to the position of the head of a household was particularly vulnerable to the estrangement of his womenfolk. He could not live satisfactorily without a woman to prepare his food and to perform the myriad other feminine tasks about the homestead. Men whose wives had left them and who could not get a female relative to help could be observed to deteriorate physically, largely because of the inadequate diet of a womanless household. In view of the power of women in a homestead it was difficult to imagine them in a servile condition. Mrs. Culwick has also expressed astonishment at the idea that women could have suffered as badly in their marriages as the first district commissioner had believed.[23] The strong possibility exists that he had been deceived by a submissive manner and by cases of abuse inflicted on some women who had lost the protection of their kinfolk in the disturbed days prior to and during European conquest. Even if a Zande man had been able to apply the strenuous measure of discipline formerly allowed, it seems most unlikely that he would have been able to force his wife to perform her duties satisfactorily.

The chiefs' meeting also presented concisely the two conflicting sets of ideas, Zande and European, on the subject of marriage. It was clear that the nature of the crucial relationships and of the stabilizing elements in Zande marriage were interpreted differently. The Europeans had consistently tried to strengthen the husband-wife relationship, while the Azande had focused upon the relationship between the husband and the wife's parents. In discussing this matter, the Azande emphasized the greater difficulty nowadays of getting husbands to perform their duties to their wives' families, calling this the greatest single cause of troubles among families. An unofficial system of fines had been started, in which the wife's parents attempted to get money as compensation from sons-in-law who had not attended funerals or who had not helped with building or cultivation.

Similarly the administration had constantly interpreted the stability of marriages in terms of the individuals involved, while the Azande had looked upon marriage in terms of allied families. The administration, in its lack of understanding of the effective

23. Culwick, 1950, p. 16.

social units responsible for the stabilization of marriages, had transferred the responsibility for marriage alignments to individuals who were evidently not capable of maintaining the same degree of stability as the Zande kin groups had been able to do. The mode of arranging marriages had been altered arbitrarily, without corresponding changes in the concepts of marriage and the accompanying standards of values and morals.

The first district commissioner has written that the result of the "Women's Charter" was a great disappointment to him, for no diminution in the number of cases of adultery was evident by the time he retired in 1932. He concluded that "anyhow we got rid of the old state of misery in which the women were living before."[24] We can see now that more was involved in the high incidence of adultery than the unfavorable position of women, for adultery and unstable marriages have continued to be of great concern to both the administration and the Azande—despite, or even because of, the changes wrought in the status of women. In 1951 the administration decided that mere talk was not enough and that drastic steps had to be taken to curb promiscuity among the Azande, and further changes were made in the marriage laws. The official statement in the Zande District standing orders declared that the "loose habits" of both sexes of all ages had become a disgrace to all Zande people. Official opinion linked these habits to widespread venereal disease, which in turn was linked to the high sterility rate and the low birthrate that was seen to be threatening the tribe with extinction. Furthermore, many marriages were interpreted in the standing orders to be merely misconduct, with the knowledge of the woman's guardians on the one hand and a "fornicating lover" on the other.

Three steps were taken to stabilize marriage unions. First, no more cases concerning marriage affairs were to be handled by the official courts unless "a legal marriage has in fact taken place." Five requirements for a legal marriage were set forth, three of which were presumed to be taken from Zande customary law: that there be mutual consent of both parties, that the bride price be paid in full at the time of the marriage ceremony, and that the bride be installed in her husband's home by her parents. Two new government requirements were added: that the girl be adult, as

24. Larkin, 1955, p. 48.

judged by the development of her breasts, and that all marriages, after March 1, 1951, be entered in the chiefs' register of the bride's parents' chief. When cases were brought to a court in which only partial payment of the bride price had been made, the bride was to be returned to her parents and the court was to investigate immediately "whether both parties have not connived at prostitution." Previous marriages that became subjects of a court case were to be registered, if they were in order.

The bride wealth was raised from £ 1.200 to £ 3. Contrary to the experience in much of Africa, where official maximum limits have been put on inflationary bride prices, the administration of Zande District found it necessary to increase the amount of the bride price in order to keep pace with the increased wealth of the inhabitants and to discourage promiscuity, presumably by making temporary unions more expensive.

The punishment for adultery with a married women was increased to six months' imprisonment or an equivalent fine, since the previous punishments of one to three months' imprisonment had clearly not served as a deterrent.

Those requirements that were said to be based on customary Zande practice actually contained two contradictions of it. First, the provision requiring consent of both parties, meaning the bride and the groom, was contrary to Zande practice, which required the assent of the bride's family and, less directly, the groom's family. Second, as already shown, payment of the bride price in full at the time of the wedding was not a Zande requirement for a legitimate marriage, nor was it necessarily considered to be a desirable condition. In contrast, one of the presumably new requirements followed Zande notions for proper marriage. The insistence on the maturity of the bride seems to have been an echo of the former prohibition on infant betrothal rather than a remedy for current malpractice, since the Azande had the definite rule that a girl was not to be married until her breasts were the diameter of a man's forearm.

In the four years in which the new marriage regulations were in effect before the end of my investigations, little change could be discerned except for a possible heightening of the confusion in the people's minds about the administration's position on marriage. Since the necessity for the marriage payment to be made in full was not accepted by the Azande, the regulations made little impact on them, other than to begin to establish two distinct categories of marriage payments—one a sort of legal fee at the time of the wedding and the other the customary payment to the bride's family. The requirement that all marriages be registered after a certain date could be met only partially because the people lacked knowledge and understanding of the new regulations and because there were not enough well-trained clerks at the chiefs' headquarters. The main tangible effect of the new regulations was the rejection of certain cases by the chiefs' courts, which meant that people became more apprehensive about taking divorce cases to the official courts and that greater numbers of cases were judged by unofficial means. The attempt to stabilize marriages by making weddings definite, recorded events had little discernible effect, since the official courts' refusal of cases involving illegal marriages was a weak sanction.

As in the case of the political organization, the domestic situation had been altered radically in some respects, but Zande values had not changed commensurately. The Azande were going through a transition period characterized by confusion and apathy. Again we can see that much of the confusion stemmed from the use of different sets of values derived from two cultures, with a mutual lack of understanding. The Azande knew that the situation had been altered, and, as we have seen in the description of the marriage procedure, they attempted to combine as much as possible of their old pattern of behavior with their version of those standards of the administrators that had been imposed upon them. The result was a good example of what has been called the "working misunderstanding." The administration constantly admonished the Azande for their loose morals. The Azande did not deny the charges. They admitted that far too much adultery existed among married people and far too much promiscuity among the unmarried, but they turned the blame back onto the administration by saying that the bad situation was due to the difficulty of controlling women and girls in their new and excessive freedom. The ability to put the blame on the government in times of uncertainty assured the Azande that they were not responsible for the instability of married life. Many seemed to have stopped trying to remedy the situation by their own efforts because they felt it had been taken out of their hands by the administration.

More than ample evidence is available here to demonstrate that administrative regulations and restrictions cannot in themselves readily change values associated with marriage. We can be sure, on the other hand, that many of the difficulties in Zande domestic life would have occurred without the "Women's Charter" or subsequent regulations. Yet the impression I gained in talking with Azande and Europeans of the three countries in which the Azande live is that marital stability was considerably greater in the Sudan than in the Belgian Congo or French Equatorial Africa. I was not able to carry on sufficient research in the other countries to make valid comparisons, but the Azande in all three were convinced that the British had weakened Zande marriages in the Sudan by their various regulations.

The desire of the administration to alleviate hardships cannot be criticized, but the manner in which this laudable motive was implemented was not effective in changing the basic reasons for the hardships. It is true that the restrictions on various abuses raised the status of women in general, but it is also true that they caused confusion in the marriage situation and thereby created different kinds of hardships. The administration wanted to eliminate brutality, which cannot be done by regulations alone. Basic Zande values and ideas had not been changed.

CHANGES IN
THE SUBSISTENCE ECONOMY

In this chapter I will attempt to determine how Zande production for livelihood has been altered since pre-European times, by surveying the essential activity within the subsistence economy and then assessing the significance of the imported goods purchased for money. The introduction of money will be seen to be one of the most important factors tending to change the subsistence economy.

In pre-European days each family, consisting of a man with his wives and dependents, was a largely self-sufficient economic unit, producing most of the things it consumed in ordinary life. Little exchange seems to have existed among households, although iron tools and spears made from locally smelted ore had a limited application as a medium of exchange, being used primarily for marriage payments. Everyone was directly dependent upon the production of the household to which he belonged. The only division of labor was based on sex, and there was no full-time occupational specialization. Also there was a remarkable absence of special goods designed for display or differentiation. The wealthiest chiefs simply had a great deal more of everything possessed by ordinary persons. Wealth was primarily in the form of perishable agricultural produce. Little else could be accumulated, and by tradition the property of an individual was destroyed after he died. Let us now survey briefly the subsistence activities as observed in the period from 1952 to 1955, to learn what changes had taken place during the European administration.

SUBSISTENCE ACTIVITIES

The center of Zande economic activity is the homestead (*kporo*), the domestic establishment of one man with his wife or wives, their children, and other dependents. A considerable portion of the productive energy of the Azande goes into the construction and maintenance of their courtyards and buildings. The forces that tend to destroy the neatness and effectiveness of a Zande homestead are constantly and rapidly at work, and the inroads of natural vegetation and animal and insect pests, such as termites, can be counteracted only with constant care.

Very considerable differences in the neatness of Zande homesteads could be observed. Even as a stranger I was impressed with the remarkably better order and state of repair of some homesteads compared with neighboring ones. As I became accustomed to the Zande way of looking at other people's homesteads, I discovered that the condition of courtyard was an extremely important criterion in their eyes and that much could be learned by analyzing the physical features of a courtyard. In my visits to Zande homesteads I found myself playing a game with my companions while waiting in a courtyard for the occupants to come in from the fields. We would try to work out the composition of the family, the age of the homestead, the state of food supplies, the handicraft specialties, and the general industriousness of the male and female heads of the household. After our departure the Azande with me would also make comments about the characteristics of a homestead and about the occupants. Their tendency to analyze courtyards as reflections of the inhabitants, particularly the head of the household, was not confined to other people's homes. The Azande were aware of the impression their own homes made on visitors. I received a number of apologies from the heads of households about the state of their courtyards, with full explanations for the deficiencies of which they were ashamed.

Two basic types of buildings, houses and raised grain stores, were the minimum required. There also might be reception shelters, separate kitchens, guest houses, or smaller versions of the raised store, used to house chickens at night. In areas where cotton was grown, separate small stores for cotton might also be erected. All were variations on the basic buildings, which were built of mud, wooden poles, and grass. Temporary buildings might have grass or cane walls, but more permanent ones had walls of mud mixed with chopped grass. All buildings were thatched with a common grass *(Imperata cylindrica)*, called *bingba* by the Azande.

Only two changes or additions in the traditional building technique of the Azande were detected. First, most houses had doors fitted with hinges, hasps, and locks. The doors were usually made of boards and flattened-out gasoline tins. Very seldom was the traditional door made of canes, since hinges, hasps, and locks were sold in even the smallest and most remote shops. Another variation, a square or rectangular ground plan for houses instead of the circular one, may have been an innovation in the time of European administration. The circular plan allows for the strongest and most economical form of wall that can be devised, but the interior of a round house is awkward to arrange, especially when it must contain beds and other items of non-Zande furniture.

The form of Zande buildings and the other features that make up the ordinary courtyard appear to have changed very little during the time for which records about the Azande are available. In fact no important differences could be seen in the appearance of courtyards in the three countries in which the Azande live, even though there were other variations, such as in style of clothing. Despite differences in settlement patterns and economic development, the courtyard, along with most of its activities, remained much the same in the three countries.

The kitchen gardens and any field cultivations adjacent or near the courtyard would be included in a Zande's general reference to the *kporo*, or homestead. If need be, cultivations could be specified by the term *ati* or *abino*, meaning clearings, fields, or cultivations. Fields at some distance were usually distinct from the main homestead in Zande terminology. Quite often temporary shelters would be constructed at more distant fields.

The Azande cultivated a relatively wide variety of crops, including various cereals, roots and tubers, oilseeds, leafy foods, other vegetables and fruits, of which cassava, eleusine, peanuts, maize, bananas, and sweet potatoes formed the largest part of the diet. Sorghum, sesame, bulrush millet, yam, taro, rice, and various pulses and cucurbits were of less importance and less regular distribution. A high degree of uniformity in basic agricultural practice was found from one homestead to the next, as well as a striking similarity in the inventory of types of crops grown in all homesteads surveyed. A homestead only a few months old would contain specimen crops of virtually everything being grown in the oldest and best established homesteads. About 30 different types of cultivated plants were found in virtually all homesteads; additional types were grown more occasionally.[1]

Upon the establishing of a new homestead, it was natural to make all cultivations near the courtyard first, then to go farther and farther away for field cultivations. The crops grown in the courtyard or in the garden around it may be roughly classified as perennials and miscellaneous, to distinguish them from the field crops, which were mostly annuals and which furnished the bulk of the food supply. The Azande regarded the garden around the courtyard much as we do a kitchen garden, a place to get a bit of food for immediate preparation, whereas the field crops usually required large-scale harvesting, processing, and storage. In the courtyard and the garden around it were found most of the cultivated trees and other perennial plants, many of which had been introduced relatively recently, such as pineapple, papaya, citrus, oil palm, and mango. The Azande seemed quick to appreciate new additions to their stock of perennial plants.

The mango deserves special mention as the most successful of all newly arrived plants. Within the time of British administration the first seeds were brought to the Sudan from the Belgian Congo, whence the tree had been introduced from East Africa and India. Since about 1918, mango trees had become an outstanding feature of the countryside in Zande District. All buildings, whether Zande or official, were surrounded by mangoes. The trees had grown to great height and gave enormous quantities of fruit. Because the

---

1. De Schlippe, 1956, lists the varieties, pp. 48–77; Culwick, 1950, gives an excellent list of Zande crops, pp. 79–111.

fruit ripens at the end of the dry season, when food tends to be scarce and fresh food is very rare, the large harvest of mangoes was a welcome and excellent addition to the diet of the Azande. Large quantities were consumed, some individuals and even families virtually living on them for days at a time. A particularly cynical Zande observed that the introduction of the mango had been the most important contribution of the Europeans to Zande welfare. In some areas more of the fruit was produced than could be consumed, despite the amount eaten. During the resettlement the population was removed from the old stands of mangoes along the roads, but the Azande planted mango trees in their new homesteads. (These, incidentally, were useful as guides to the ages of the homesteads.) The mangoes seeded themselves very successfully and were spread by baboons, monkeys, elephants, and other animals that ate the fruit.

Eleusine had the reputation, backed by the accounts of earlier observers, of having been the staple crop. It was still the most important cereal and the favored ingredient in porridge and beer, but it had been displaced by cassava, in greatly varying amounts according to locality and situation, because of the ease in which it could be cultivated and processed into food. Cassava is not critical of soil, is highly drought and insect resistant, requires little care aside from rough weeding, and keeps well in the ground. It is an almost perfect famine reserve crop and had been encouraged as such in Zande country, though the danger of famine was not as great there as in other parts of Africa. The processing of cassava into flour was done in two stages: The tubers were fermented in a pool or stream for three to five days, and then the resulting lumps were dried, pounded, and sifted. The process entailed much less work than the flailing, winnowing, and grinding required of eleusine. The nutritional value of cassava flour is low, however, compared with that of flour prepared from eleusine or other grains.[2]

Zande preferences coincided with the nutritional findings. They preferred most other foods to cassava, for while it was the cheapest and most available food, it was also one of the least desirable. The amount or proportion of cassava in the diet of a household provided a rough indicator of stability, since it was

2. Culwick, 1950, p. 8.

used as a substitute when other foods were not available. It was rarely eaten unmixed with other food, except in what might be considered abnormal situations: after resettlement of the entire population of an area, in urban situations, or in homesteads lacking the services of a woman.

The Azande regarded themselves as good and industrious agriculturalists, able to choose the best land and knowing the requirements of their various crops. They practiced what is usually referred to as shifting cultivation, involving the clearing of forest for small fields that were useful only for two to four years, after which they had to be allowed to regenerate the natural vegetation. It has been difficult for outsiders to detect any system underlying Zande agricultural practices,[3] and to the European eye their procedures seemed wasteful and erratic. Therefore the system of agriculture has undergone direct changes imposed by the administration.

The most recent resettlement interfered with the traditional practices by preventing the normal selection of fields for cultivation. The administrators and agriculturalists failed to distinguish between shifts in cultivations and shifts in residence, assuming that courtyards were shifted as a result of shifting the fields. The Azande, in contrast, implicitly made a distinction between residential and agricultural shifts. They regarded themselves as residentially sedentary, maintaining that they were willing to travel considerable distances from a courtyard in order to find suitable land for cultivation. The administration's attempt to stabilize the population on the land by assigning fixed plots resulted in overcultivation of portions of the plots. Chapter V goes into the relationship between residential and agricultural practices more fully.

On the whole, the Azande still managed to practice their traditional system of agriculture while I was there, but under difficulty. They consistently complained of interfering distractions, such as work for the government and for the chiefs, the labor of constructing paths and new homes in the resettlement programs, and the cultivation of cash crops. The planners of the development scheme had hoped that cotton would become ab-

3. De Schlippe, 1956, contains some codification of Zande agriculture, but as most of his information was gathered at secondhand, he tended to oversystematize Zande agricultural practices.

sorbed into the routine of Zande subsistence cultivation, but this absorption did not occur because the people regarded cotton as a nuisance and complained of the time required for its care. The important matter of cash cropping is discussed in Chapter VI.

The Azande did not keep livestock, except dogs and chickens, and had no pastoral traditions. The chickens were used largely in the poison oracle, and the dogs were valued as pets and for hunting. The Azande were without a significant domestic supply of meat, of which game was virtually the sole source. Hunting and fishing ranked high among Zande pursuits for two reasons: They were interesting activities, and they were the only means of obtaining animal food products for most of the population. The Azande are always classified as agriculturalists, but if one were to judge from the talk of the men, one would think of them as almost exclusively hunters. Even the women talked more about hunting and fishing than about agricultural matters, for while agriculture was undoubtedly important, it did not seem to be a popular topic of conversation.

Large-scale hunting was done in the dry season when the tall grass withered and dried or was burned over, for at other times visibility was virtually nil. That season was also the time, of course, when agricultural work ceased, after the harvests. During the dry seasons many families traveled to the uninhabited areas for weeks at a time in order to lay in stores of dried meat and fish for the year. Most Zande hunting was done with nets, the game being driven into them and then speared by men waiting in hiding. The nets were made in various sizes, weights, and meshes for various types of game. Several nets were erected end to end on slender poles, arranged so that the animals would cause the nets to drop and become tangled in them. Animals were driven into the nets by fire, dogs, or human trackers and beaters. A pair of good hunting dogs, male and female, were among the most valued possessions of the Azande.

Various restrictions on hunting practices were originated by the European administrations and to a considerably greater extent in the Sudan than in the other two territories. In the Sudan traps were forbidden, as was the use of fire for hunting purposes. Also there were restrictions on the numbers of elephants that might be killed in each chiefdom, and the use of nets was illegal from December through March, in order to reduce the killing of pregnant and newly born animals. Firearms were carefully registered, and permits for guns were difficult to obtain. The Azande found these restrictions hard to understand. They saw no danger of depleting the game in their country, since they regarded the reserve of animals in the uninhabited areas to be limitless. This reasoning was enhanced by the very considerable trouble they had with animal pests of all kinds in their cultivations. The only time I saw Azande lose their polite demeanor with European administrators was at a chiefs' meeting in which the district commissioner was asked why the Sudan game laws were so much more restrictive than those of French and Belgian territories. When the district commissioner replied that these regulations were designed to prevent the depletion of animals, the assemblage broke into a roar of amusement at so completely strange an idea. The administration in the Sudan had always been concerned to conserve the game, but the Azande saw in the restrictions only a major nuisance and the curtailment of their supply of meat.

Two main types of fishing were practiced. The first was done by men with strong, conical basket traps set in rapids, particularly during the dry season when the level of the rivers was low. The other type was done primarily by women and involved the damming of streams in the dry season into a series of pools. (Men might assist in the building of larger dams.) The women emptied the water out of the pools by hand, using all manner of vessels as dippers. When the pools were drained many kinds of fish, snakes, and crustacea could be picked up. Fish might also be caught by using a variety of poisons[4] known to the Azande. Some fishing was done with spears and nets, but these methods were of minor importance.

Termite collecting was a source of both excitement and food. Various kinds of termites swarm in large numbers at different intervals and at different times of the year. The Azande gave high priority to the gathering of certain kinds, such as the large ones that fly at the end of the dry season. Some termites were eaten uncooked, but the most important kinds were roasted. A fine cooking oil extracted from certain varieties was in great demand— a demand that did not seem to be at all satisfied in the days when

4. Culwick, 1950, p. 88, gives Zande and botanical designations.

I was among the Azande. The appeal of termite hunting was so great that the administration had tried to get the cotton sown early enough so that the picking would be finished by the time the major flights of termites took place. The avidity with which the Azande ate termites seems to be justified by an analysis of their nutritional components,[5] which include considerable fat and protein. Thus termites may be regarded as a source of animal food, although the exact nature and relative food value of their protein and fat are not known.

The Azande also ate other insects, such as certain types of caterpillars that were found at times in large numbers in the forests. Nothing else of insect origin, however, held the appeal of termites.

Certainly the most important item of gathered produce was the chilli pepper (*Capsicum minimum*), generally found in a semi-natural state near Zande courtyards or fields where it had been sown by bird droppings and kept clear of competing vegetation by the Azande. Since the bushes are perennial, clumps of them could be seen being cared for on the sites of fields long abandoned. The Azande sometimes attempted to sow peppers broadcast, usually along with cereals, but they said that there was very little return from pepper seeds sown in this manner. The pepper bush is evidently a recent introduction from the west. The arrival of the naturally sown bushes was observed about 1932 in the Meridi area just to the east of Zande District.[6]

These peppers were sometimes used in the food of the Azande but only in negligible amounts compared with the supply available. The peppers were gathered sporadically, whenever enough ripe ones appeared on a bush or a clump of bushes; they were dried in the sun for two or three days and stored until a trip was made to a shop where they could be sold. This activity was a casual but important part of the money economy. The total amount paid for peppers in Zande District varied tremendously from year to year, but often it was comparable with that obtained for all cotton grown in the district, even in a good year for cotton. In the estimation of the Azande, gathering chillies was a far better and easier way to make money than was raising cotton.

5. *Ibid.*, p. 140.
6. Catford, J. R., 1953, p. 157.

Next in commercial importance were beeswax and honey. These products were taken from wild hives in the bush and forest. The Azande did not erect hives as did some of their neighbors, but they would at times prepare hollow logs and other containers for possible use by wild bees. The gathering of honey and wax was particularly popular in the drier regions in the north of Zande District, where the bush affords myriad blossoms of many varieties from which bees suck nectar. Both the amount of honey gathered and the prices secured for it varied from year to year.

Little else of commercial value was obtained in Zande District. Some spices and rubber are available in the deep forest, but none of them were collected in appreciable quantities.

Numerous natural vegetative products, by contrast, were sought out for domestic use. What seemed at first glance to be a minor category of Zande life proved on closer examination to be relatively important. The Azande are excellent woodsmen and are familiar with a great variety of plants in the forest and bush that yield many products vital to the Zande economy. These can be classified as follows: (1) fibers for construction and cordage, (2) wood for carved articles, (3) firewood and charcoal, (4) materials for baskets, sieves, winnowing trays, mats, and hats, (5) timber for all construction, (6) thatching grass, (7) food and seasonings, (8) medicines and poisons, and (9) cosmetics.

Fibers were obtained from many different plants. In a short time I collected a list of 34 plants that yield fibers in common use by the Azande. Of these, only five—*Ficus* for bark cloth, sisal, Deccan hemp, banana, and pineapple—were cultivated. The fibers from wild plants were used in much greater quantity than those from cultivated plants. Fibers for construction (often bark simply stripped from plants) and for cord making consumed the greatest amounts of fibers, although plaited articles such as baskets and mats also accounted for relatively large quantities.

Even a momentary consideration of how much timber was used for construction and carving as well as for fuel indicates the important part forest timber plays in the life of the Azande. Because of its ready availability, it was generally taken for granted by Azande and outsiders alike.

Natural food products had no great value for the Azande, except in times of exceptional food shortages. They had knowledge of various vegetable products with which they would eke out their diet in times of shortages, but the reserves of cassava and sweet potatoes obviated most of the need for forest food products. The oilseed-bearing trees were the most significant uncultivated sources of food in normal times.[7] Other natural food products included a wide variety of fungi and various fruits, but none of these were collected in quantity or in a regular fashion. The private fungus beds referred to by previous observers[8] seemed to have lost their usefulness, perhaps because of the various moves of the population.

Many varieties of cultivated and natural plants were burned and the ashes dissolved in water, strained, and evaporated to obtain the chemical residue, which was used as a seasoning and had the same function and name, *tikpo*, as commercial salt. Most Azande bought commercial salt, but some women still made their own to use in conjunction with it or as a substitute.[9]

Finally, natural plant products were also used for medicinal and cosmetic purposes as well as for fish, arrow, and bee poisons. These are discussed in other works[10] but do require amplification in this study.

The Azande had no occupational specialties; that is, no one except chiefs earned his living, or expected to do so, by work other than agriculture. Most men had some skill that they might or might not practice regularly, and some spent much more time at handicrafts than did others, but none viewed his craft as we view an occupation. The occupations of the Azande would be best described as agriculture and hunting, while the handicrafts can be regarded as avocations. They may be classified as follows: (1) traditional woodworking, (2) carpentry, (3) ironworking, (4) pottery making, (5) plaiting and basket making, (6) string and net making, and (7) bark cloth making. Some of these categories obviously include more than one craft or skill.

Certain crafts were specialties of small numbers of individuals; others—mainly those in the last three categories—were nearly

7. Culwick, 1950, p. 102.
8. Seligman, 1932, p. 499.
9. See Culwick, 1950, p. 85, for a list of salt plants and pp. 111–12 for the mode of preparation.
10. DeGraer, 1929, pp. 220–51 and 361–408; Culwick, 1950, pp. 112–14 and 88–91; Evans-Pritchard, 1934, pp. 49–57.

universal. In the pre-European days, when communications were more limited and each cluster of homesteads was probably nearly self-sufficient, most of the articles needed in daily life were produced there. In my time, many of these articles were made to be sold as well as to be used in the household. All handicrafts were carried on exclusively by men, with the exception of pottery making, which could also be done by women. It might be said that the women's crafts had to do with the care of the courtyard and the preparation of food, which included beer making, a most important activity that had many of the attributes of a handicraft. Beer making was the principal means by which women could make money of their own. They also sold flour and other food products, but the most effective way to turn subsistence produce into money was to brew beer.

One major traditional craft has been lost: the smelting of iron. This was no longer practiced nor was there anyone left who knew the process. The knowledge seems to have disappeared as soon as trade goods entered the area, for iron articles were introduced by Arab traders in pre-European times. The Azande assured me that the British had deliberately stopped the smelting of iron, but there was no record of such a prohibition. Most other skills had survived to the time of this research except for the manufacture of shields, which were forbidden by the early British administration.

Two distinct categories of woodworking appear in the above list. The first includes the traditional methods of hewing articles from solid blocks of wood and of joining cylindrical sections of wood, without the use of metal fasteners, by piercing some pieces to receive the ends of others. These woodworking techniques seem to have changed little since pre-European days, and most of the articles described and illustrated by early European explorers around 1870[11] were still being made, though the more elaborate versions were difficult to find. Most wooden articles were produced for ordinary household use, so that stools, bedsteads, large wooden bowls, and wooden handles on iron tools and weapons were found in every home. Zande musical instruments were basically wooden, as exemplified by the slit gong (*gugu*), skin-covered drum (*gaza*), and harp (*kundi*).

---

11. For examples see Schweinfurth, 1878, Vol. I, p. 293.

The second category of woodworking, carpentry, was the only new Zande craft of any importance. Recently introduced articles such as tables, chairs, boxes, and house doors were made, some of them from boards obtained from packing cases but many more from boards laboriously adzed from logs. Nails might also be taken from packing cases but were on sale at most shops. Tables, chairs, and storage boxes were used mostly by the more sophisticated Azande of the centers; however, tables and chairs appeared to be considered increasingly desirable in ordinary Zande homes.

Blacksmithing had undoubtedly declined as a craft among the Azande since pre-European days, for the earliest imports included spearheads and hoe blades. During my time hoes, axes, and some types of spearheads were most often purchased from the larger shops, while knife blades, certain forms of spearheads, the butt pieces of spears, and other special articles were made locally. The large spears that had long served as a medium of exchange among the Azande and that were still used to express the bride price were also a major source of iron for local ironworking. They were broken up by the blacksmiths and manufactured into smaller articles. In some parts of Zande country blacksmiths were rather rare, but plenty were to be found in the more remote regions.

Bark cloth must have been made in almost every home in the old days, but it had been almost entirely supplanted by woven cloth at the time of my study. However, in remote regions where cloth was not easily available or where money was scarce, some bark cloth was still made. It was cheaper than woven cloth but less durable and could not be washed. It was sometimes used as bed-covering material and as a wrapping for bodies prepared for burial, as well as for men's breechcloths.

Leather working has not been listed because only raw skins were in general use. These were made into bags and coverings for harps and drums. Sometimes skins were also used for the seats in chairs, particularly folding chairs of the European pattern, as an alternative to woven rattan cane. Occasionally sandals were fashioned from raw buffalo hide as well as from old automobile tires.

A few other crafts, such as weaving, the tanning of leather, and the turning of wood and ivory, were practiced by some individuals, but these recently introduced skills played a negligible part in Zande life. The very small-scale production of clay and wooden figures and of baskets and plaited chairs, for tourists and other Europeans, was usually confined to the stations and was regarded by the Azande as the work of daily laborers for the government.

Only a few techniques, mainly carpentry, had been added to Zande crafts, and only one important skill, the smelting of iron, had been lost. The local handicrafts still produced the bulk of the articles used in daily life. Pottery making, string making, plaiting, and basketry were important activities, producing a variety of universally used articles, such as cooking utensils, storage and carrying containers, sleeping mats, and hunting nets. However, an influx of various imported goods supplemented and partially replaced items of local manufacture. The range of these goods, associated with the advent of the European administration, needs to be surveyed, to ascertain the part they played in Zande life.

IMPORTED COMMODITIES

The largest single category of imports into Zande country was piece goods. The most common garb for men was a shirt and shorts, for women a simple frock or blouse and skirt. Numerous variations in costume and even more in the state of raggedness of the clothes were observed. Most women at work did not wear much clothing, but it was unusual to see a young woman wearing only the traditional costume of leaves, one bunch in front and one at the back. Some cloth usually appeared in her costume, perhaps no more than a small piece on a string around her waist, either as a substitute for leaves or in addition to the leaves she might be wearing. In the more remote regions, or on old men, one could still see the traditional men's loincloth, but even then it was usually made of a piece of textile and rarely of bark cloth.

Clothing in the new styles was important to the Azande, but for reasons not easy to define. Coverage was not an important factor, for the Zande notions of modesty, to which they adhered strictly, had not markedly changed and still required, in general, that only the groin be covered. Warmth was a reason often put forth by Azande to explain their desire for European-styled clothing, but they used relatively few woolen garments, such as sweaters, nor did they wear blankets, which would have been the cheapest way to keep warm. Though they were universally concerned with the notion of keeping warm, particularly while sleeping, I found that they would usually buy clothing for use during the heat of the day rather than blankets for the cooler nighttime, if there was not enough money for both. Hence the common-sense virtue of warmth obviously was not the primary reason for the desire for clothing.

The most important reasons would seem to have been social ones, for the Azande quickly grasped the idea of wearing clothes for display and for prestige. Even in remote regions, where the daily working dress was very simple, almost everyone would appear in shorts, shirts, and dresses for dances and other social occasions. Most people had only one good outfit of clothing, which was carefully preserved for such affairs. The younger generation, however, particularly near the towns, liked to wear European-type clothing all the time, for work and play. The result was severe wear and tear on their clothes, for most of them could not buy more than one outfit at a time. Not only the constant wear but the often weak materials combined to make clothing short-lived and, consequently, a large item in the Zande budget.

European dress had become a necessity for social occasions, but as a prestige symbol it had rather negative implications. Little desire to outdo others, to be more conspicuous or outstandingly dressed, could be noted. Rather the desire seemed to be to conform to a certain minimum standard of dress, below which one felt himself an object of ridicule. A Zande would have a sense of shame and deficiency if he did not have a nice outfit of clothing to wear to a dance, for example.

One of my employees once came to me to borrow money. He had already drawn a considerable sum in advance because of difficulties with his wife, who had returned to her family. He was embarrassed to ask for more money, and I had heard from others that he had tried desperately to borrow elsewhere. But he said he needed money to buy a new shirt, for his only one was torn. He wanted to go to his wife's father to negotiate for her return and, he said, it would be no good going on such a mission in a torn shirt. His father-in-law would sneer at him and refuse to let his wife return to a man who couldn't manage his affairs well enough to possess good clothing.

The need for clothing, in fact, formed one of the main expressions of tension in marriage. Wives often complained that their husbands did not provide sufficient clothing for appropriate occasions. Husbands complained that their wives were continually making unreasonable demands for clothes and that women were prone to wander from husband to husband, acquiring "gifts," mainly clothing, as they went.

The prices for cloth and clothes provided one of the primary standards by which the Azande judged the adequacy of financial returns. This, as we shall see, was a major factor in the course of the development scheme.

Second only to imported cloth was the demand among the Azande for imported household utensils. In every courtyard could be seen cooking and eating utensils of enamelware, aluminum, tin plate, and glass. Along with Zande-made pots on the cooking fires were imported pots and kettles. The locally produced wooden and pottery food bowls had been replaced almost entirely by enamelware; vessels made of calabashes had been replaced by glass bottles; and gourd cups by enamel, tin, and aluminum cups. Five-gallon gasoline tins often served as containers for liquids, though many large locally made pots were still in use. Large, shallow tin basins were used, by those who could afford them, for washing clothes.

When asked why they wanted all these utensils, the Azande had a ready answer: The imported articles were stronger and lasted longer than equivalent items of their own manufacture, since containers made of clay are extremely fragile and those made of wood or gourds are liable to termite damage as well as breakage. But imported utensils had the great disadvantage of high cost. A white enameled bowl 10 inches in diameter cost about 35 piastres and a 15-inch one cost about 60 piastres, whereas a locally made porridge bowl of clay or wood, from 12 to 15 inches in diameter, cost only three to five piastres. Even so, most Azande ate from enameled bowls and plates. Great numbers of native water pots, beer pots, and cooking pots were still in use because the larger imported vessels were prohibitively expensive for the Azande. As the costs of imported goods rose, locally manufactured articles sometimes came into use again. A woodcarver who was making a large wooden bowl for washing clothes told me that he had not made any of these bowls for years, but because the prices of large tin basins had recently increased women were again asking for wooden ones. Aside from a desire to have nice imported utensils for the use of guests, most of the demand for imported household equipment was based upon the practical qualities of greater usefulness and durability.

One of the largest categories of imports was blankets. They were not so noticeable as other things in the homesteads, but their universal presence in shops gave an indication of their importance to the Azande. The blankets available to them were generally cheap cotton ones, selling from 45 to 75 piastres each. Because woolen blankets cost from two to five pounds they were much too expensive for all but a few Azande, although most persons with whom I discussed the matter were well aware of the greater warmth of woolen blankets. Blankets did not last long, for those usually purchased were of the weakest fabric and since the Azande do not generally have sheets or mattresses, the blankets were used on sleeping mats laid upon the earth floors of houses. Often they lasted less than a year, and hence the cost of blankets was a large item of expenditure.

A universal concern about blankets and a desire for more blankets was expressed by all the Azande with whom I spoke. I found quite a few persons, however, who did not have any at all and had to rely upon the fire in the center of the hut to keep warm at night, as all of them had done before blankets were available. But in my time most Azande were not content to do without blankets, and a common way of complaining about the unsatisfactory level of cash rewards was to state that members of the household had to sleep without blankets. Even those who had one or two said they needed about four to keep properly warm at night. Quite often the head of the family would express the ideal of having spare blankets for the use of guests. To be able to offer a guest blankets was a fine gesture of hospitality. The number of blankets in use in a household gave, I found, a good measure of its prosperity.

The imported articles mentioned so far were relatively low in cost, but bicycles and guns were also much desired by the Azande. When discussing imported goods, they often did not mention these items, but I learned that many households were saving most of their money toward the purchase of a bicycle. Whenever the question was asked, "If you happened to find 20 pounds, what would you do with it?" the answer, with very few exceptions, was "Buy a bicycle."[12] Some men would have preferred to buy a gun first, with a bicycle as a second choice. Compared with East Africa there were few bicycles in Zande country, but the number was mounting all the time. As cash incomes grew larger with the recent increase in commerce and trade, thousands of bicycles were sold in Zande country. Some people saved a pound or two each year for years in order to purchase one.

Bicycles were in demand because they provided a much desired increase in mobility. Whenever a Zande was asked why he wanted a bicycle or why he had bought one he would invariably reply that a bicycle enabled a person to travel more quickly. Visits could be made with little loss of time, and one was able to fulfill social obligations, such as participation in a funeral, with ease and rapidity. Bicycles also made it possible to earn money in itinerant trade or hauling produce to market. The bicycle was the only vehicle directly under the control of Zande merchants and traders, and a considerable portion of the goods bought and sold at their shops was carried on bicycles. Sometimes they traveled over 100 miles, with loads up to 100 pounds in weight on the carriers of their bicycles. The peace imposed by European rule had opened vast tracts of Zandeland, and the Azande considered the bicycle to be a fortunate accompaniment to this widened scope of travel. Also the demands of a new kind of life, such as regular wage earning, could be fitted in with the traditional Zande social obligations more easily if one had a bicycle.

Since most Azande knew about the strict control on firearms, their expressed desire for guns was usually tempered in accordance with the availability of licenses. Nevertheless, the desire was constant and universal. Those who possessed guns cherished them above all else because of their effectiveness, as compared with spears, in hunting. Most of these weapons were very old, but any gun that fired was an asset. Powder and shot were more readily available in the Belgian Congo and French Equatorial Africa than in the Sudan and formed items of local trade.

---

12. A bicycle costs about £15, or $43.

Other items in demand included simple oil lamps, nails, hinges, hasps, locks, salt, soap, matches, cigarettes, and kerosene, none of which were as important to the Azande as the categories already noted.

Another class of products was purchased by the more sophisticated and wealthy, including such luxury items as wristwatches, pressure lamps, phonographs, radios, suit and uniform jackets, long trousers, and raincoats. The demand for these products was still confined to clerks, technicians, teachers, traders, and young chiefs. Most Azande said that they would not buy these things if they could afford them. Rather, they would buy extra cotton clothing, woolen coats and sweaters, blankets, bicycles, guns, more household utensils, and more furniture. They wanted their children, however, to belong to the class that could buy wristwatches and phonographs.

So far, money has been mentioned only in connection with imported goods. Since the introduction of money and wages may well be the most important change in the economic organization of the Azande, let us review briefly the commercial history of Zande District and then investigate the influence of money on the subsistence economy.

COMMERCIAL DEVELOPMENT

Zande District contained no valuable natural resources. It was remote, communications were poor, and transport was expensive. In other areas in Africa, these disadvantages have often led part of the population to migrate in order to earn money, but this had not occurred to any appreciable extent with the Azande. True, a few individuals had left the district to find work. Indeed as early as 1920 a tendency was noted for some young men to go to Wau and even to Khartoum in search of jobs.[13] I have met Azande in Khartoum and Kampala and heard of individuals working in Egypt, Kenya, and Tanganyika. They were few in number, however, and tended to stay away for many years. The relatively small number of migrants from Zande District was probably largely due to the difficulty of traveling back and forth and the lack of possibility for employment within any convenient distance. The Azande them-

13. Larkin, 1955, p. 6.

selves stated that they did not go away to work because they were fond of their own country. This sentiment is not unique to them, but because there was no shortage of land they were not forced to go away to earn money for taxes and for the few imported things they needed.

Money and trade followed the advent of European civil administration and the opening of roads, but the economic development of the area remained at a relatively low level. Considerable export of ivory took place in the first years of British administration, for many elephant tusks had been hidden away during the previous disturbed years.[14] After the surplus of ivory had been disposed of, the only source of cash for many years was the sale of small amounts of forest produce and the wages paid by the administration. When taxes were introduced in the 1920's, many men were not able to pay five piastres (then worth about 25 cents) a year in cash, but worked on the roads for five days in lieu of payment. The development of a small trade in chilli peppers gradually provided enough money for most men to pay their taxes in cash, and with a boom in the sale of peppers in the early 1930's, poll-tax labor became scarce. In 1932, the year in which the first district commissioner retired, the export of chilli peppers from Zande District totaled 70 tons, and by 1934 it had jumped to more than 600 tons. The influx of money had immediate effects on the number of shops in the district. Whereas only six "bush" shops were licensed in 1931, there were 17 in 1932 and more than 100 by the end of 1934.[15] All these small shops in outlying regions were operated by Azande, most of them working as agents of the Greek and northern Sudanese merchants who owned large shops in the towns. An increased demand for imports, including cotton cloth, hats, shoes, and bicycles, was reported,[16] and the second district commissioner was concerned lest there might be an unsettling temporary increase in wealth. However, the demand for chilli peppers and the price dropped sharply in 1935, and Zande District was depressed by the effects of the world economic slump for a number of years. During this period activity was confined to maintenance and to minor administrative changes.[17]

14. *Ibid.*, p. 49.
15. Zande District Handbook, 1936, pp. 82–83.
16. *Ibid.*, pp. 69 and 73.
17. *Ibid.*, 1954, p. 8.

The vigorous expansion of the road system stands in contrast to the weak commercial development of the district. The roads were necessary for the regular sleeping sickness inspections of the entire population, and by 1934 about 1,500 miles of all-weather earth and gravel roads had been constructed in Zande District. Motor vehicles had penetrated to the district in the early 1920's and had become the sole means of transport, eliminating porterage as a means of earning money among the Azande. Administration and medical services were motorized from the early 1920's on. In 1934 over a dozen private motor vehicles, mostly trucks belonging to the merchants of the towns, were licensed in the district.[18]

A big change came with the beginning of the Second World War, which coincided with the relaxing of most of the sleeping sickness restrictions in Zande District. The war years brought great commercial activity to the province. Much military equipment and personnel were shipped across Africa and down the Nile to the forces in Egypt. The cutting off of the ordinary routes through the Mediterranean and the Red Sea made it necessary to use the more difficult trans-African routes, which concentrated on Juba, the southernmost point of navigation on the Nile. The road link with the Belgian Congo was greatly improved, and an entirely new route was constructed to Juba from the railhead in northern Uganda. Equipment also moved by road across Zande District from French Equatorial Africa.

The entire province was affected. Large numbers of men were needed as laborers, and others joined the military forces. In 1942 alone, 2,365 conscript laborers were provided from Zande District, and 539 Zande men joined the Pioneer Corps.[19] The laborers were needed in Juba, 300 miles and more from their homes. The men in the military forces went as far afield as Eritrea and Burma. Almost all of them returned home, but Zande country had become less isolated through the improvement of communications and through the knowledge its people had gained of other places.

For the Azande, along with the other residents of the province, payments for labor and service brought an increase in cash income during the wartime period of great activity about Juba. The amount of currency introduced into the province was almost nine

18. *Ibid.*, 1936, p. 78.
19. Wyld, in Beaton, 1949, p. 33.

times greater in 1942 than in 1939. When the enemy forces were defeated in Libya, the activity on the Nile rapidly diminished, and by 1944 the figure dropped to about twice that of 1939.[20] The improvement of the roads in Equatoria Province during the war contributed to a higher level of commerce in Zande District than in prewar years, which meant a considerable increase in money coming into the district even before the beginning of the development scheme in 1946. Prosperity was then enhanced by the construction work required for the Zande Scheme and by the increasing returns for cotton. Most of the development money was spent in Zande District, but the rest of the province benefited, too, particularly those regions lying along the routes traveled by trucks transporting goods from Juba to Nzara.[21]

FIGURE 7
CASH INCOME FOR ZANDE DISTRICT, 1931 TO 1951*

Year	A Paid to cultivators for cotton	B Total paid for produce (includes A)	C Total money put into circulation (includes A and B)
1931	‡	‡	£ 1,000
1936	‡	£ 3,000	11,000
1942	‡	17,000	‡
1943	£ 370	19,200	27,700
1944	950	21,800	29,500
1945	500	22,200	33,700
1946	1,100	26,600	55,400
1947	3,900	29,000	95,900
1948	22,600	43,900	122,600
1949	21,600	48,500	138,300
1950	85,000	120,000†	190,000†
1951	64,500	130,000†	‡

*Beaton, 1949, p.32; Zande District annual reports, 1936–52; and Wyld, 1949, p. 52.
†Approximation
‡Not available

Figure 7 shows the marked increase in the amount of money available to the Azande in the years following the start of the Scheme. Chillies, honey, and beeswax were in demand, and the

20. Beaton, 1949, p. 181.
21. An example of this is the temporary increase in the trade in grain at Meridi; see Catford, 1953, pp. 158–59.

favorable prices held firm. Cotton also became a major source of cash in 1948 and brought relatively large sums of money to the Azande in the following three years. Wages paid for labor, however, put the largest amount of money into circulation. The total figure can be somewhat misleading, in that the amount paid to the individual Zande was not great, either in his estimation or in fact; but since the total amount of labor performed *was* great, the money disbursed was considerable. A corresponding increase occurred in the imports of the district, particularly as goods became more available after severe wartime shortages of consumer items.

In earlier times little money had flowed into Zande country, even in comparison with other parts of Africa. Nonetheless the Azande had been using money for about 50 years and were familiar with it as a medium of exchange. Virtually all economic transactions among themselves, as well as those with the outside world, involved money. But to them money had a different role or, more accurately, a different set of roles than in more industrialized societies. These roles should be amplified.

THE ROLE OF MONEY

What did money mean to the Azande? When they were asked why they wanted money, they would first say that it enabled them to pay their taxes and buy the goods available in the shops. On further questioning they would mention expenditures for marriage payments, costs of feasts, gifts, and finally savings. The Azande saw money primarily as a special commodity required in the shops for the exchange for certain goods that could not be manufactured in their subsistence economy—chiefly clothing, blankets, various household utensils, bicycles, and guns. These things were not indispensable, but they had been a part of Zande life for a long time. The people expressed a desire for the imported articles and in order to acquire them they had to exchange subsistence goods for money or enter into relationships that would provide cash rewards for labor performed. Questions as to why food and other articles were being sold in the markets or why individuals were working for wages inevitably were answered in terms of the need for money to buy imported goods. When I asked a woman why she was selling flour in a market, she replied, "I am selling it for money." When I asked why she wanted money, she pointed to the shops and said they were full of things she needed. The Azande, far from resenting the intrusion of imported goods into their lives, resented only their inability to obtain a greater quantity and variety of these goods. So everybody wanted more money.

Despite this preoccupation with money and imported goods, these goods satisfied only a small part of the total needs of a family. The subsistence economy was still extremely important, and the productive activities of the individual household had changed relatively little in contrast with the profound changes in the political organization and territorial distribution of the Azande. By far the greatest portion of the subsistence goods consumed by any family at the time of my observations was produced by its members, and most of the productive economy of the Azande was not involved in any exchange or money transactions.

The importance of subsistence agriculture in the economy of the Azande is immediately obvious when one considers that the ordinary Zande almost never bought food, except perhaps salt, as a regular procedure. He might buy an occasional cup of beer, a piece of meat or some fish, but these were luxuries. For at least 95 per cent of the population—that is, for people other than daily laborers, traders, teachers, and clerks—virtually all the food consumed was grown locally, usually by the household that consumed it. This fact was the tacit basis for the development of Zande District. Even the permanent laborers depended heavily on the food that they and the other members of their households could raise. The special cases, representing a tiny fraction of the population, were those people who had to live on what they could buy or, more frequently, supplemented their diet by purchased food. The difficulties of this group resulted not only in a poor diet but in a profound dissatisfaction with their rates of pay. The best solution, not always possible, for one of these persons was to attach himself to a homestead as a temporary or permanent member, sharing in its subsistence economy.

Since the subsistence economy still produced most of the things required for daily life and, in a pinch, could produce everything essential, we can say that the Azande had a "pin-money" economy. They wanted money primarily to buy extras, not to live on. A consistent characteristic of the Zande use of money emerged from the investigation of cash expenditures: Almost nothing was spent for daily subsistence, even among families with members earning regular wages. This principle was verbalized by the Azande who stated that they did not like to spend money on food or shelter. Even town laborers regarded money spent merely to live as "wasted."

The pin-money economy is illustrated by the manner in which the Azande made most of their money before the introduction of cotton as a cash crop. The gathering of forest produce was a sideline that did not interfere with the ordinary work of earning a living—that is, cultivating, hunting, gathering, working on crafts, and doing housework. The chilli pepper was perfectly appropriate to the money it earned: It was sown largely by the birds, then casually tended, harvested, and sold as a minor part of household activities. The money received played a correspondingly minor role in the life of the household.

The pin-money aspect of Zande economy can also be demonstrated by an examination of the cash income figures for Zande District. If the figures for 1936 and 1950 in Figure 7 are divided by 50,000, which is the approximate number of households in Zande District, the average cash income for one household was about 22 piastres (about $1.10) in 1936 and 380 piastres (about $10.85) in 1950. The European administrators usually stressed this enormous increase in cash income, but if the prices of goods in the shops are considered, even the higher figure is of little significance. It is of still less significance if the potential cost of the subsistence of a family is considered. No method has yet been devised for assigning monetary value to the things produced by a subsistence economy, but a hypothetical figure will suffice to make this point: Thirty cents a day per person yields a total cost of about $110 per person per year, or about $385 per year for an average-size household in Zande District. This minimal figure illustrates the importance of the subsistence economy in relation to money income.

Here, then, was the Zande view: Money was a special commodity, a sideline to ordinary life. But this was only a part of the story of money in the Zande economy. Money played an important role in the subsistence economy—one not grasped clearly by the Azande themselves. Investigations into the cash income and expenditure of households in various parts of the district revealed that the cash income varied greatly from one household to the next and from one region to another. The biggest regional difference was related to the proximity or remoteness of towns, since the cultivators close to the towns often augmented their cash income by selling produce in the town markets. For households close to the towns the sale of agricultural produce, plus forest produce, provided more money, almost without exception, than did the sale of cotton. In the remote regions, on the other hand, the sale of cotton accounted for more of the cash income, although the total income tended to be smaller. In a sample of 25 households in a subchiefship between Yambio and Nzara, the income ranged from £2 to £18 per year, with a median figure of £8. In a similar sample 20 miles west of Nzara, the household incomes for one year ranged from £1 to £9, with a median figure of £2. In all but three of these 50 households the expenditures for food were less than £1 each a year. For the most part meat was usually the largest item of food bought for money. In the three cases in which greater amounts of money had been spent on subsistence items, food and beer had been purchased for funeral feasts. The amount of cash income had little relation to the amount of money spent for subsistence commodities, since the latter expenditure was generally determined by the social obligations of a household rather than by the amount of its income.

No family, I found, spent all its cash income for goods in the shops. To my inquiries about cash expenditures, the first responses always had to do with the amounts spent for taxes and for imported goods. Further probing was usually necessary to bring out expenditures for marriage payments, contributions to feasts, and gifts. A distinction is implicit between the subsistence goods used for ordinary life within the household and those required for broader social purposes. While money should not be used for ordinary needs, it could be expended to meet social obligations.

Along with this distinction we can note a certain hierarchy of exchangeability[22] in the Azande's use of money. They believed it commendable to convert subsistence goods into money, but they did not want to reverse the process. Money could be freely exchanged for imported goods but not for subsistence goods unless—and this is important—these were needed to meet some social

22. I am indebted to Steiner, 1954, and Bohannan, 1955, for the exposition of the principles of exchanges and related ideas used here.

obligations. This same sort of limited exchangeability can be seen in the former use of spears for marriage payments. The father who received the spears at the marriage of a daughter could, in theory, use them as he pleased. He could, if he wanted, exchange them for subsistence goods for his own use, but he was in fact morally bound to use them for arranging other marriages, especially if he had sons. If he squandered the spears he met with the disapproval of the community. An alternative approved use of spears was for the purchase of food and beer for a funeral feast or some other social obligation.[23] Marriage payments were never cited as income, in my experience, although they were often mentioned as expenditures—which would seem to demonstrate the irreversibility of the spheres of exchange.

Money has now been substituted for marriage spears, but the money payments are still referred to as "spears." However, money cannot be said to have been a simple substitute for spears, as it had a much wider range of exchangeability and was much more generally available than spears had been. Not only were spears scarcer than money, but they tended also to pass more exclusively through certain channels. In effect, spears had a narrower range of uses than money, which was a common denominator in all kinds of exchanges. This more general nature of money had far-reaching implications. For example, the introduction of wages and the substitution of money for spears as marriage payments had contributed to profound changes in certain family relationships, particularly the father-son relationship, as described in Chapter III.

Money differed from anything else in the Zande economy in the relative ease with which it could be accumulated and stored; spears were scarcer, were socially marked, and could not be hoarded as readily as money. In my time surplus money was converted into silver coins and buried away, and such hoards were not destroyed upon the death of individuals. Discrepancies between income and expenditure were most often explained by savings, but when families were questioned about the disposition of their cash incomes, they mentioned savings last. Almost all families were found to save money when possible. Some said that they were saving for large purchases, usually bicycles; others, that they were

23. Seligman, 1932, p. 513.

saving for social emergencies. Savings seem to have become markedly greater, while cash expenditures in the shops had not risen with the recent increases in cash income reported for the district in general.

Increased savings seemed to be accompanied by increased use of money for social purposes. Contrary to all expectations, including those of the Azande, larger cash incomes had not resulted in correspondingly larger expenditures for imported goods. The Azande themselves had assumed that when they had more money they would use it to buy more European goods, thereby becoming more like the Europeans. Instead, there seemed to be a distinct tendency to substitute money for the goods and services required for social obligations. The special nature of money was clearly illustrated in that it had become a preferred form of gift to relatives and friends. In any relationship in which gifts were exchanged, a small present of money was considered to be most appropriate. Even the chiefs expected gifts of money from their followers, which appeared to be given and accepted in the same spirit as gifts of goods and services. But money, by its very nature, does not force the redistribution of wealth as do grain, beer, and other perishables. Similarly, money was often given in lieu of beer or food contributions to feasts sponsored by relatives, so that the sponsor could make the necessary purchases for the feast. I know of some occasions when money contributions were specifically solicited, particularly when meat was required and could be obtained most readily by purchase, either from the butchers in the towns or from the Azande of French Equatorial Africa, who had more time for hunting and greater surpluses of meat. Another use of money in the realm of social obligations appeared when a man came to borrow money from me, explaining that he had not attended the funeral of a relative of his wife and therefore had been "fined" 20 piastres by his father-in-law for failure to perform his obligatory duty as son-in-law. Such obligations could weigh heavily on the Azande, and they found it convenient to have reserves of cash with which to meet social emergencies.

In comparing the cash expenditures of the 50 households mentioned above, I found that those in the subchiefship between Yambio and Nzara used money in the purchase of commodities needed for feasts or for ordinary hospitality more than did households in the lower income area. Money was also used more often as gifts to relatives and for contributions, in lieu of subsistence commodities, to the feasts given by relatives. In the higher income area there was more local trade in subsistence commodities. The persons who sold grain, flour, meat, or beer to someone else for use in the execution of social duties presumably exchanged the money they earned for either imported goods or other subsistence goods. This indicated the beginning of a trade based upon money, which ultimately could have had a wide influence on the Zande way of life. As of 1955, however, the acceptance of money as a medium of exchange had not created a dominant money economy, for Zande usage imposed limits on the use of money, especially for everyday subsistence items. Therefore, despite an increase of trade in subsistence goods—in connection with social obligations—little occupational specialization had developed, and the subsistence economy remained one of the least altered aspects of Zande life under European administration.

The use of money as a medium of exchange does not mean that the Azande had taken over all European ideas about money. Not even its specific nature was yet appreciated, as demonstrated in the use of money as gifts among kin and others. It was not good, according to the Azande, to specify the time or the amount of the return for a gift or service. Nor was it expected or desired that the return be exactly the same as the gift or service. Probably almost everyone kept mental notes of the exchanges in the relationships in which he participated, but it was generally considered bad taste to verbalize the accounting. While money seemed to be becoming more and more the accepted form of gifts as cash incomes increased, the very preciseness of its value was an awkward feature because the amount of the gift could be too easily recalled in cases of friction and dispute.

In Chapter III it was noted that the appearance of the Zande courtyard had been altered hardly at all from the pre-European form. Now it is possible to state that the activities associated with it had also changed little since pre-European times, despite the introduction of wages, money, and imported goods. A point of no return had not yet been reached in subsistence activities, in my judgment, because there had been no change drastic enough to prevent a relatively easy reversion to almost complete self-sufficiency in each household or cluster of households. The household's subsistence activities still produced the major part of all goods consumed in that establishment. Although certain changes have been stressed, they have been relatively unimportant in the total subsistence economy.

There seems to be little doubt, however, that if observed trends had continued and the money available had been increased, Zande society would eventually have been profoundly affected by the nature of money. As we have seen, it had already wrought some changes in a number of different aspects of Zande life. Chapter II describes its effect upon the patron-client relationship and the associated standards of material returns. Chapter III discusses the effect of money and wages upon the father-son relationship, the significance of the marriage payment, and the importance of imported clothes in marital friction. And Chapter VI notes the importance of money as a gauge of adequacy of rewards. Money is one of the most pervasive themes in this report, despite its relatively slight effect on the subsistence of the Azande.

V

TERRITORIAL CHANGES

In social studies of tribal peoples, information about residential patterns and territorial distribution is generally regarded as essential. But at the beginning of my research among the Azande, I could see that little could be accomplished by this kind of investigation, since the Zande people in all three countries had been moved from their traditional homes. In the Sudan they had been moved as many as four times, the last move resulting in a completely arbitrary settlement. In time, however, it became evident that the reasons for the difficulties inherent in the latest resettlement of the population of Zande District of the Sudan would have to be investigated in order to throw light on the residential requirements of the Azande. I attempt to do this by reviewing the traditional residential organization and summarizing the moves the population has undergone, while comparing the assumptions of the European planners with Zande notions about residence.

Although the resettlement program came to be regarded as a necessary and inseparable part of the development scheme, it is best for our purposes to consider resettlement separately from the introduction of cash crops. This chapter will deal with the effects of resettlement from the point of view of changes in residential patterns, and the development scheme proper will be reserved for the following chapter. This separation is not as arbitrary as it might seem to one accustomed to the mode of thought of the later years of the Zande Scheme. Resettlement was not included in the original proposals for the Scheme, nor has it been found necessary for similar types of cash cropping in other parts of the Sudan or in Uganda.

PRE-EUROPEAN TERRITORIAL ORGANIZATION

The Azande had been agriculturalists with no clearly defined residential organization. Their original pattern of settlement had been along the streams that abound in the territory. They did not form multiple units or extended households, and in pre-European times, as in my time, the basic unit was the household of one man with his wives, children, and dependent relatives. In pre-European times clusters of homesteads, each at some distance and well screened from the others, were located along the abundant streams. No kinship theme was discernible in this grouping, although there was a tendency to settle near relatives, either affinal or consanguineal.

Zande memories appeared to be quite short, and no one could be found who had clear recollections of life before the population was first moved by the European administration about 30 years before my inquiries. But the consensus was strong, if probably quite idealized, that things were very different then, mainly because sons were much more dependent on their parents. A young unmarried man had depended upon his mother for food and therefore usually lived in the homestead of his father, either in the main courtyard or in an adjoining one, and he had been dependent mainly on his father for the acquisition of the spears needed for his marriage payment. Young men had married much later than they did at the time of my investigations and had lived with their parents longer. A boy had lived in his father's home and had worked for him until he became a warrior. The eldest son would be second to the head of the household and would probably make his homestead near at hand when he got married. My informants told me that there had been no rules as to where a man would settle but that usually some of the sons of a household would make their homes nearby. Others might go farther away, though probably not any great distance since they would be expected to return to help their father in his building work and his cultivations. At the same time the Azande stressed the freedom of choice a man had had in selecting the site for his homestead and cultivations. When a man married, he might settle down near his father, or he might choose to live near another relative or a friend.

A girl had lived in the homestead of her father until she married, visiting the home of her future husband at intervals. She had retained a strong attachment to her parents and siblings, visited them a good deal, depended upon them to take her part in case of difficulties, and moved back to her father's home if the marriage broke up.

The Azande, with the exception of the ruling clan, did not trace their descent for more than three or four generations, and they did not have lineages or descent groups of any importance. They had patrilineal clans, literally hundreds of them, and each person was a member of a certain clan.[1] The clans, except for the ruling one, were exogamous units, and kinship terms were extended to the members of one's own clan and of one's mother's clan. A tradition of reciprocal hospitality existed among clan members. The Azande said that members of certain clans used to live together, but such concentrations no longer existed. The clans had had no corporate functions or activities other than reciprocal hospitality. Their members were scattered widely over Zande territory when I studied them.

If the clans had ever had much function or importance in the political or territorial organization of the Azande, it has been replaced by the centralized political organization under their chiefs. The choice of locale for the homesteads of young men was probably influenced by the personalities of individual patrons as well as by kin. That is, although a man would tend to be oriented to his father's house, his choice of locale might also be influenced by preference for a certain important man as a patron.

My informants' reconstruction of the past seemed so vague and unsystematic that I doubted their memories, but a survey of the literature showed that the traditional Zande territorial distribution had indeed been as diffuse as I had been told it was. Early explorers found no regular concentrations of population,

---

1. Evans-Pritchard, 1956(b), 1956(c), 1959, 1960(b), and 1961, gives much information about clans and their totems.

such as villages or towns, in Zande country. They wrote that the homesteads of single families were separated by cultivations and forests, though neighbors were often relatives. A chief's deputy selected a site near a stream, and along its banks in the vicinity were located the homes of his relatives and of his clients.[2]

SUMMARY OF THE MOVES

The original distribution of the Zande population was changed by a number of events in recent history. The first direct changes came as a result of the discovery of sleeping sickness in the area. During the 1920's the population was resettled along the roads in order to facilitate medical inspection and get the people away from the tsetse fly, which carries the disease but does not travel more than about 300 yards from the dense forest along the streams. The roads were on high ground, which is generally free of the fly. Clearly, in all three countries administrative advantages also accrued from this resettlement of the population. Members of the administration and the medical corps in the Sudan believed that the benefits of the move outweighed the difficulties,[3] although they recognized the disruption it brought to the life of the people. The Azande in the Sudan, in addition to being removed from their preferred locations along the streams, were forbidden by a forest conservation ordinance to cultivate within 150 yards of a stream, thereby being deprived of the land they considered most suitable for cultivation.

The next change in the Sudan came in 1940 when the sleeping sickness precautions were relaxed because of the decrease in the number of cases of the illness. The results of this change are extremely difficult to assess. People were no longer required to live along the roads, but no records are available to tell how many of them moved and whether they moved to other places on the roads or into the forest. Although the official version was that there was merely a relaxation of regulations, the Azande recall it as an enforced move away from the roads and designated it by the English

2. See Schweinfurth, 1878, p. 287; Seligman, 1932, pp. 498–500; Evans-Pritchard, 1937, p. 14.

3. Larkin, 1955, pp. 56–57; Larkin, typescript notes, Tembura Subdistrict file No. 60; Maurice, 1930, p. 236.

expression "number two," i.e., the second movement of the population under British administration. Evidently a good deal of confusion prevailed. Chiefs have told me that they had a hard time
keeping track of their people during this wartime period, when the
region played an important part in supplying the campaigns in
northern Africa. The second district commissioner, who had taken
the post in 1932 and was interested in agricultural development,
expressed deep concern at the time that the scattering of the population would produce great difficulties for agricultural supervision.[4]

By 1943 Zande District was designated as the scene of an experiment to test the possibilities for social and economic development in the southern Sudan. At early planning meetings the
second district commissioner broached the subject of how cotton
was to be grown and advocated the resettling of the 15,000 families that were to cultivate cash crops on the model of the three
"community farms" he had organized during the Second World
War. The purpose of such resettlement was to facilitate the supervision of cotton cultivation and to insure conservation of soil and
forests.[5] At the same time he was in favor of separate family cotton
plots and opposed to communal plantations because of the greater
danger of plant disease and soil erosion in large fields. The governor of Equatoria Province approved of the general idea of "mod-
ifying the existing social system and some resettlement on a village
basis," in order to provide for "rational use of the land and forest." At the same time he viewed the matter of "villagization" as
distinct from the main problem of development and suggested that
separate files be set up for the two subjects.[6] The district commissioner, however, proceeded on the assumption that "villagization" was an indispensable requisite to development and cotton
growing, and went ahead with the resettlement of 5,000 homesteads in the Yambio area during the dry season early in 1946. He
was highly gratified with the response of the Azande to his appeals
and noted that the work had gone more quickly than he had dared
hope.[7] Since other officials did not share his enthusiasm, he issued

4. Letter, Zande District file No. 2.M.2, 28 January 1941.
5. Ministry of Agriculture file No. Z-1, Vol. 1, pp. 84–87, and letter, Zande District
file No. 2.B.3/1, 7 August 1945.
6. Letter, Equatoria Province Headquarters file No. 2.R.1, 12 July 1945.
7. Letter, Zande District file No. 2.B.L/1, Yambio, 9 March 1946.

a firm statement that resettlement was necessary in order "to comply with the fundamental principle of the Scheme that there should be no expansion of cotton growing without adequate agricultural supervision."

The governor again gave his support, maintaining that the policy of resettlement was based on agreements made at the earlier meetings, though not recorded in the minutes of the meetings. He was convinced that the Zande Scheme could be successful only if the agricultural activities were adequately supervised from the start and that this would be possible only if the Azande were regrouped into "manageable units."[8]

The provincial senior inspector of agriculture objected at this point to the manner in which the need for resettlement had been described. He disapproved of the implication that Zande resettlement was being undertaken purely to facilitate agricultural supervision, for he believed it was being carried out as much for administrative purposes as for agricultural purposes. He granted that there should be adequate supervision of cash-crop cultivation and, further, that resettlement would simplify supervision. He maintained, however, that "adequate supervision is quite possible without resettlement" if sufficient well-trained staff were available. He pointed out that there had not been any sort of resettlement during the development of rain-grown cotton in the Sudan in the previous 20 years. He was convinced that cotton cultivation should not be confined to those Azande who had been resettled.[9]

The issue came to a test in the meeting of the Equatoria Projects Provisional Working Committee, held in Yambio in March 1946, when the district commissioner submitted the proposal that cotton growing should be confined to areas which had been resettled. The director of agriculture, as chairman, reminded the meeting of the utmost importance of soil conservation and stressed the need for careful siting of cotton plots; he considered that supervision would be most effective in resettled areas. The committee agreed to the policy and, with this, resettlement became wedded to the Zande Scheme.

The district commissioner had his way on this subject thereafter, although there is record of disagreement from time to time

---

8. Letter, Equatoria Province file No. 2.R.1, Juba, 5 February 1946.
9. Letter, Department of Agriculture (Juba) file No. ZE/2.M.1/4, 19 February 1946.

with his policy of resettlement. Nothing came, for example, of an observation made by the inspector of agriculture for Zande District at the end of the first year of resettlement: that it would have been better to allow the people to choose the land for cultivation within the unit area, while assigned regular places for the homesteads, than to restrict each family to a specific strip of land.[10]

More than 5,000 families had already been resettled at the time of that controversy, some on areas that had been chosen for plantation crops such as sugar cane, coffee, and oil palm. As it happened, this contradiction of stated plans did not cause much difficulty, for the planners showed little enthusiasm for cash crops other than cotton. Cotton was introduced into the areas originally intended for other crops, so that the people already resettled would not be left without a cash crop to cultivate—which was, after all, the stated reason for resettlement. Any lack of coordination between plans for resettlement and for cash cropping was resolved in this manner, after the resettlement of a portion of the population.

The district commissioner's plan was to form "villages" on an "H Plan," each based on three roads or paths and containing 50 families. Each family was to be assigned a 40-acre plot of land with a frontage of 150 meters on one of the roads or paths forming the H, as shown in Figure 8. Each village was to have a headman living at the center, and a central location was to be selected for a "village green and meeting place."[11] The H Plan village could have become, according to an enthusiastic observer, a centralized village community with its own register, a collecting center for cotton, and possibly a school and dispensary.[12] A system of crop rotation and fallow, followed in a set sequence by each householder, was to be directed by the agricultural staff.[13] About four acres would be under cultivation in the average homestead when it was fully established, with the rest of the plot in fallow or unbroken ground. The cultivation strips were to be across the slope of the land, with grass strips between them to prevent erosion. As conservation measures, all rocky hills and outcrops were to be

10. Zande District file No. 2.B.3/1, pp. 180–82.
11. Zande District file No. 2.B.3/1, pp. 38 and 52.
12. Wright, 1947.
13. Letter, Zande District file No. 2.B.3/1, 25 January 1946.

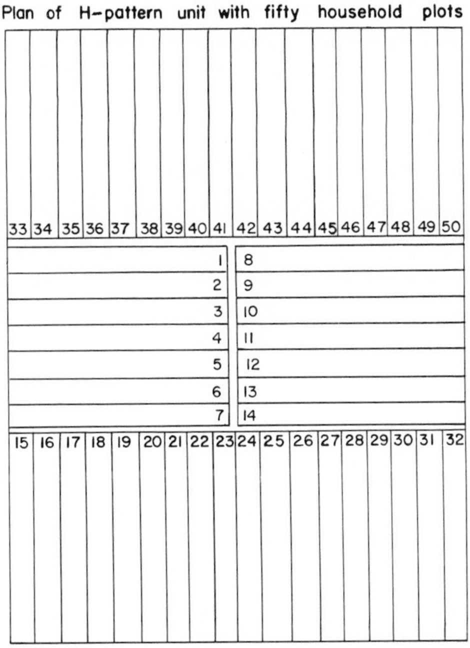

Plan of H-pattern unit with fifty household plots

Plan of straight-line unit with fifty household plots

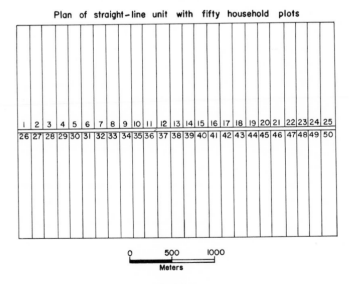

FIGURE 8

FIGURE 9

allowed to vegetate naturally, no cultivation was to be permitted within 150 yards of any stream, and forest reserves were to be set aside. A program for growing trees to be used for building poles was suggested. Its purpose was to improve the supply while reducing the drain on forest reserves.

Resettlement on this general pattern proceeded in the area southeast of Yambio during the dry season of 1945–46. It was necessary, owing to the lack of information and accurate maps, to cut long, straight lines from the roads for distances of as much as 15 miles. After the distances along these lines to the principal natural features, such as hills and rivers had been measured, the district commissioner called meetings of the subchiefs and headmen to allocate, after discussion with them, the sites for that area. It was found convenient to use the long lines cut through the bush as pilot lines on which to base the new "villages." Each pilot line was assigned to one or more subchiefs, and the units under them were based on the pilot lines rather than on existing roads, as had been envisaged.

Difficulties in applying the H pattern became evident during this first season of resettlement. Many deviations occurred from the standard plan, either through misunderstandings or because of irregularities of terrain. A number of units were found to be overlapping, and confusion had arisen about the length and relationship of the unit lines. Some homesteads had been placed outward from the village boundaries rather than from the paths, and the ultimate limits of these homesteads were difficult to determine. When some of the units had been laid out as a series of straight lines, either to follow the courses of streams or by error, a straight-line plan was found to be more convenient and more readily understood than the H pattern.[14] The plan for the resettlement of the rest of the district was changed to a straight-line pattern, with 50 family plots arranged along a straight bicycle path, 25 on each side, as in Figure 9. This was done because of greater speed and ease of layout, with less likelihood of errors. It also meant less work for the people, although the administration recognized that there might be more difficulty in finding suitable water supplies. No provision was made for a community center in the straight-line pattern, as there had been for the H

14. Zande District file No. 2.B.3/1, pp. 180–82.

pattern. After the first year, the term "resettlement" was used almost exclusively. The term "villagization" was dropped, and terms such as "compact," "closeness," or "concentration," which had been freely used in planning the resettlement, were employed less and less.

The district commissioner who had been almost solely responsible for obtaining the official approval of the policy of mass resettlement was to have a predominant role in putting the policy into practice; he personally directed the resettlement of most of the population of Zande District. The governor of Equatoria Province considered the second district commissioner to possess a virtual monopoly of knowledge about the Zande people as a result of service in the district since 1932. Therefore the governor appointed him resettlement and liaison officer for four years beginning in mid-1946, when he was relieved of administrative duties and another district commissioner appointed.

The justification for resettlement was that no one should grow a cash crop until the proper agricultural supervision was assured, but the resettlement policy was altered gradually from a preparation for the development of cash crops into a universal move for the population of the district. By the spring of 1950 almost 50,000 families had been resettled, comprising the entire population of the district aside from a few families in the northernmost areas. The original development plans, however, had called only for about one fifth of the families of the district to cultivate cotton. The area of resettlement greatly exceeded the original area designated for cotton cultivation—i.e., land within a 50-mile radius of the ginnery—and extended far beyond the recognized limits of regions suitable for the cultivation of cotton. Resettlement was supposed to be a preliminary step to the introduction of a cash crop, but since cotton was the only peasant cash crop developed, there was a tendency to introduce it throughout the district, reinforced by the spectacular increase in the world prices for cotton. Even so, many resettled Azande in areas definitely unsuitable for cotton were to be left without a cash crop.

The second district commissioner, who had conceived and carried out the resettlement, summarized the motivations for "this apparently drastic measure" in a lecture in London in 1951:

. . . At the earliest meeting on the matter it was decided that safeguards for the countryside and the soil must be provided through the provision of adequate agricultural supervision to insist on methods of good husbandry. This naturally included the protection of forests. It appeared immediately that no form of agricultural control could be imposed without an impossibly large staff of both British and native supervision if the people were allowed to dwell at their own sweet will, scattered through the unmapped forest. Advantageous use must be made of the most fertile land and natural water supplies. Forest reserves must be created.

The object throughout has been to interfere as little as possible with the people's own way of life. Before S.S. [sleeping sickness] measures were imposed, the Zande lived in scattered groups (not by clans) often widely separated and with little intercommunication. The problem therefore was to retain this natural group system but to make the groups more accessible, to ensure that each family had adequate land of good quality as far as possible and adequate water, without constant shifts. The operation of resettlement had to be one that could be carried out by the D. C. [district commissioner] with the assistance of locally trained personnel under the control of the chiefs, subchiefs, and headmen. It was obvious that such an operation could only be carried out with the support and cooperation of the chiefs and the good will of the people.[15]

This and other statements implied that the best features of the old and new systems were to be obtained for the Azande. They were to be regrouped in a manner similar to their traditional distribution, but their homesteads would be more accessible and arranged in an orderly fashion. They were to have a cash crop but were to be protected from exploitation and the evils of commercialism. Agricultural methods were to be introduced to improve, but not to disturb, the traditional system of agriculture and to obviate further moves to find land. The protection of natural resources was to be ensured, while utilizing the best soils and water supplies. In addition, a better system of registration of the population would be developed, medical facilities established, and other public health measures introduced. These laudable intentions were, however, difficult to put into practice. From the start of my research in Zande District it was evident that something was seriously wrong with resettlement from the point of view of those affected by it.

15. Wyld, 1951, p. 8.

REACTIONS TO RESETTLEMENT

A traveler's first impression of Zande District after resettlement was very different from what it would have been before. No demographic information is available for the period when the people were living along the roads, but it has been related that in some cases the roads had to be made longer than necessary in order to accommodate the local population and in other cases new roads had to be constructed just for settlement. A British official recalled in conversation that, when he traveled through Zande District in the mid-1930's, he seemed never to be out of sight of habitations. Travelers on the same roads during the time I was there, from 1952 to 1955, were often under the impression that they were traveling through uninhabited country. The population had been evacuated from the roadside settlements and dispersed throughout vast areas of the geometric resettlement pattern. Figure 10, a diagrammatic map of a portion of the district, shows the "lines" on which the new settlement pattern was based. There were almost 1,000 lines in Zande District, each with about 50 families on separate plots, 20 to 40 acres in area. The density of population in the resettled areas was about 50 persons per square mile, and some homesteads were more than eight miles from a road. The arguments for resettlement had stressed compactness and regularity as aids to agricultural supervision and had hinted at greater social concentration,[16] but only the aspect of regularity survived in the final distribution of the resettled Azande.

Particularly important was the uniformity of dispersion of the population. The homesteads were built on the individual plots, usually near the central path. The frontage of these plots was 150 meters along the path, and they were from 600 to 1,200 meters long. The homesteads were separated by considerable and uniform distances. In only very few cases was it possible for the people of one homestead to see other homesteads, either across the central path or along the path, because of the dense bush. Thus resettlement did not mean continuous habitations or cultivations. Figure 11 is a diagram of a portion of the central path of an actual line with homesteads and paths.

16. Letter, Equatoria Province file No. 2.R.1, Juba, 5 February 1946, and Equatoria Province Annual Estimate, 1947, proforma B(1).

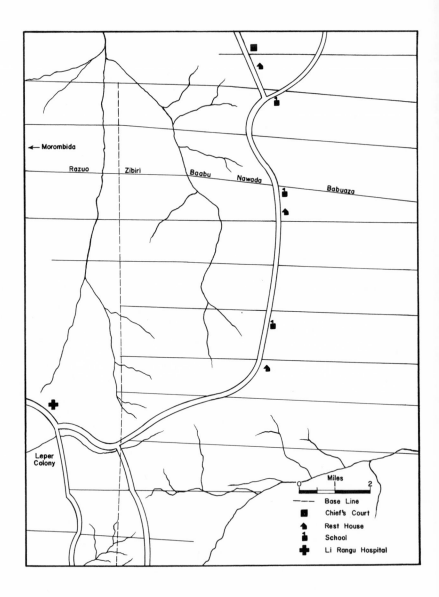

FIGURE 10
DIAGRAMMATIC MAP SHOWING "LINES" FOR A PORTION OF ZANDE DISTRICT

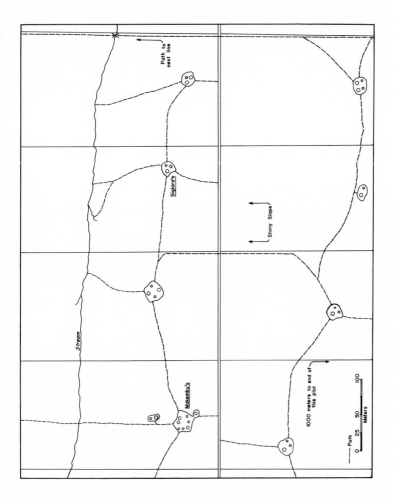

FIGURE 11

DIAGRAM SHOWING PART OF THE CENTRAL PATH OF AN ACTUAL LINE

There were, in fact, no aggregates of population. Even the town dwellers had been resettled on lines around the towns. The plots of land in these urban lines were not as large as those outside the towns, but they had been established on similar principles. Only in Nzara, the industrial center, was there any concentration of people. There many of the clerical staff and the semiskilled laborers lived in the middle of the town, while most unskilled laborers lived on four-acre plots outside it. In the other stations the permanent laborers had been resettled on lines in which the size of the plots ranged from half an acre to 12 acres.

This lack of communities made observation for social study difficult. Following the anthropological principle that the best way to study a people is to live among them, I took over an abandoned homestead in the lines to the north of Li Yubu, expanded it for my use by having more buildings constructed, and arranged for the cultivation of the usual food crops. But because of the dispersion of homesteads the benefits of this arrangement were not as great as I had hoped. While I gained rapport and information that I could not have obtained otherwise, I found myself quite effectively isolated in my courtyard, which was out of sight and sound of other nearby courtyards. Of course, visitors came to my homestead, other Azande worked for me in the construction of my buildings and cultivation of my crops, and I could visit other homesteads. But there was no feeling of a neighborhood, and everyday life could be observed only intermittently. In time I was able to observe the entire daily routine of the Zande homesteads, but the process was much more discontinuous than it would have been in a village compound or even in the Zande roadside settlements in the Congo or French Equatorial Africa.

The inconvenience for my work caused by the new settlement pattern had its counterpart in the experience of the people. At the time of my first inquiries among the Azande, in the autumn of 1952, a great deal of discontent was evident among them. They continually complained of difficulty in getting enough food. There were frequent shortages of important grains, accompanied by an increased use of cassava, which was not considered to be a desirable food, either by the Azande or by nutritionists who studied their diet.[17] The primary cause of food shortages, according to

17. Culwick, 1950, pp. 38 and 251.

the Azande, was the large amount of time and energy that had to be spent on work for the government, in which they included moving for resettlement and cotton cultivation, in addition to labor on roads and public works. Resettlement, forced cotton cultivation, and poor returns for the cotton were discussed with much grumbling. As soon as they came to know my neutral position, they expressed freely their disappointment at the way in which the development scheme was being conducted. But it could be seen that many of the difficulties had been occasioned by resettlement, as distinct from the introduction of a cash crop, for they asked many questions about why they had been moved and made many complaints about the trouble caused by the moves. Almost without exception the people said they would have preferred living on the roads to the new life in the lines.

I spent my first year in the remote western area that had been the last to be resettled, and there I was able to observe the vast amount of work involved in setting up new homesteads. The Azande were capable of building temporary quarters in a relatively short time, which gave the impression that they could move and settle into new homesteads with little trouble. But temporary buildings alone do not make a homestead. It takes time to clear the courtyard, to put up more substantial structures, to establish the kitchen gardens, to make completely new clearings for field crops, and to do the many other things that go to make up a homestead. Much traveling back and forth was necessary to bring unharvested crops, stores, and equipment from old to new homes. The people in my area did not have to plant cotton until the second year in their new homes—in contrast to the people of most of the rest of the district, who had to plant cotton during their first few months in the new plots. That they had been successful with their first crops speaks well for their industry, for even without cotton cultivation the people I observed were busy constructing new buildings and cultivating new gardens and fields. No Zande would have agreed that the displacement of his homestead involved little hardship.

The ease with which a Zande family can move had been underestimated in another respect: There is vast difference between moving the entire population of a region and moving single homesteads within a population. When only one family moved, friends, relatives, and neighbors could help by supplying labor and food. But if everybody moved, no such help was available. No family could borrow food or eat at another homestead. Even building materials for houses became scarce near the locale of the mass movement. Men had to travel as much as half a day into the forest to find, for instance, sufficient binding materials—the bark of certain trees, which usually could be found close at hand. Re-settlement, then, had been much more trouble than was antici-pated and the Azande were tired from the work of moving. They had done it willingly on the assumption that there would be commensurate returns. The trouble and work had raised their expectations from the government and deepened their disappoint-ment in its failure to provide what they had hoped for.

Hardships in making new homes were not the only complaints of the Azande. They often objected to the isolation into which they had been forced by resettlement. Having become accustomed to living on the roads, they missed being able to see people coming and going and to hear the latest news. I noted a marked tendency among the Azande, after resettlement, to gravitate toward the towns, despite regulations. Constant vigilance was necessary to keep down the number of "visitors" and squatters in the plots closest to towns. A survey of selected lines showed very few vacant plots in the lines near the towns, in contrast to those in remote places. Furthermore, the lines near the towns often had a waiting list of applicants for vacancies. Many of these applicants, while waiting for plots of their own, were living in the homesteads of relatives or illegally doubling up in plots already occupied. The greater and more regular spacing of homesteads produced by re-settlement had indeed yielded no benefits, in the estimation of the Azande. Instead they complained about the distances they had to travel to shops, courts, schools, and particularly hospitals. Fre-quently I heard remarks to the effect that "the people will die in the lines," meaning that the delay in getting to a hospital could be fatal for a seriously ill person. Vague fears were also expressed of the wilderness and of epidemics, as well as unhappiness at being cut off from the centers of communication.

The discomfort caused by isolation may seem strange when we recall that the traditional settlements were scattered throughout the forest. But the new type of settlement had no features that re-

minded the people of the older mode of residence, and furthermore they did not want to live in that manner. Almost without
exception, they yearned after the life on the roads. When they had
lived on the roads they had still been able to arrange themselves,
in most cases, as they had wished, but once each family had had to
take a permanent plot in the lines, adjustment was difficult. A very
common Zande complaint was that they could no longer live in
the manner normal to them—that is, with their relatives. Histories obtained from some families showed that in the roadside
settlements sons often lived next to their fathers, and brothers
lived adjacent or very near to each other, in some cases with married sons at hand. Although the pattern emerging from the actual
histories was not so well defined as idealized statements suggested, the layout of the previous homesteads indicated a distinct
tendency for kin to live together.

When asked why they had not selected the plots they wanted
when the lines were laid out, my informants explained how arbitrarily the plots had been assigned. A clerk came, with a policeman or two, to register them. He sorted out the people of a
subchief according to the headmen of the new lines. Then each
group was taken down its line, and a man was assigned to each
plot, with little hesitation or question. Two brothers and their
father, for example, had lived close together on the road and
wanted to have three adjoining plots on their new line. They were
afraid to say anything at the time of assignment, for fear of the
policeman's cane, and so were scattered throughout the line. A
headman of a line, whom I got to know well, explained that even
he had had trouble arranging for his plot to be next to the road
and for his wife's father to be on the other side of him. He had
been afraid to request any further arrangements for fear of losing
what he had already gained from the clerks and police, on the one
hand, and, on the other, of angering his people by getting too
many favors for himself when they had none. The situation was
made even worse by the assignment of unmarried men to plots of
their own because they were taxpayers. The administration tried
to avoid such assignment, but it happened often enough to cause
considerable distress.

We may be sure that this degree of arbitrariness was unin-
tentional. The second district commissioner had been alert to

such dangers, but he was busy with the enormous task of arranging the resettlement of an average of 10,000 families in each dry season for five years. He had more than enough work ensuring that the chiefs and subchiefs knew what to do and that the best land and water supplies were utilized for the lines, as well as checking to see that the lines were laid out properly. Thus assignment of plots and attendant details was left to the subordinate staff. The original plans had included the inspection of all plots and lines after the families had moved, but not enough senior staff was available even to begin this task, and even if inspections had been possible it would have been extremely hard to undo the difficulties caused by arbitrary assignments to the plots.

What could be done in the way of adjustments after the assignments? Any move between two chiefdoms after resettlement required the approval of both chiefs. Such approval was not easily obtained because no chief wanted to lose his people. Moreover, one of the purposes of resettlement was to reduce the movement of homesteads. Even a move within a chiefdom required the approval of the chief and his census clerk. This meant spending a great deal of time making inquiries and waiting to be seen by the chief's clerk, who tended to regard applications for permission to move as burdensome. Then, too, there was the problem of finding a vacant plot in or near the desired place. An applicant had to prove that such a plot existed, generally by bringing the headman of the line to the chief's clerk. The tendency during the original assignment had been to fill up each line with its full quota of homesteads, since usually only enough lines had been cut to meet the needs of each chief or subchief. The most desirable plots, in terms of distance from water, quality of soil, or proximity to roads, had been taken. If there were any extra plots, they were located at the ends of the lines or on poor soil. So there was little hope of adjusting the population within the system of lines, and the result was much tension and illegal moving. Some families maintained two homesteads, one in the assigned plot and one elsewhere.

Another complaint was that animal pests, such as antelope, guinea fowl, and wild pig, were causing a great deal more damage to crops in the lines than previously. When I asked why predators should be more troublesome in the lines than in the old cultivations, Azande explained that when the courtyards had been near the roads, the continuous settlement had kept animals away; that fields away from the courtyards had been selected with animal pests in mind; and that when several families had been able to cultivate together, guarding duties could be shared. I myself had observed such arrangements in French territory. Furthermore, my own cultivating experience confirmed the seriousness of animal marauders when cultivations were dispersed piecemeal throughout forest country. I lost a whole field of corn to a pack of baboons in one afternoon, while the field was temporarily unguarded. Animal depredations were officially acknowledged to be an important problem in the resettled areas in the Zande District Annual Report of 1952. In a publication of 1954 two former British inspectors of agriculture in Zande District recommended that the game laws be altered to allow the Azande to contend better with animal pests.[18]

Other disadvantages of resettlement appeared when the situation in the Sudan was compared with that in French and Belgian territories. Informants assured me that travel had been made much more difficult by resettlement, since it was hard to find food and accommodation now that the roads were deserted. Clerks and teachers had much more trouble finding food for sale than they had had when the people lived along the roads. Also it was no longer safe to travel at night.

While the chiefs agreed in general with the observations of the people on resettlement, they could see one advantage in the arrangement: They now knew better where people were living than prior to resettlement. Some chiefs said that the resettlement system had made more work for them by separating kin. For example, they explained, suppose a man beat his wife. If his brothers lived nearby, they would try to persuade him to modify his behavior before he got into trouble. But when brothers were separated, they could not readily influence each other, so more trouble occurred and the chiefs needed to hear more cases.

Some minor chiefs and subchiefs had been adversely affected by the resettlement because they could not get their people to contribute work and gifts as readily as when they had lived on the roads. One particularly weak subchief complained to me that his grain stores were depleted and his buildings in poor repair be-

18. McCall and Lea-Wilson, 1954, p. 10.

cause his people were so busy growing cotton, building new home-steads, and working on government projects that they were not willing to help him. He had to be careful, he said, in ordering work to be done, because cotton defaulters might use their work for him as an excuse for poor cultivation of cotton. When they had lived on the roads, he recalled, his grain stores had been full, he had been able to give food and beer generously, and he had had little difficulty in attracting people to work for him.

The educated Azande were uniformly bitter about resettle-ment, even though most of them were not required to live in the lines. Their views were stated in a letter written in 1948 to the district commissioner by a boy attending an intermediate school outside the district:

. . . I heard that these lines are made to provide good fields of cotton, and the planters are going to live there forever. Is that true? Sir, Zande people had been living in the forest for many years, and you came to Africa, big roads were made for them. Now they are used to it and forget about the life of the forest. We are also born to this life and are used only to it; I think we shall find it very difficult to live there.

Zande land seems to be very fertile. Sir, could you not leave them along the main roads and divide to them as much as you could those fields? Sir, you are our chief, our father, have mercy on us. If you order them to live again in the forest like that of long ago, they will never be civilized. Those boys who are now in school will find it difficult to go back to their land and settle down to do all what they learned at school, in order to show his countryman how to lead a new life. Citizens and foreigners will find it difficult to obtain food in Zande country, because, they are all in the forest. Therefore roads will be bad because they do not take much care about them. Then they will not unite with the people of another kingdom. Through this terrible life, the peasants will really never be happy.[19]

When I met the writer, six years after he had written this letter, he was working as a clerk in the Equatoria Projects Board office and was still of the same mind about resettlement. The edu-cated Azande often expressed themselves as being suspicious of the motives of the administration in resettling the population, be-lieving that there must have been some hidden purpose behind this inexplicable policy. A group of clerks and hospital attendants

19. Zande District file No. 2.B.3/15, p. 98.

once engaged me in a discussion of resettlement policy. When they asked why the people had been resettled I explained that I knew only the usual agricultural reasons. They were not willing to accept any of the stated justifications, and one vigorously affirmed that the real reason had been the second district commissioner's concern about the "morals of the young girls" in the roadside settlements. Several others agreed that he had "spread the population out in the forest" in a misguided effort to reduce sexual promiscuity. They were scathing in their judgment of the validity of such a maneuver.

The lack of sympathy of the educated persons for the second district commissioner was reciprocated. The commissioner consistently supported the chiefs and their traditional authority against the educated elements, recommending frequently that all action be taken through the chiefs and not "their paid employees." He was aware of the educated persons' resistance to resettlement even while it was being carried out. In an official communication he wrote that resettlement had unfortunately emphasized "the superficial desire for schooling" among the Azande and commented upon the "meretricious outlook" of many teachers who avoided the resettlement staff "in case it might involve them in any personal effort."[20]

From the point of view of the Europeans also resettlement had not produced the desired results. Educators uniformly denounced the effects of resettlement. According to the missionaries in charge, the entire educational system had received a severe setback. Resettlement had sometimes left the previous schools without populations to serve, and new schools had had to be constructed. Many children stopped coming to school because they had to help in the building of new homesteads, and even after the initial period the school population was deficient because of great distances to schools from remote lines. Moreover, the registers of the resettled units were not as accurate as the planners of the resettlement program had expected. The lack of sufficient well-trained clerks for the chiefs and subchiefs made for poorly kept records that did not tally from one department to another. (The records were among the best in rural Africa, at that.) The only public health measure introduced into the resettled areas

20. Zande District file No. 1.C.8, p. 23.

with any success was the digging of pit latrines in the new home-steads. A considerable fraction of them, however, were never used.

The notions of strip cropping and fixed rotation of crops had failed in application. By the time I arrived in 1952, the work of the agricultural staff was largely confined to laying out government plots for cotton and supervising its cultivation and purchase. The Azande were required in the early years to put their cotton plots on new ground each year. Later cotton was ordered to be put into second-year land. This merely meant that an additional plot had to be laid out, to be used for food crops for the first year and for cotton the next. But even this simple portion of a rotational scheme could not be applied uniformly, partly because of lack of adequate supervision and partly because of a lack of understand-ing on the part of the Azande. The degree of misunderstanding of just what the government wanted was serious. In one extreme in-stance the people of a line complained bitterly that the govern-ment was preventing them from cultivating sufficient eleusine for their needs. I assumed they were referring to the distractions of outside work, but they asserted that they were being specifically limited in the size of fields to be sown to eleusine. Investigation revealed that the demonstrators had been ordered at that time to lay out in each plot two fields of one-half acre each, one for groundnuts and eleusine and one for cotton, so that cotton could be grown on second-year land, following the food crops. The Azande interpreted the arrangement as meaning that cultivators could not plant more land to eleusine than the designated field. They reasoned that the government would not have interfered with their food crops except to limit them. Since they did not want to grow cotton, the government made them cultivate a cer-tain minimum amount. Conversely, since they wanted to grow as much eleusine as possible, they reasoned that if the government laid out a plot for it, the motive must be to limit food cultivation. Any administrative move was immediately suspected of being con-trary to Zande interests.

Perhaps most disappointing of all was the fact that cotton cul-tivations within the lines were far from easy to supervise. The supervision of cotton planting and cultivation was carried out by European inspectors of agriculture, working through junior agriculturalists, all southern Sudanese, who were in charge of the Zande agricultural demonstrators, who lived in the lines, and each of whom supervised the cotton cultivation for some 100 families. The supervision was more difficult than might be visualized from a neat diagram of 50 homesteads along two sides of a central path. The fields were scattered throughout the bush and forest at varying distances from the central path, from where they could be seen only occasionally. The demonstrators usually managed to lay out the cotton plots and to see that they were weeded, but they could do little else. Both British and Zande agricultural staffs were often heard to complain about the difficulties involved, and no one would agree that residence in the lines had conferred any advantages in this regard.

RESETTLEMENT IN THE LIGHT OF ZANDE REQUIREMENTS

In order to account for the disparity between the intended benefits of resettlement and the actual effects, let us recapitulate the assumptions made by the administration about Zande territorial distribution. The salient points that had made resettlement seem feasible and desirable to the administration can be summarized as follows: (1) Available land had been exhausted along the roads, and fresh land was required for food and cash crops. (2) Moving involved little hardship for the Azande. (3) Shifts in residence were frequent anyway, because of deaths, the threat of witchcraft, and the search for new land. (4) Since each homestead was an independent unit, any arrangement of homesteads would work. (5) The Azande dreaded close contact and would welcome being spread out in a manner resembling their original distribution. (6) Careful supervision was vital to successful introduction of cash crops and agricultural reforms as well as to conservation of soil and water. (7) Future shifts of residence could be avoided by restraining random moves and by substituting crop rotation for shifting cultivation. (8) Orderly settlement was necessary to avoid haphazard settlement in inaccessible places.

In the above discussion of the reaction to resettlement, the errors in some of these assumptions have already been pointed out. The comments of those involved suggest that the need for fresh land could have been satisfied without resettlement, that the ease of establishing new homesteads had been grossly misjudged, and that the new pattern had been found by the Azande to be inflexible and isolating. In addition, an unforeseen element of arbitrariness had developed in the assignment of plots, and a good deal of confusion had arisen about the aims of resettlement.

These assumptions had to be tested further, in the view of the writer, since some had not been directly commented upon by the persons involved. Inquiry into the rate of movement of homesteads, the importance of witchcraft in residential practices, the influence of shifting cultivation upon shifts in residence and requirements of Zande territorial grouping—all needed examination in the light of the administration's reasoning.

The Rate of Movement of Homesteads

Outside observers usually believed that Zande homesteads were frequently abandoned and that there was much movement of households. To the question, "Is it true that you people are always moving?" the Azande would agree readily, especially the chiefs. But if one then pointed out that some homesteads had been occupied for 20 or more years, they would explain that the persons who moved were unmarried men and newly married men. When a man and his family found a good place, as proved by the presence of offspring and the lack of misfortune, they would develop it into what they considered to be a permanent home. This stage was marked by the planting of trees and other perennials. In French territory and in the Belgian Congo old homesteads could be seen that contained mature trees and other plants of many useful and ornamental varieties. When the head of a household had a good place, he would build larger and better buildings than before and settle down to a lifetime in the homestead. Of course, if disaster struck, as might happen at any time, the homestead might have to be abandoned, but such a possibility was considered to be relatively unlikely. An understandably greater tendency was also observed for a household to try to stay in a well-established place rather than in one that was only partially developed. The Azande considered it to be most unfortunate to be forced to leave a well-established homestead, whatever the reasons. The few Azande in the Sudan who had managed to stay in their old homesteads in spite of the resettlement felt themselves very lucky and, like the members of old homesteads in French Equatorial Africa and the Belgian Congo, wanted to stay in their present homes for the rest of their lives. If death or some other misfortune forced them to move, they regarded this as a very great hardship.

The impression that all Azande are more or less continually on the move seems to have been derived from observance of only a portion of the population, usually the younger adults who had not yet settled down. The whole population was never at any time on the move. Quite to the contrary, a distinct feature of Zande settlement practice involved the settling down of a family in what they considered to be a permanent homestead. But this settling-down process required a certain amount of mobility and freedom to choose a suitable locale.

When a man's wife died he usually abandoned his homestead and moved to another place. A good deal of variation occurred in the nature of this move, depending on the composition of the homestead, particularly the number of wives. After resettlement the government ruled that a man should simply move toward the rear of his own plot when his wife died, building a new homestead instead of transferring to another plot. The rationale here was that, since the woman was buried in the homestead of one of her relatives and not on her husband's land, he did not need to move. The Azande, when questioned on this point, agreed that this reasoning was quite logical and that the rule could be followed in all cases. But in making a detailed inquiry into the reasons for moves in four widely separated lines, I found that most of the men who had moved out of those lines had done so because of the death of wives. I found only one case in which the man had stayed in his plot after his wife died. But he himself had died within two months. When confronted with these findings, the same people who had agreed at first that the ruling was logical and should be followed pointed out that in each case of a move the man had found that it would not be good for him to stay, usually by consulting the oracles.[21] He had then asked the oracles where he should move, and it happened that each man, except for the

---

21. Evans-Pritchard, 1937, contains full descriptions of Zande oracles and their applications.

one who stayed and died, had found it best to move elsewhere in the same line or even farther away. Though the people were willing to comply with the rule, most widowed men found that it was for them better to move. And the moves had been made, despite the difficulties imposed by the new system.

In the event of the death of the head of the household, the household could not possibly stay in the same plot, for the wives returned to their families and the dependents went with their mothers or to other relatives. The settlement in lines produced a problem in this connection. The plots had been demarcated so definitely that the Azande associated an entire plot with the courtyard and cultivations within it. Previously only the courtyard and cultivations of a dead person were avoided for as long as they could be seen or remembered. Cultivations soon lost their social identity, since their original appearance was changed by fast-growing vegetation. Courtyards, with their more durable structures, retained their identity longer, but since they occupied relatively little space, avoidance of them was no great hardship. After the resettlement, when a homestead was abandoned because of death, the entire plot was regarded as abandoned. I noted that others were reluctant to move into such plots, although in the more desirable locations, especially near towns, some were re-occupied. Discussion of the problem revealed uncertainty; Zande ideas about it were not clearly formulated.

The implicit hope that the Azande could be made into sedentary cultivators was actually more confounded than assisted by resettlement, because the crucial point of continuity of settlement from generation to generation had been overlooked. Formerly, some of a man's sons probably lived near him—particularly the eldest, who was usually second to the father. This pattern had been followed in the homesteads along the roads before resettlement in the Sudan, and could also be found in French and Belgian territory during my study. In the event of the father's death, his courtyard was usually abandoned, but the sons might stay in their own courtyards nearby and cultivate the same general area used by the previous generation. But when kin were scattered, through assigning each taxpayer his own plot wherever available, all hope of real stability on the land was lost.

View of a courtyard, showing screening effect of vegetation.

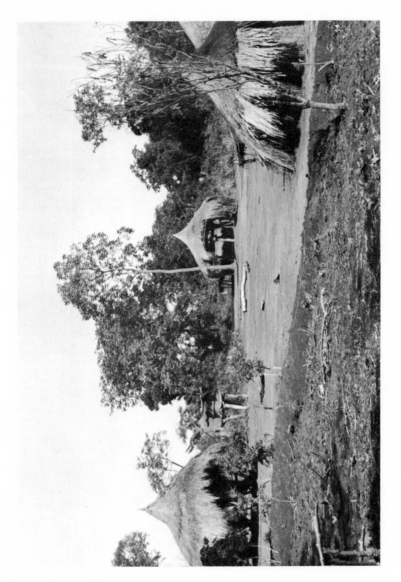

View of a courtyard with a recently cleared portion in the foreground.

Woman weeding with a hoe.

Women and children fishing in the forest.

Old man bringing cotton into market.

Packing cloth into bales in the Nzara mill.

Weighing cotton at a market.

A family cleaning cotton under a grain store.

The Influence of Witchcraft on Residence

The assumption that the Azande would welcome a change which would locate them farther from their neighbors and thereby give them greater freedom from the threat of witchcraft as well as greater privacy was only partially valid. While most Azande were still concerned about witchcraft and believed it to be most effective at close range,[22] the notion that the mere possibility of witchcraft could cause the abandoning of homesteads was faulty. Concern about witchcraft was touched off by misfortune; only then were the oracles or diviners consulted. And only after failure to stop the operation of witchcraft, as evidenced by the continuation of the misfortune, would the Azande leave a homestead. Thus their reason for leaving was the incidence of misfortune, not residential proximity.

Observers at the time of the first roadside settlement[23] mentioned the horror that the Azande expressed about the possibility of witches close at hand. But ideas had changed, for in my time the Azande living in towns and along the roads maintained that they did not mind living close together. For a generation they had known only the life on the roads. Their desire for personal privacy could be satisfied by screens or hedges, and they had learned by experience that survival was possible with many close neighbors. When I mentioned to Azande in French roadside settlements that they were supposed to be afraid to live close together (as they were doing) because of the threat of their neighbors' witchcraft, they merely shrugged their shoulders. They could live anywhere, they said, and were not worried so long as no one in their families became ill.

Both French and Sudanese Azande spoke of the advantages of having two homes. For one thing, in the event of misfortune, the afflicted person or the whole family could move to the other home to get away from the source of witchcraft. But restriction on the choice of locale for cultivations in the Sudan lines made it difficult to have such a retreat at a time of danger. The spacing out of homes during resettlement had done nothing to reduce the possibility of witchcraft, in the view of any Zande family. Probably their apprehensions in this and other respects had increased be-

22. See Evans-Pritchard, 1937, for an account of Zande beliefs in witchcraft.
23. Larkin, 1955, p. 57.

cause the families had been settled arbitrarily, could not move freely, and were deprived of the immediate comfort of nearby kinfolk.

The Relation of Shifting Cultivation to the Movement of Homesteads

Members of the administration and other Europeans assumed a direct connection between shifting cultivation and the shifting of homes. Yet the Azande did not see that the need for new land necessarily entailed a change of residence. Accordingly they did not understand why it had been necessary for them to move in order to grow cotton. Many appreciated the advantage of having fresh soil to cultivate, but they could not believe this was the reason for the move, since they would have been able to find good soil without such inconvenience. They knew that plenty of land was available and would have been willing to go considerable distances to cultivate either a cash crop or their food crops. They often recalled their large fields in the days before resettlement. In response to questions about how far it might be to suitable land when they had lived on the roads, they explained that they used to travel up to approximately seven miles, building temporary shelters at their fields in order to live there when work was heavy and crops required protection. They insisted that they had cultivated much more grain when they lived on the roads and could choose the land for their cultivations. According to their estimates, as laid out on the ground for me, it was not unusual for a man with two or three wives to cultivate fields of groundnuts and eleusine about three acres in area. This area was larger than all but a few plots that I found in the lines, but how much exaggeration had been brought on by nostalgia could not be estimated.

It was easy, however, to compare these Azande with the Azande in French territory, who lived along the roads as they had for many years past. As one crossed the border from the area in the Sudan which had just been resettled the difference was striking. In roadside villages in French Equatorial Africa one felt an air of stability and social activity which was painfully lacking in the Sudan. The houses along the roads were well built. Many mature trees had been planted in and around the homesteads, and everything appeared well established.

I immediately noticed that there was little cultivation near these old homesteads in French territory, except for the perennial crops and a few stands of cassava bushes. The land around the communities had been cultivated beyond its capacity, so everybody cultivated at some distance, either along the road between communities or in the forest away from the road. The preferred places were along the streams, I was told, and use of this land was not prohibited as in the Sudan. During times of heavy agricultural work the homesteads in the villages were mostly deserted or attended only by children or old persons. Most of the able-bodied people stayed away for long periods.

When I asked to see the fields, I was never taken to any in the forest, only to those along the road. The usual reason given was that the cultivations in the forest were too far away. The real reason, I was informed by my Sudan friends, was that the French Azande were careful not to reveal the extent of their homesteads at the outlying cultivations. Almost all families seemed to have had town houses, which were their official residences, and country homesteads at their cultivations. Professor Evans-Pritchard told me that when the people in the Sudan lived along the roads, most of them had temporary houses beside distant cultivations. I was not able to determine by observation the relative importance of their two homesteads to the families in French territory, but I was told that there was great variation in the nature of the outlying homesteads. These ranged from temporary grass shelters to fully developed homesteads that were, in fact, the primary homes of their families. Tales of "lost villages" being found by the French *commandant* had reached the Sudan. These, I learned upon inquiry, were occasional groups of homesteads of families that had neglected to keep up their roadside homes and had in fact made shifts in primary residence.

Zande agriculture is usually described as shifting cultivation. The term is quite correct in so far as it means that they did not practice any fixed system of crop rotation, incorporating a fallow period. It is also true that the cultivation of most land was limited to three or four years, in common with most tropical agriculture. But the system of agriculture must be distinguished from the system of residence. It is *not* correct to assume that Zande homesteads were constantly changed because of the search for new cultivatable land. Evidence existed in roadside settlements that a household might occupy one courtyard for many years, cultivating at a distance and utilizing secondary homesteads in conjunction with these cultivations. An extremely large household might have had to shift its locale quite often in order to find sufficient new land. But a household with one to three wives, like most Zande households in modern times, could find sufficient land for cultivation within walking distance to last for an indefinite period. The assumption that shifting cultivation is coterminous with shifting residence is clearly not applicable to the Zande situation—nor, probably, to many others. The ability of the Azande to utilize secondary homesteads for purposes of cultivating at a distance from primary homesteads was not appreciated by the administration and therefore not taken into account in the attempt to stabilize the population on the land.

The second district commissioner had hoped to obviate the need for further moves by the introduction of strict rotational methods (including long fallow periods) in the assigned plots, which were designed to be large enough for the needs of each family for an indefinite period. But the most elementary agricultural reforms planned as part of the resettlement program had not been introduced. Even the most rudimentary rotation of crops had not been achieved. Nor had such innovations as antierosion bunds or grassy strips between fields been accepted by the Zande cultivators.

Most courtyards were placed near the central path, even if unfavorable locations had to be used. The focus of the resettlement was the central path. The Azande either assumed—or in some cases were told by the junior staff allocating the plots—that they should stay close to these line paths, which were regarded as substitutes for the roads on which they had lived previously. Even after they became accustomed to the plot boundaries and to the idea of confining their cultivations to their own land, most of the Azande used the land adjacent to the central path for cultivation and for courtyards. They continued to cultivate this land longer than was considered wise, either by them or by the agricultural supervisors, while the land to the rear of the long, narrow plots was not freely used. The effect was, in most cases, the same as if the families had been assigned to overly small plots without the possibility of looking for fresh land in the usual manner. Thus within the confines of their narrow plots overcultivation became common.

The lack of success of the rotational schemes and the overcultivation near the lines worried the agricultural section of the administration. In 1953 an agricultural officer suggested a plan for ensuring that the Azande make use of new land at frequent intervals. The essence of the plan was that every courtyard be moved completely every four years to a newly designated place within the assigned plot. This plan, which would have been devastating for the Azande, was never considered. The administration had become aware of the resentment of the Azande toward arbitrary resettlement, and great care was being taken not to start a rumor that there might be another move.

Residential Requirements

The tensions produced by the arbitrary settlement served to highlight certain features of Zande territorial organization. I suspect that after they had been restrained from choosing their locations the Azande themselves became much more aware of the importance of the grouping of homesteads than they had been before. Although the freedom of choice of individual householders was consistently stressed, it was always stated in terms of living *with* someone. Complaints about not being able to live where desired were put in terms of not being able to be near certain other homesteads, usually those of relatives. Despite the fragmenting and individualizing influences of recent years, there was still a need for homesteads to cluster together. So arbitrary resettlement had attacked Zande social organization at its weakest point—the grouping of homesteads.

The simplicity and flexibility of Zande local organization had led to the belief that it could be easily changed. This belief had a good deal of truth in it. If the Azande had had more definite ideas about where they should live, certainly trouble would have occurred in the course of resettlement, despite their high degree of compliance with authority. The system was flexible because each head of a household individually selected the locale for his homestead. The traditional system permitted a wide range of choice, and in the former life on the roads a large degree of selection had still been possible. But the resettlement plan was based on the implicit belief that the Azande could be transformed into stable peasant cultivators by assigning them definite plots of land. The flexibility of the social structure was exploited in accomplishing the resettlement. Afterward, however, the system was made rigid and arbitrary. It did not allow for adjustment and grouping, although the need for moves had greatly increased.

Regular geometric distribution had not conferred the advantages of the pre-European system, which, in any event, was no longer wanted. And the imposed rigidity of territorial distribution worked against Zande needs. The people did not plan to move and considered themselves to be stable, but only by permitting a certain amount of mobility could stability have been achieved. If sufficient freedom of selection of sites of courtyards and cultivations had been allowed, the population could have been stabilized to a remarkable degree, as demonstrated by the presence of old, well-established courtyards near the roads in the Belgian Congo and French Equatorial Africa. And if the Azande had been given a certain amount of free choice within limits prescribed by the administration, they would have settled down in accessible places, since they preferred to live along the roads.

Judging from the Azande's recollections of life on the roads in Zande District prior to resettlement and from observations of roadside settlement in Belgian and French territories, the Azande evidently had been able to adjust satisfactorily to the changes in their residential patterns first imposed by the European administrations.[24] Zande ideas about residence clearly had changed in at least two important respects: They preferred to live along the roads, and they seemed to have become accustomed to living in close proximity to other homesteads. Roadside settlement gave them a choice in their immediate residential arrangements, which the geometric settlement pattern in the Sudan did not.

The administration's use of such terms as "haphazard" in reference to the residential pattern indicates that Zande behavior was being judged by European values. The notion that the geometric spacing out of homesteads was similar to the traditional

---

24. See also the judgment by Evans-Pritchard, 1947, p. 15, that the roadside settlement had not produced any great change in the life of the Azande.

distribution and the refusal to allow the Azande to locate themselves according to their "own sweet will" reveal a lack of awareness of Zande residential characteristics, perhaps even a lack of
awareness of the need to inquire into Zande ideas on the subject.
The residential needs of the Azande had been misinterpreted. The
diffuse nature of their original settlement had led to the assumption that each household could be treated as a unit, fitted into a
geometric pattern, and stay fixed. The mass resettlement of Zande
District seems to have caused more unrest than any other recent
change in Zande society. Toward the end of my stay, the system of
fixed family plots in the resettled areas had clearly begun to break
down, and the government had adopted a policy of tacitly permitting the movement and adjustment of homesteads.

MOTIVES FOR RESETTLEMENT

Ideas on resettlement cannot, however, be put into a European-
Zande dichotomy. The senior inspector of agriculture of the Equatoria Projects Board and the second district commissioner, both
British and both with long experience in Zande District, disagreed
about the necessity for introducing various aspects of resettlement
and cash cropping and about the reaction of the Azande to these
measures. As far back as 1949, the senior inspector of agriculture
had expressed concern to the Zande District Local Advisory
Council about how the introduction of individual holdings and
cash crops affected the Azande. Individual holdings in the lines,
he believed, did not permit the most effective use of the land. He
proposed, as he had three years before, that the homesteads be
laid out on a regular pattern but that the people be allowed to cultivate anywhere within the area designated for the resettled unit.
Resettlement meant "great upheaval in Zande life," he said. He
recommended that an administrative officer be appointed to give
full time to the consolidation of the resettled Azande, since they
had then only the haziest ideas about the aims of the administration. He felt that resettlement had been only superficial but that
its consolidation was far beyond the capabilities of the available
agricultural and administrative staff. He feared that the Azande
would "rapidly become unsettled" unless a concerted program,
involving years of patient work, were undertaken to make the re-

settlement program function as planned. To change the Azande from shifting cultivators to stabilized peasant farmers by the device of assigning each of them to a plot of land could not be done, he warned, without changing deeply rooted ideas—a process requiring much time and sympathetic effort.[25]

The district commissioner challenged these statements. He felt that the problem of constriction within the individual holdings was being exaggerated and that the solution lay in the selection of the best sites within plots. He disagreed about the inconvenience to the people involved in resettlement. The Azande could easily move their homes, he said, and recommended that each family build a temporary home near the central line and later erect more permanent quarters on the best site within its holding. He was firmly opposed to any changes in the rules prohibiting cultivation outside the individual plots, lest the system disintegrate before it had ever been consolidated. At this early stage, he admitted, neither he nor anyone else could do more than speculate as to whether the system of individual holdings was a means to an end or an end in itself. But he expressed the opinion that "the mathematical precision" of the resettlement system was "the scaffolding on which we hope to build a settled population of peasant farmers with sufficient share of the best land available, and living in an accessible and rational manner, not as beasts in the wilderness." He also flatly contradicted the senior inspector of agriculture's statement that cotton was not a popular crop.[26]

The district commissioner won out in most of the disputed points, but the evidence now indicates that he saw the situation less clearly than did the senior inspector of agriculture. Probably because he dealt with the people only through their chiefs, the district commissioner had insulated himself from the ordinary cultivators, whereas the senior inspector of agriculture seems to have had more personal contact with them. When the district commissioner alluded to "the personal touch and the paternal manner" he was referring to his relations with the chiefs and not with the people. Before resettlement was started in any chiefdom, he met with the chief, his subchiefs, and their headmen. At these meetings the planned benefits of development and resettlement

25. Zande District file No. 1.C.9/3, pp. 72–77.
26. Letter, Zande District file No. 1.C.8, 15 October 1949.

were explained and investigation was made of the areas and water supplies preferred by each headman. The tremendous work of re-settlement was, in fact, accomplished by telling the chiefs to order the people to move. The chiefs, as noted in Chapter II, were less interested in expressing the views of their people than in not of-fending the administration. The report of the first year's resettle-ment shows that the chiefs could not have understood well what was going on, for the subchiefs and hangers-on of the chiefs proved to be the most difficult to move. Although the chiefs were presum-ably informed, they were actually not so much consulted as ordered to act. Their opinions were solicited only on minor details and, in my observations, they often did not grasp what was required of them and their people. At no time were the people themselves con-sulted; they had only the vaguest idea of what was happening and what their roles were to be. The administration failed to under-stand the difficulties in communicating with the chiefs and, even more, the ineffectiveness of the chiefs in communicating with the people.

Furthermore, the district commissioner appeared to lack any real faith in the ability of the Azande to fend for themselves. He invariably insisted upon close supervision and was consistently worried about possible loss of control over the Azande. Even when protesting his confidence that the Azande could produce what was needed for success in the development scheme, he ended with, "provided only that sufficient enthusiasm and well-planned guid-ance is imparted by the supervisory staff." His very praise of the Azande was circumscribed in a similar way:

The character of the people as a whole is good natured and amen-able, they can understand a simple argument and they have a sense of humour. On the other hand while enthusiasm for novelty is easily raised, they are apt to become quickly bored. The will for sustained ef-fort needs constant impetus by interest taken and encouragement given, by the supervisory staff.[27]

Really close supervision by Europeans would have been im-possible, because of the expense and large staff involved. Even if it had been possible, vital questions of how long such super-vision was to be carried on and how it was to be terminated had not been considered. The second district commissioner's notion of

27. Zande District file No. 1.C.8, pp. 22–24.

supervision was to have a few Europeans working through what he saw as an effective hierarchy of chiefs and headmen. He does not seem to have been aware of the decline of the chiefs' authority, which was further weakened by their role in compelling the unpopular resettlement and cotton cultivation. As it was, too little supervision was available, and too little supervision was much worse than none, especially since it introduced the taint of tax labor to the cash crop. The Azande disliked the supervision more than they did cotton; they often spoke of their distaste for being "run after." The second district commissioner's insistence upon close supervision accords poorly with the experience elsewhere in the Sudan. In the quite similar conditions in the Nuba Hills, a minimum of change in the way of life of the people was required for successfully introducing rain-grown cotton as a cash crop. It also fits badly with the basic spirit of the development scheme drawn up by Dr. J. D. Tothill, who had been associated with the very successful development of cotton as a cash crop in Uganda. There it had been left largely to the peasant farmer and private enterprise, particularly at first, with no direct European supervision or any overt compulsion.[28]

The phenomenal amount of work in resettlement, which was accomplished with alacrity, attested to the Azande's high degree of amenability to authority and also to the enthusiasm with which they accepted the idea of development. But the large amount of work they had to do heightened their rather unrealistic expectation of returns, as seen in the discussion of notions about rewards in Chapter VI. Their initial enthusiasm was accepted as the norm and led to administrative misjudgment of what was to follow.

When the early resettlement proceeded at a pace beyond anyone's expectations, the second district commissioner had waxed enthusiastic about the program, which he saw as a panacea for the ills of the Zande way of life. He wrote in his annual report for 1946 that the resettled areas had produced better food crops than had Tembura Subdistrict,[29] despite the lower demands on the labor of that region. He attributed the failure of food crops in the Tembura area to "indifferent chiefs and headmen, exceptionally

28. Wrigley, 1959, p. 15.
29. Zande District was then composed of three subdistricts: Yambio Subdistrict in the center, Tembura Subdistrict to the west and north, and Iba Subdistrict to the east.

lazy people, and lack of administrative staff time, and agricultural staff to stimulate their efforts." He forecast the extension of the resettlement program into this area, which was never considered favorable for cotton and in which it later proved to be infeasible, by stating that "the sooner 'Resettlement' reaches that area the better it will be for all concerned."[30] When Yambio Subdistrict, in the second season of cotton growing, produced a markedly higher yield per acre than Iba Subdistrict, where cotton was still being grown under the older, pre-Zande Scheme conditions, Iba Subdistrict was included in the resettlement program. The district commissioner was confident that the closer supervision made possible by resettlement would improve the yield in the Iba area.[31] But the hoped-for effects did not take place. The yield of cotton per acre fell after part of the area was resettled in the next season,[32] and dropped even further the following year after the entire subdistrict had been resettled.[33] Resettlement and closer supervision were obviously no antidote to the unpopularity of cotton in Iba Subdistrict. But the program to resettle the rest of the district went on unabated.

Resettlement had been pushed for reasons other than the officially stated purposes of expediting the supervision of cash crops and agricultural reforms. The determination of the second district commissioner to resettle all the Azande seems to have stemmed largely from a sincere fear of harming them through urbanization.

The greatest threat and menace to well being and decency in an African community is urbanization [he wrote]. Much of the evil of urbanization can be avoided by careful planning. At Yambio we set our minds against the usual native lodging area composed of blocks of huts in tiny compounds on narrow streets. Such abominations are mere slums and are bound to breed every vice and become a festering disgrace to the community. Instead we made wide sweeping perimeter roads on which to locate the dwellings of employees in a natural manner.[34]

Mass resettlement seems to have been an extension of the experience at Yambio, based upon a dread of anything smacking of

30. Zande District Annual Report, 1946, p. 2.
31. *Ibid.*, 1948, p. 3.
32. *Ibid.*, 1949, pp. 1–3.
33. *Ibid.*, 1950–51, p. 21.
34. Wyld, 1951, p. 10.

urbanization. It was carried out with singular determination by the second district commissioner, over the protests of other officials, because he was convinced of its ultimate benefits to the Azande and because he felt the need to protect them against the ill effects of industrialization. As is shown in Chapter VI, his approach to the development of the Azande was philanthropical, as opposed to the commercial bias of the Equatoria Projects Board, and he consistently defended the Azande against any kind of exploitation.

Good intentions were not enough, however, to overcome the effects of poor communication with the people, a lack of understanding of their needs, and inadequate planning. That the plans for resettlement had not been fully thought out is evidenced by the claims for compactness in what was actually a dispersed form of settlement, by the unauthorized shift from villages on an H plan to a straight-line pattern with no community facilities, and by the unapproved expansion of resettlement from a portion of the district to the whole district.

When the change was made to the straight-line pattern of resettlement in 1946, a disadvantage accorded to it was that it was less compact than the H plan. Comparison of Figures 8 and 9 shows, however, little difference in compactness. Any unit containing 50 plots of land 40 acres in size will have a total area of at least 2,000 acres. The distance from the center to the outside end of any of the paths, measured along the straight paths, is the same in both types of units. Only if each homestead in the H pattern had its own shortcut to the center of the unit would there be any saving of distance and, therefore, any more effective compactness in the layout. As such an arrangement is not the usual pattern for Zande paths, the H plan could not have had a greater centralizing influence than the straight-line plan. Moreover, there is little point in reckoning distances to the center of the unit if nothing is at the center. The belief that the H pattern would be compact enough to lead to community centralization was based only on speculation, it seems. The H-shaped units that had been occupied during the first year of resettlement were still to be seen in later years. Observation revealed no difference between the life of the Azande on these H units and those living on the more common straight-line units. Thus there was nothing inherent in the H plan that, had it been applied to all of Zande District, would have produced more community spirit or more centralized social life.

The change to the straight-line pattern was not as important in itself as was the accompanying change in policy, which dropped all planning for community facilities within the units. The promise of community centers, centralization, and compactness for the people appears to have been based largely on the desire to obtain approval for resettlement. No provision was ever proposed for expenditures on community facilities, and the talk of compactness and "villagization" seems to have been entirely in the realm of slogans, which were very persistent in their appeal. Early in 1946 the second district commissioner began to try to reverse the impression that had been built up about the compactness of the resettled units. He explained to the governor that the term "village," which had been applied previously to the resettled units, was not an accurate description of groups of 25- to 40-acre farms.[35]

By 1948 he had to combat the notion that the resettlement was producing urbanization, an idea most repugnant to him, as we have seen. At this time he stated that the resettlement was not resulting in urbanization because the resettled units covered areas of about two square miles each and the homesteads were dispersed on 25- to 40-acre farms.[36] Earlier he had stated that resettlement would not result in a "scattered" pattern because it "concentrated" the people on the best land. The nature of resettlement was not well understood by persons on the outside, however; the literature on the Zande Scheme continued to contain references to villages. As late as 1954, an author writing from an agricultural research station in the northern Sudan used the anomalous term "dispersed villages" to describe the units resulting from the resettlement of the Azande.[37]

An administration that could force mass resettlement upon people without realizing the difficulties and defects involved was certainly out of touch with those people. Yet it felt itself to be in close contact with them. The extent of this illusion is illustrated by the use made of the Zande word *gbaria* to designate the resettled

35. Letter, Zande District file No. 2.B.3/1, 25 January 1946.
36. *Ibid.*
37. Ferguson, 1954, p. 9.

units. This same term had been applied by the administration to the former government settlements along the roads in the days of sleeping sickness population controls, because of the similarity in the method of demarcating the settlements to that of making the original *gbaria*, a roughly circular hunting area surrounded by a path. The newly resettled units after 1946 were also known as *gbarias* to the administration, though not to the Azande, to whom the form of the new settlements was quite different from their meaning of the term. When speaking English they used the word "line" to designate both the central path and the entire unit of 50 families. This word was taken over into the Zande language. *Lai-ni*, or *rai-ni*, as it was pronounced, meant the entire area of the unit, while *gene laini* designated the central path (*gene* = path). The administrative use of *gbaria* became jargonized to the extent that it appears in the Arabic glossary of a 1954 publication of the Sudan Ministry of Agriculture with the definition "clan; clan area."[38]

In 1954 a former general manager of the Equatoria Projects Board told me that in his personal opinion resettlement had been more of an obstacle than an aid to the development of the Azande. His view was virtually universal at that time among the officials in the administration and in the Board. Clearly, in retrospect, the resettlement program had been put through for reasons not directly linked with the development scheme. Unrecorded or even unexpressed motives may have existed, but whatever the motives, resettlement was regarded as a burden by the people who were to benefit from it. Despite undoubtedly sincere desires to help the people, despite assertions that their way of life was not to be changed any more than was necessary, it was changed in a most drastic manner by arbitrarily altering and attempting to fix residential patterns.

By 1954 the governor's office was trying to find some way to get the Azande into homes of their own choosing without giving them the idea that the government was ordering another move. A small step was taken by putting the permanent road gangs back into houses along the roads, away from the lines on which they had been resettled previously. But at this point an impasse was reached. There seemed to be no way of moving the remainder of

38. McCall and Lea-Wilson, 1954, p. 14.

the population without arousing still more resentment about administrative interference, for every action of the government in this regard was immediately viewed with apprehension by the Azande.

VI

THE
DEVELOPMENT SCHEME

In this chapter we come to the part of the Zande situation which was the area of my primary concern and to which the foregoing chapters are in a way introductory. The Azande had begun their work under the Zande Scheme with great enthusiasm, but had slackened off to the point of putting the Scheme in jeopardy. Why they had reacted in this manner was of interest both to the Sudan government and to my academic research. It was soon apparent that I could not understand the situation in which I found the people without studying the policies behind the development scheme and that such investigation required a review of the history of colonial administration, since so much of the Scheme's orientation had been derived from earlier policies and attitudes. Also it was necessary to summarize the changes that had occurred in Zande life in the colonial period before the Scheme in order to evaluate the changes brought on by the Scheme itself. The preceding chapters have been devoted to that summary. This chapter will discuss the effects of the introduction of cash crops and other aspects of the Scheme.

To evaluate the reaction of the Azande to the Scheme, I shall go back to its beginnings. After a brief background, the original proposals and their modifications will be presented, along with

140

the division of opinion that developed regarding the official plans for the Scheme. The work of construction, the sales of manufactured goods from the Scheme's factories, and cotton production and prices will be examined to discover their effects upon the Azande. The ideas of the Azande about appropriate rewards for their work will then be compared with those of the Europeans in charge. Finally, explanations will be sought for the paradoxes that appear.

Since the reconquest of the Sudan in 1898, the southern Negro provinces had been administered under a policy designed to protect the population against commercial exploitation. This protectionism, combined with the remoteness and poverty of the region and with a lack of capital investment by the administering powers on anything beyond bare strategic essentials, had produced an economic situation that, even by African standards, was undeveloped. This is clearly shown by the cash incomes cited in Chapter IV. During the 1920's cotton as a cash crop had been introduced into Equatoria Province on a small scale. Zande District was not included in these cotton projects until 1931. At that time, by an administrative reorganization, Iba Subdistrict, where cotton had been cultivated since 1926, was added to Zande District. Cotton had not been a popular crop in Equatoria Province, and results had been good only when direct compulsion had been employed. Both the administration and the people regarded cotton as a crop which merely allowed men to pay their taxes.[1] In 1935 trial plots of cotton were grown in the Yambio area and plans were considered to extend the cultivation of cotton to the rest of the district.[2] These plans were delayed, however, pending the formulation of a program for the development of the entire southern Sudan. The need for a change in policy in regard to the South was felt in Khartoum in the mid-1930's, and the program of development was started in 1937 with the appointment of an ecologist to make a preliminary botanical and ecological survey of Equatoria Province (which then included the present Bahr el Ghazal Province).

In 1938 Dr. J. D. Tothill, who as director of agriculture in Uganda had been closely associated with the development of

1. Catford, 1953, pp. 153–60.
2. Equatoria Province, file No. 2.M.2 1/2, 3 February 1936.

cotton as a cash crop there, was appointed to the post of director of agriculture and forests in the Sudan. Directed by the governor-general to study the possibilities of agricultural development in the southern Sudan, Dr. Tothill made an extensive tour of Equatoria Province in 1939 and submitted proposals for development of surpluses of oilseeds, dried meat, and clarified butter. He suggested that the economic stalemate of the region might be attacked by stimulating internal trade and improving trading and transport facilities. In addition, he made specific observations about each of the various regions in the province and stated that cotton would be the most profitable crop for Zande District because of its similarity to good cotton-growing areas in Uganda. He did not believe the road distance of 300 miles to a river port to be an insuperable obstacle, nor did he consider the previous unpopularity and poor production of cotton in the province to be worthy of concern. Although cotton had been successfully grown in parts of the province, he gave several reasons why it had never been developed commercially: poor prices, the suspicions aroused by the forcing and regimentation of the crop, the necessity for siting ginneries before proving the crop in particular areas, the reduction of marketability by poor ginning, and cultivation of a variety of cotton that was shorter and harsher in staple than competing types. Of these, the first, he felt, was most important. In the past, prices had been far below those paid in Uganda. A guarantee of an attractive price would mean, he believed, that regimentation could be replaced with "active propaganda," which would include encouraging the people to live on good land (without reference to roads), to improve domestic water supplies, and to grow cotton in the ordinary food-crop rotation.[3]

The Second World War then diverted attention, personnel, and money away from all development plans. The ecologist continued his work despite the war but was killed in a road accident in 1942, before he had submitted a final report.

THE BASIC PROPOSALS
FOR A SOCIAL EXPERIMENT

At the end of 1943 Dr. Tothill submitted a new memorandum, obviously based on his first proposals for agricultural development

3. Ministry of Agriculture, Khartoum, file No. 2–1, Vol. 1, pp. 50–54.

in Equatoria Province but a good deal more specific. He entitled it "An Experiment in the Social Emergence of Indigenous Races in Remote Regions"[4] and assigned as its goal "the complete social emergence and the social and economic stability of the Zande people."[5] The experiment, he believed, could lead toward possible further large-scale development of other parts of the Sudan and indeed all the remoter parts of British Africa. The arrested development of "the neolithic cultures" of these interior regions seemed to him a challenge "in an age of machinery and wireless and awareness of the rights of the common man." The essence of his policy was self-sufficiency, for in order to plan the orderly emergence of the inhabitants of the remote areas of central Africa as "happy, prosperous, literate communities, based on agriculture and participating in the benefits of civilization," he believed it necessary to break through the impasse in development by making them as nearly self-contained as possible. They would even produce manufactured goods, achieving financial independence by marketing a sufficient surplus of such goods to obtain the comparatively small amount of money required for the few indispensable imports.[6]

He had recommended that some remote, relatively large, and well-populated area be chosen for a 30-year trial, and Zande District of Equatoria Province, with its 40,000 taxpayers and its geographical remoteness, seemed to him to be eminently suitable for the experiment.[7] A primary reason for his choice of the Zande area was that its climate was relatively favorable to agriculture.[8] Food could be reliably produced with little danger of famine—a factor not to be ignored in many other parts of the southern Sudan. Also the Azande were considered to be relatively industrious and amenable.[9]

Another factor in the choice of the Zande District seems to have been the favorable attitude of the second district commissioner. He had for some time been trying to get support for the

4. Unpublished memorandum. Reference is made to the copy seen at the Ministry of Agriculture, Khartoum, file No. Z-1, Vol. 1.

5. Tothill, 1948, p. 916.

6. Tothill, 1943, p. 1.

7. *Ibid.*, p. 2.

8. Ferguson in Tothill, 1948, p. 918.

9. Ferguson, 1954, p. 4.

agricultural development of the district. He had suggested the extension of cotton growing into the district before the war, and he had established cotton trial plots and experimental community farms, as well as a "model farm" on the station at Yambio. He had been frustrated by the previous policy of isolation and protectionism and by shortage of funds, but the new policy, allied with Dr. Tothill's ability to turn the considerable disadvantage of the district's remoteness into a positive factor, had changed the situation markedly. Little competition existed from other areas for the honor of being the scene of the new experiment, which was soon to become known as the "Zande Scheme."

The Azande were an obvious choice for this Scheme, because they occupied a considerable portion of the largest area of good rainfall in the entire Sudan. Most other areas with the favorable conditions of Zande country were considered to be too small, for Dr. Tothill had specified the need for an area large enough to be a reliable indicator. No pilot project was devised to test the feasibility of the development scheme among the Azande, partly because of Dr. Tothill's view that this Scheme was to be in itself the pilot project for a much broader program. In addition, he felt the need for a large initial effort to test the industrial experiment, which required a certain unknown minimum scale of operation. He would probably have resisted any suggestions to start on a small scale, since his plan was founded on the concept of boldness.

In unfolding his plan for the experiment, Dr. Tothill stressed the need for education. The educational system should be expanded so that 95 per cent of the Azande would be literate in 30 years' time, for he felt the Scheme was unlikely to succeed without universal education. The expansion of the educational system was to start at the bush level, with schooling available to every Zande boy and girl. He hoped that secondary schools would be established in the area and even, eventually, a university for the southern Sudan.

Dr. Tothill proposed that parts of Zande District be designated for the cultivation of cotton, oil palms, coffee, and jute. In the cotton-growing area he planned that each family should cultivate one acre[10] of cotton in rotation with the usual food crops. He esti-

10. The reference is to the *feddan*, which equals 1.038 acres; throughout this report *feddans* will be regarded as equal to acres, and only the latter term will be used.

mated that 10,000 families could produce about 6,000,000 pounds of seed (unginned) cotton annually.[11] The Khartoum area, he believed, would be a likely market for the Scheme's goods, which were to be cotton cloth, burlap sacks, soap, and coffee. The most important of these, by far, was to be cotton cloth; he hoped for a production large enough to clothe the 170,000 Azande and, in addition, to earn most of the money needed for imports and to pay the interest on a government loan for building factories. Dr. Tothill further recommended the erection in Zande District of a modern ginnery and a spinning and weaving mill, which were to be small units capable of expansion. He believed that a few mill-hands imported from Egypt, India, or the United Kingdom could, with time and patience, train the Zande people to work in the factories. Very little had been done in tropical Africa to teach natives factory work, and other officials must have had doubts about his faith in the unpracticed Azande. He admitted that he had little to go on, other than his observations that many Africans take naturally to tailoring with a sewing machine, but he could see no "*a priori* reason why the Zande people would not take naturally to the management of spindles."[12]

In addition to the four export industries, Dr. Tothill believed some industries would be required for the production of goods to be consumed locally in their entirety, such as sugar, bricks, timber, iron, and charcoal. Sugar cane, he stated, grew well in Zande country, but an export industry based on sugar was not feasible because of the high cost of transport. He judged local demand to be great enough to consume some 225 tons a year and hoped to provide cheap sugar within the district, even after imposition of the excise duty. He suggested that the taxpayers in a suitable portion of the district would be able to grow the cane in a system of small holdings. He expected locally produced bricks and timber to be used in the construction of houses and factory buildings and hoped that there might be an improvement in Zande housing inspired by the use of these materials during the construction period of the Scheme. Charcoal production he regarded as of major importance, because charcoal would supply energy for the entire Scheme. Produced from the virtually unlimited local sup-

11. Tothill, 1943, p. 2.
12. *Ibid.*, p.3.

plies of wood, it was to be the fuel for powering both factories and lorries, by means of producer gas engines.

Dr. Tothill's strong feeling about the need for the area to be as self-sufficient as possible was shown by his proposal to restrict the importing of all goods for which local substitutes might be devised. He wanted to avoid the use of as many imported materials as possible, even suggesting the use of wooden shingles for roofing, presumably to eliminate the need for imported metal roofing. Another suggestion was to revive the iron-smelting industry of the region, which had once supplied hoes, spears, and other metal objects but had expired with the importation of iron articles by the pre-European Arab traders. He listed gasoline, kerosene, metal roofing, steel girders, bicycles, and tobacco as things which should be made extremely difficult to import into the experimental area and for which substitutes should be developed in local industries. As an illustration, he suggested that an inquiry should be made into the possibility of making wooden bicycle frames and handlebars, so that only wheels, bearings, chains, and brakes would need to be imported.[13]

Dr. Tothill envisaged a controlling body, with a charter from the governor-general, to operate the various industries for the benefit of the Zande people. It was to be modeled on the Gash Board, which was composed of a number of high government officials who managed the commercial affairs of the cotton-growing scheme in the delta of the Gash River in Kassala Province of the Sudan. He noted that provision should be made for indigenous persons to sit on the Board as soon as qualified individuals would be available. Although the central government was to provide the funds, Dr. Tothill felt that the Scheme should be carried out in partnership with the Zande in order to rule out any possibility of exploiting them.

He cautioned that the whole Scheme should be undertaken in easy stages. In the educational program, for example, it seemed to him that little more than the training of teachers could be done at first. The cotton crop should be gradually expanded; the ginnery should be initially erected as a small economic unit but designed to expand with the crop. The same principle, he advocated, should be followed with the spinning mill, sugar factory,

13. *Ibid.*, p. 5.

sawmill, and coffee factory. He suggested that the first steps should nonetheless be bold ones and that the controlling Board should be provided with a capital of about £250,000 to be able to establish the pilot industries, start teacher training, and plan the expansion of the whole experiment.[14]

It is important to have these basic proposals in mind, since they set the direction of the development scheme. It is important also to know how they were modified, in order to understand the ultimate expression of the Zande Scheme and evaluate the reaction of the people to it. Because of illness, Dr. Tothill was not able to make further detailed plans. A number of very important changes were subsequently made in his proposals, although the spirit of his work continued to be referred to throughout the planning and operation of the Scheme.

MODIFICATION OF THE BASIC PROPOSALS

In 1944, the year following Dr. Tothill's proposals, reconnaissance was made of parts of Zande District by technical members of the Department of Agriculture and Forests, and a number of committee meetings were held to discuss plans and estimates of costs. Early in 1945 an ad hoc planning committee[15] met in Zande District to discuss the general principles of Dr. Tothill's proposals. It decided that the prohibition of imports was not desirable because the administrative machinery needed to enforce it would be colossal and smuggling across the borders would be likely to increase. The committee reasoned that Azande in the Sudan would feel aggrieved if they were denied cheap and desirable articles available in neighboring countries. The committee further decided that local building materials were not always satisfactory for all purposes and their exclusive use might lead to delays and to additional expense, both capital and recurrent. The committee resolved, therefore, that the principle of self-sufficiency should be

14. *Ibid.*, pp. 6–7.

15. This committee was composed of the director of agriculture and forests, the governor of Equatoria Province, the director of the Board of Economics and Trade, the superintending engineer of the Department of Agriculture, the senior inspector of agriculture of Equatoria Province, and the province medical inspector, with advisers consisting of the district commissioner and assistant district commissioner of Zande District, the inspector of education (south), four other members of the Department of Agriculture, the government geologist, and the local medical inspector.

applied only in so far as local produce and locally made articles could compete with imported goods.

The policy of self-sufficiency was gradually vetoed by early committees, although it had been the basis of Dr. Tothill's proposals for the industrial development of a remote region. The retaining of the industrial aspects of the Zande Scheme, while supporting ideas were eliminated, resulted in the establishment of a costly industrial experiment in an uneconomic location. The factor of remoteness remained in the Zande Scheme, but without the justification inherent in Dr. Tothill's proposals. Nor was any compensation for the remoteness of Zande District devised by the planners who followed him. Along with the theme of self-sufficiency he had advocated a general improvement of communications, including the shortening of the line of both road and river transport by building a new road to the northeast and the developing of a new port on the river at Adok. This proposal was soon defeated on the grounds of economy. Because the new road was to run through swampy and sparsely inhabited country, the usual practice of using locally recruited labor for road building and maintenance could not have been applied, and the importing of labor would have meant increased costs. At the time when the idea of the new road was abandoned, a committee member made the point that the existing road to Terrakeka, a small Nile port 50 miles north of Juba, was not much longer than the new road to Adok would have been and might well be improved, but this suggestion was not followed. Instead, the existing and relatively indirect road to Juba was widened and improved to all-weather standards and its bridges were rebuilt.[16] The distance from Zande District to Juba by this route is about 60 miles longer than the most direct trace would have been and about 100 miles longer than the distance to Terrakeka. But it was cheaper to improve the existing road to Juba than to build new sections of road or to improve the port facilities at Terrakeka. The wisdom of this immediate economy was questioned many times in the following years, in view of the additional fuel costs, the higher rate of wear and tear on vehicles, and the difficulty of navigation in the river near Juba at times of low water. This sort of making-do with existing facilities went

16. Minutes of meeting, Equatoria Projects Provisional Working Committee, Yambio, 6–8 March 1946, pp. 1–2.

against one of the main aims of the Zande Scheme—to transcend high transport costs. In this and other ways the boldness was taken out of Dr. Tothill's proposed experiment.

One of the 1945 ad hoc committee's advisers, Dr. Greene of the Department of Agriculture, made a strong case for the postponement of the cotton scheme in favor of the development of tree crops. He considered these to be far more suitable for Zande country than any annual crop—especially one like cotton, which required clean weeding—because of the danger of serious erosion. The committee accepted his views in principle but decided to carry on with the cotton program because the limited cotton-growing area and the smallness of the plots would allow adequate supervision to ensure that correct antierosion measures would be taken. Furthermore, no crop promised as quick a return as cotton did. This occasion, in fact, was the only one on which anyone challenged the suitability of cotton as the primary crop for the Zande Scheme.

Major changes were made in Dr. Tothill's proposals for multiple peasant cash crops. Oil palms, coffee, and sugar cane were to be developed in the form of plantation crops controlled by the governing Board. The reasoning was that the administration knew too little about the crops at the time to ask the native cultivators to take them into their local economy. The maximum areas for these crops were reduced drastically to 350 to 500 acres each.[17] Even this reduced acreage was not approached in practice, for no other cash crop was ever to compete with cotton in the Zande Scheme. By mid-1945 Dr. Tothill's proposals for several cash crops had been simplified into a one-crop project. While cotton had been the single most important feature of his plans, he had hoped for a broader base of three or four peasant-grown cash crops, with attendant processing industries. Only cotton survived the initial committee meetings. The fiber and sack industry was never discussed; after 10 years fewer than 100 acres of sugar cane and fewer than 20 acres each of oil palms and coffee had been planted, all as plantation crops. In comparison, Zande cultivation of cotton was to exceed 20,000 acres in some seasons.

17. Ministry of Agriculture, file No. Z-1, Vol. 1, pp. 84-87. Minutes 1 and 2 of meeting of ad hoc committee, Zande Projects, Yambio, 22-28 February 1945.

Dr. Tothill's emphasis upon a modern gin to avoid damaging the cotton lint was countered by the purchase of antiquated machinery. This was used until 1955, when a modern gin was installed. A familiar longer staple cotton was to replace the higher yielding, short-staple variety that he had suggested for the Azande.

The principle of an attractive price to the cultivators in lieu of direct compulsion, which Dr. Tothill held to be vitally important throughout his proposals, was largely ignored in practice, as was the corollary of keeping prices at favorable levels relative to those in adjacent territories. Instead, compulsion was relied upon to produce adequate amounts of cotton. Each Zande family was required to cultivate at least one-half acre of cotton as a public service; failure to do so was punished by various means, usually by assignment to labor on public works. Apparently there was little need to enforce this regulation at first, but when cotton production began to decline after the bumper crop of the 1950–51 season, more and more direct compulsion was exercised and more attention was given to the punishment of cotton defaulters.

Still other suggestions made by Dr. Tothill were extinguished in the early planning meetings. The use of wooden shingles, which had been part of his scheme for the exclusion of imported articles, was firmly vetoed by the local administration, and his suggestion for the revival of the iron-smelting industry received little support. Similarly, the proposal to use local fuels for motor transport—specifically, charcoal-gas-driven trucks—did not survive discussion. It must be pointed out, however, that part of the latter concept survived, for the main electrical generating station at the industrial site has been largely powered by charcoal gas derived from local wood supplies. The local production of building materials, mainly stone, bricks, and timber, was also carried out successfully, although an important range of imports—mainly metal roofing sheets, steel girders, and cement—was also used in building, contrary to Dr. Tothill's desire to restrict these imported materials.

Dr. Tothill's basic plan of providing facilities for the universal education of the Azande within 30 years received some preliminary consideration. The number of teachers and schools that would be required, how additional teachers were to be trained, and the problem of getting girls to attend schools[18]—all were discussed. Then the whole idea was abandoned, on the assumption that the proposed expansion of educational facilities for the entire Sudan would provide enough teachers within 28 years for all Zande children to get an education of village school standard.[19] The actual increase in educational facilities during the first 10 years of the Scheme did not suit the Azande, however, nor can it be judged to have approached Dr. Tothill's intentions.

Nothing came of his suggestions for "partnership" for the Azande or for participation of Zande individuals in the administration of the Scheme. Throughout the 10 years of the Scheme there was no deviation from former practice; policies and decisions were made solely by the Europeans of the governing Board and the district administration.

Dr. Tothill's major suggestions concerning the financing and administration of the Scheme were carried out. The capital was furnished by the government, free of interest, and the governing body was a Board of high government officials. In June 1945 the governor-general's council in Khartoum approved in principle the modified Zande Scheme and the setting up of the Equatoria Projects Board to administer it.[20] This Board, after some changes, consisted of six directors and a secretary. Three of the directors were ex officio: the director of agriculture and forests, the director of economics and trade, and the governor of Equatoria Province. The other three directors were selected from three central governmental agencies in Khartoum: the Department of Agriculture and Forests, the Finance Department, and the Board of Economics and Trade. The secretary was furnished by the Department of Agriculture and Forests. The chairman of the Board was at first the director of agriculture and forests and later the governor of Equatoria Province. The abbreviation EPB and the word Board were used interchangeably by those persons involved in the Zande Scheme to designate the Equatoria Projects Board in all its aspects. In this report, "EPB" will be used to refer to the organization developed to administer the agricultural and commercial

18. Education Department, Khartoum, file No. 9.9.22, Letter 11, January 1944, and Resident Inspector of Education, Lalyo, file No. 1.C.2/1, 20 January 1944.

19. Minutes of meeting of ad hoc committee, Zande Projects, Yambio, 22–28 February 1945, pp. 7–8.

20. Letter, Finance Department, Khartoum, 341, 1, 3 July 1945.

aspects of the Scheme, which was located in Equatoria Province, while "Board" will refer to the Board of Directors that met periodically, usually in Khartoum, to make policy decisions. The local organization became a large and important feature on the Zande scene, but people on the ground did not clearly distinguish—as we should do in an analysis of policy—the local organization from the policy-making body.

The original proposals were also modified by two important additions: the policy of resettlement, which has been detailed in Chapter V, and a trading function for the EPB. The first mention of trading activities associated with the Zande Scheme came from Dr. Tothill's successor, Mr. G. F. March. He believed that the Azande would have little incentive to work under the Scheme unless they "attained a desire for money," which would happen only if they could expect to buy desirable goods with the money they earned. He felt that the shops were too few and far between to give them a "realization of what money can do for them." He saw great objections to development of trade on either the Uganda pattern, with its Indian merchants, or the West African pattern of large private companies handling all import and export trade. He stated that it was incumbent on the government to train some of the local inhabitants to become shopkeepers and petty traders immediately by establishing a number of shops supplied from a central wholesale store in Juba. The second district commissioner pointed out at the time, at a committee meeting in July 1944, that Zande District had a shortage of capital rather than of shops. Upwards of 200 shops were already in operation in the district, but, according to him, consumer goods were lacking because of too little capital and too little initiative on the part of the merchants.[21] Despite this cogent observation, Mr. March's idea was put into practice.

A good deal of time and energy was consumed by the early planning committees in the deliberations about these trading activities. When the Equatoria Projects Board was established, it contained two parts, a production division and a trading division, both under a manager who was stationed at Juba, the province headquarters. Later, in 1948, the charter was revised to make the

21. Ministry of Agriculture, file No. Z-1, Vol. 1, pp. 150-51.

two parts more independent of each other and to give each part a manager. The production division headquarters then was moved to Nzara, the industrial center in Zande District, while the head office of the trading division remained in Juba.[22] The trading division was a province-wide organization, while the production division's activities were concentrated within Zande District. In contrast to the production division, the trading division consistently operated at a loss. It had relatively little effect on the Azande and will receive correspondingly little attention in this report.

DIVISION OVER POLICY

Instances in which immediate economy was decisive show a lack of agreement by other planners with Dr. Tothill's concept of boldness for the Zande Scheme. He had not elaborated on this concept in his proposals for the Scheme, nor did he make explicit what practices or ideas he was opposing with his stress on boldness. It is evident, however, that he had been reacting to the caution and economy that had been influential in maintaining the conditions he wished to alleviate in the remote parts of Africa. Divergences of opinion about policy for the Scheme are summarized here, because the outcome of these disagreements had definite effects on the nature of the Scheme and its meaning for the Azande.

From the start not all officials were in agreement about the basic aims of the Scheme. In 1944, for example, the draft charter of the Equatoria Projects Board was changed, at a meeting of the Board of Economics and Trade in Khartoum, to alter the wording in the clause, "The general policy of the Board shall aim at the social emergence of the peoples of Equatoria Province, and the purely commercial aspects of its undertakings shall be subordinated to that aim." The last four words were changed to read "in conformity with the aim."[23] The ad hoc committee on Zande projects then had qualms about possible commercial tendencies in the Zande Scheme and asked that the change be either rescinded

22. Minutes of eighth meeting, Equatoria Projects Board, 19–20 July 1948, pp. 3–4.
23. Minute 131 of twenty-seventh meeting, Board of Economics and Trade, Khartoum, 21 December 1944.

or modified. The committee formulated a cautionary statement stating that the Zande Scheme had as its basic aim not just the economic development of the people but their concurrent social emergence, including the betterment of educational opportunities, diet, and health. Concern was expressed that "without simultaneous and synchronized advance along the three main lines of social emergence, viz., economics, medical and education" unforeseen evils might follow to produce "disadvantages for the people whose welfare is the main objective."[24]

Strongly opposed opinions were also held among the officials about the feasibility of the industrial aspect of the Scheme, producing a crisis early in 1946 during a committee meeting. The assistant financial secretary stated that his office seriously questioned the financial soundness of the proposed industrial program, particularly in light of the threefold increase in estimates for the cost of machinery. He could not see the necessity for the spinning and weaving mill and could not understand why it was referred to as the core of the Scheme. He pointed out that only about 400 people were to be employed in the mill and, further, that the price of cotton was then high enough so that Zande cotton could be profitably exported as lint. Other members of the committee countered with the opinion that the financial aspects of the Scheme should not be allowed to override its social aims and that the spinning and weaving mill was a central feature of Dr. Tothill's original plan to increase the Zande level of self-sufficiency and thus aid their social emergence. The governor of the province indicated that he would withdraw his approval of the Scheme if it were to be only a cotton-exporting project; he noted that two such projects for the Azande had been disapproved previously. The district commissioner expressed himself even more strongly, contending that the withdrawal of the spinning and weaving mill would be a breach of faith.[25] He threatened to resign his post if the policy were changed to remove the industrial program from the Scheme and thereby produce "a shabby and worthless substitute" in the form of a cotton-exporting program.[26]

24. Minutes of meeting of ad hoc committee, Zande Projects, Yambio, 22–28 February 1945, p. 6.

25. Minutes of meeting, Equatoria Projects Provisional Working Committee, Yambio, 6–8 March 1946, pp. 6–12.

26. Letter, Zande District file No. 2.B.3/1, Yambio, 9 March 1946.

The estimates of costs were then recast and received the approval of the financial secretary; the capital grant was increased to £500,000, since the estimated cost of the spinning and weaving mill alone was about £250,000. Later the grant was increased to £750,000[27] and ultimately to £1,000,000 (about $2,900,000).

Some officials continued to be fearful of inefficient operation of the Scheme if there should be much deviation from accepted commercial practices. A new director on the Board in 1947 expressed the opinion that the Scheme had been "launched at a time rendered wholly unpropitious by world conditions and that the technicians had been allowed to rush ahead before the administrative machinery had been manned and put in working order."[28] In the next year another director, new to the Board, expressed similar doubts about the bold approach to the Scheme, saying that too much rush had cost more money than need have been spent and that the remedy lay in good management, which was not possible without "ruthless bookkeeping and auditing."[29] Others, particularly the province and district administrative officials, objected vigorously to what they saw as overly commercial tendencies and had to adopt strong counteractions in order to retain the philanthropic direction of the Scheme.

At the time of these early crises the officials were already aware of factionalism. The chairman of the Board, in proposing increased cotton production, referred to opposing arguments as those of "the administration." The district commissioner allied himself with the "sociological" faction, as opposed, presumably, to the commercial faction. By the end of 1948 the second district commissioner concluded that the time had come to implement the wider aspects of the Scheme. With the resettlement of some 100,000 people and the production of the third cotton crop, he felt that the stage was set in the greater part of the district for the furtherance of the sociological and economic aspects of the Zande Scheme.[30] Fearing the aims of the Scheme, which was taking years to put into operation, might be obscured by daily routine and change of personnel, he drafted an "Aide Memoire" to reempha-

27. Minutes of sixth meeting, Equatoria Projects Board, Khartoum, 14 December 1947.
28. *Ibid.*
29. *Ibid.*, eighth meeting, 19–20 July 1948, pp. 1–2.
30. Zande District Annual Report, 1948, p. 19.

size the original purposes of the Scheme and show progress to date. It would be a tragedy, he wrote, if the enthusiasm and ideals that had inspired the Scheme were to be lost through the tedium of its implementation. He summarized it as an experiment on a grand scale, designed "to bring progress, prosperity, and the reasonable decencies and amenities of contemporary human existence to the Azande." He alluded to the division of opinion over policy when he stressed that the underlying principle had always been "development and not exploitation" and that "the sociological side of the scheme transcends the economic side, but the economic side must be sound as it forms an essential foundation of the scheme." Agricultural development, education, improvement of public health and diet, and preservation of soil fertility and of water supplies, he stated, were all of equal importance to the development of the Azande.[31] At the same time the district administration complained of the unsatisfactory supervision of agriculture, which was a function of the EPB. Qualified staff had not been recruited in sufficient numbers. Furthermore, the complaint continued, the available senior agricultural staff was largely occupied with supervision of the buying of cotton and spent too little time supervising the planting and cultivation of that crop, let alone giving assistance to resettlement or doing anything to improve food crops.[32] The district administration seems to have held up the expansion of cotton growing in this year, for of the 13,000 families resettled by the beginning of cultivation in 1948, only about 2,500 planted cotton during their first year, as had been planned for all. The district office attributed this limitation to the lack of supervisory staff,[33] but there seems to have been another reason for this delaying tactic, in addition to a desire to highlight the inadequate assistance being received from the EPB agricultural staff: resistance to Board pressure to expand cotton growing indefinitely.

The Board, along with its local organization, tended to become more autonomous as its policies were opposed, and a new element of secrecy can be noted in its operations. For the first time the minutes of its ninth meeting, early in 1949, were not

31. Zande District file No. 1.C.8, p. 22.
32. *Ibid.*, pp. 23–24.
33. Zande District Annual Report, 1948, pp. 1–4.

given wide distribution, as were those of previous meetings. Following this meeting, the district commissioner for resettlement of Zande District found it necessary to write a letter to the governor requesting that an administrative note be published outlining the aims and purposes of the Zande Scheme. The relationship of the EPB to the Scheme should, he suggested, be clarified and a local interdepartmental committee, headed by the district commissioner and composed of heads of local departments in the administration and the EPB, should be established to officiate in further implementation of the Scheme.[34] He was upset because the EPB's charter had been reinterpreted so that the social emergence of the Azande was to be realized only after the commercial program of the Scheme had provided the means. He maintained that it was absurd to consider social emergence separately, since it was not possible to shelve issues which had been raised by the impact of the Scheme, and he felt that any attempt to delay social development would undermine the whole Scheme. The EPB had been at pains to emphasize that social development along the lines of the mass resettlement was the function of the province administrative authorities and not of the EPB itself. The district commissioner asserted that such efforts of the administration did not justify placing a new interpretation on the official definition of the Scheme. He pointed out that the Zande Scheme was of basic importance as the first large-scale development experiment in the southern Sudan and that the confidence of the people in the administration and in themselves would be affected by its success or failure. He foresaw dangers in the future unless a local authority was established which would have coordinating powers at the local level. He believed that the interests of the Board should be subordinated to those of the government.[35]

The governor recognized a need for "a more deliberate coordination of effort than can be expected through undefined cooperation, however enthusiastic," but his acceptance of the proposal for the local committee was qualified by the provision that its function should be only advisory. Thus the Zande District Local Advisory Committee (ZDLAC), as established, was not the powerful body the district commissioner had hoped for. It had

34. Letter, Zande District file No. 1.C.9/3, 16 February 1949.
35. *Ibid.*, 1C.9/9, 8 April 1949.

an active but short existence, meeting some 16 times in the two years following December 1949. Although a great deal of discussion took place in its meetings, its recommendations had few tangible results, although quite possibly it may have had indirect influences on policy. For the governor the committee acted mainly as a sounding board of local officials' opinion. For the purposes of my investigation, the minutes of ZDLAC meetings gave useful information about the attitudes of various officials toward the Azande and the state of knowledge about them.

After these objections, the EPB intensified its efforts toward autonomy by identifying itself as a commercial enterprise independent of the local administration. This action was not easy to take in a territory like Equatoria Province, where most services and facilities were directly under the control of the administration, but the EPB was large enough to be able to maintain considerable autonomy; it had funds to provide for itself essential services, such as transport and labor, and essential materials, such as fuel and water. The local EPB organization itself was staffed largely with seconded government officials, so the orientation of operations differed little from established governmental practices and the directors of the Board continued to be high government officials acting in commercial roles for the Board. Nevertheless the permanent staff of the EPB in Zande District insisted on the fiction that it was an independent commercial concern. The tendencies toward secrecy, already noted, were intensified. Early in 1951 the Board agreed to a proposal made by the manager of the production division that copies of the division's budget not be issued in the future, because he considered it inadvisable "for too much information concerning the Board's processing costs, techniques, etc., to be made public."[36] This isolation, justified in terms of maintaining business privacy, added to the poverty of effective communication between the people and the policy-forming agencies that characterized the Zande Scheme. The aloofness of the EPB from local affairs strengthened the Azande's suspicions about the machinations of the Scheme; and the Board's commercial bias proved in time to be based on inapplicable premises.

---

36. Minutes of fifteenth meeting, Equatoria Projects Board, Nzara, 28–30 March 1951, minute 34(o).

As the local staff of the EPB withdrew into itself as much as possible, there was a consequent lack of identification with the philanthropic aims of the Scheme and with the populace. Those of its activities that overlapped the functions of the administration, such as the cultivation of cotton, were generally handled by the offices of the district commissioner and the manager of the production division. Common policies were discussed at ZDLAC meetings, attended by members of the administration and the EPB. The governor of the province was the only person serving on both the administration and the Board. The original charter of the Board remained under revision for years, but, judging from actions taken, the policies formulated by the Board at its ninth meeting, which had so disturbed the second district commissioner, remained in effect. As late as 1955 the secretary of the Board made the statement that the office of the financial secretary had decided earlier that the EPB was to make certain of economic stability in the Scheme before attempting social development among the Azande and also that the social development of the Azande was primarily the responsibility of the administration, not of the Equatoria Projects Board.[37]

CONSTRUCTION FOR THE SCHEME

While the above policy matters were being discussed, construction work was going on. Let us go back to the beginnings of the Scheme, in order to review its more tangible aspects. When the Zande Scheme was approved in June 1945, little had been accomplished in the 18 months since Dr. Tothill's proposals, other than the location of some suitable sites for plantation crops and the siting of a sawmill. But with the approval of the Scheme, the attendant allocation of funds, and the return to normalcy in trade after the war, the construction phase of the Scheme and the introduction of cotton as a cash crop began.

Along with the work of resettlement and the introduction of cotton, a great deal of other activity took place in Zande District during the construction phase, from 1946 to 1952. The building program included a large number of houses for the additional

---

37. From notes made at a meeting of the committee to advise the governor on the expenditure of the Social Development Fund of the Equatoria Projects Board, 1955.

staff. About 25 new houses for British staff and more than 100 for Sudanese clerical and artisan staff were constructed in Zande District in this period. Numerous other buildings were also required: the industrial buildings at Nzara (about 14 miles northwest of Yambio); post offices in Yambio and Nzara; office blocks at Yambio, Nzara, the experimental farm, and the agricultural training center; trading division shops in Yambio and Nzara; and various stores and workshops. The industrial buildings at Nzara included the spinning and weaving mill, oil mill, soap mill, and power station as well as cotton stores, other stores, and workshops. Since there was nothing at Nzara, all basic utilities and amenities had to be provided for an industrial center and its community, including water supply, electrical power, police accommodation, dairy, dispensary, and recreational facilities for about 1,500 workers and their supervisors.

The building program was slow in getting started, owing to shortages of materials, labor, and artisans, but by the end of 1946 the district office reported that the EPB works officer had "finally succeeded in virtually transforming the face of Yambio." Construction was in progress at Nzara and at the agricultural research center about one and one-half miles east of Yambio.[38]

The rising costs of materials and equipment caused numerous recastings of the estimated budgets, and shortages of materials and delays in deliveries harassed the builders throughout the construction work. One of the most severe shortages was that of corrugated metal sheets for roofing. Records indicate that houses could not be completed owing to lack of roofing sheets and, more serious, that 1,800,000 pounds of cotton were spoiled by rain early in 1948. This instance illustrates the combination of factors which hampered work: The ginnery, an old one that had been moved from east of the Nile, could not be made to operate; the unginned cotton was stored in the open because the roofing sheets for the storehouse were not available; the cotton could not be transported to the Meridi ginnery, as had been done with the previous crop, because there was a shortage of gasoline following a strike on the Sudan Railways; and the rains were unusually early.[39] The loss of

38. Zande District Annual Report, 1946, p. 2.
39. Minutes of the eighth meeting, Equatoria Projects Board, 19–20 July 1948, p. 13.

the cotton was an important reason for shifting the office of the manager of the production division from Juba to Nzara.[40]

Most of the artisans in the district were put on the new construction work and more were recruited from the outside, but because of the acute shortage of southern artisans, by 1947 160 northern Sudanese artisans were employed by the EPB in Zande District.[41] It was difficult to get northerners to work in Zande District, however, as shown by a statement made during a Board meeting that a certain contractor had been allotted contracts without competing bids because he alone had been able to obtain northern artisans and to vouch for them.[42]

Most of the factories constructed at Nzara were completed by the end of 1950, and the installation of the machinery proceeded under the guidance of engineers from manufacturing firms in the United Kingdom. The most promising Zande workers were selected from the erection and installation crews and were trained as operators by British textile experts employed by the EPB. The oil mill was in operation by the beginning of 1951, producing cooking oil from the cotton seed from the ginnery; the first year's production of 40 tons[43] of oil was increased to 90 tons in 1952, all of which found a ready local market. The soap mill began operations on an experimental basis at about the same time, but there were various difficulties in the production of salable soap.[44] In July 1951 the power station, which was the third largest in the entire Sudan—smaller only than the municipal power stations at Khartoum and Port Sudan—began to furnish electrical power for the works. The spinning and weaving mill began to produce cloth in November 1951, but the cloth was not to be sold, both because of the policy that training was to take precedence over full production and because of the desire to accumulate stocks of cloth before putting it on the market.[45] The industrial center of Nzara was officially opened on March 18, 1952, by Mr. J. F. Tiernay, governor of Equatoria Province and chairman of the Equatoria Projects

40. *Ibid.*, pp. 12–13.

41. Zande District Annual Report, 1947, p. 12a.

42. Minutes of the eighth meeting, Equatoria Projects Board, Khartoum, 19–20 July 1948, p. 14.

43. Annual Report, Equatoria Projects Board, 1951–52, Appendix I, p. 3.

44. Progress Report, Equatoria Projects Board, Nzara, February 1952, p. 1.

45. Annual Report, Equatoria Projects Board, 1950–51, pp. 1–2.

Board. In about six years, despite numerous difficulties, a complex factory had been installed at the confluence of two streams
where only bush had existed before.

The sugar plantation, southwest of Yambio near the Belgian
Congo border, had been planted to the extent of 35 acres by May
1946, and about 100 pounds of sugar a day were being produced
by the middle of 1947. This product was a dark brown sugar, obtained by extracting only water from the cane juice. By the end of
1947 production had increased to 130 pounds of sugar a day, but
the machinery proved to be far too small to cope with the crop.
The mature cane on about 20 acres was lost when it had to be cut
down to allow the cane to shoot again for the next year. Larger
pressing and boiling machinery was obtained at second hand
from the Belgian Congo and was installed during 1948; by the end
of the year sugar was being produced in small, wrapped blocks for
sale by the trading division.[46] By 1952 production was up to 64
tons annually.[47] Local demand for this product was good, although it was not widely distributed.

Another phase of the construction period was the improvement of the roads of the district. Toward the end of 1946 the reconstruction of the main road from the Lingasi River eastward
through Nzara and Yambio to Meridi was begun. This involved
widening, straightening, improving the surface, and building concrete and steel bridges to replace the older wooden ones. About
125 miles of main road were brought up to all-weather standard
under the Public Works Department by 1949, and the remaining
approximately 150 miles from the Lingasi River to the northern
boundary of the district were improved under supervision of
the district administration in the years 1949 to 1951. In addition,
a program to improve the side roads being used by trucks hauling
cotton from buying points to the ginnery was undertaken in a
major part of the district. Plans were drawn up to improve the
surface, to replace major log bridges with steel and concrete
structures, and to cut back overhanging mango trees on more than
1,000 miles of side roads.[48] This program proceeded at the rate
of 200 to 300 miles of roads each year.

46. Zande District Annual Report, 1948, p. 5.
47. Annual Report, Equatoria Projects Board, 1951–52, Appendix I, pp. 2–3.
48. Zande District Annual Report, 1949, p. 6.

Other minor projects were undertaken in the construction period, such as the erection of a telephone line from Yambio and Nzara in 1947 and its relocation in 1951. Originally it had been located some 100 yards from the road, in accordance with regulations based on conditions in the northern Sudan, but maintenance work was found to be too difficult in the dense growth of Zande District. Also, extensive rebuilding of schools and other public buildings was necessitated by the resettlement of the population.

All in all, an enormous demand for labor was put upon the Azande. Prior to the beginning of the Zande Scheme government labor in the district had been obtained by requesting one or more chiefs to supply certain numbers of men; the chiefs had usually divided the numbers among their subchiefs, who selected the laborers. This system was based on the assumption that each able-bodied man should do one month's work each year for the common good. The wage of 30 piastres, or 85 cents a month, was not much of an inducement for the men, who were not provided with food. Conscripted laborers generally did the work required of them and returned home as soon as possible. The conscription system under which the roads, rest houses, district administration buildings, and other public works had been constructed and maintained was expanded to meet the increased labor requirements of the Scheme. A labor shortage existed throughout the construction period of the Scheme. Already in 1947 there had been a general shortage, because the very area in which most of the construction was going on was being resettled. The men who were being resettled were exempted from public service in their first year, and the resettlement program was generally given precedence over labor requirements. The shortage of laborers in Yambio Subdistrict in the early years was met by requesting men from some of the chiefs of Tembura Subdistrict. An effort was made in 1947 to increase the number of available laborers by increasing the monthly pay to 45 piastres ($1.30) a month for volunteer laborers and those from outside Yambio Subdistrict.[49]

The district commissioner, in reviewing the labor situation at the end of 1948, found that the construction had required more than 1,000 conscript laborers monthly and that, in addition, for

49. Zande District Annual Report, pp. 15 and 19.

each of the first four months of 1948 an average of 725 laborers had been conscripted for roadwork by the Public Works Department alone. These demands were over and above those for laborers needed for normal maintenance of public buildings and grounds. The provision and control of labor had become one of the largest tasks of the district administration. The commissioner proposed a new policy that would restrict the use of conscripted labor to Public Works Department road gangs, mission stations under certain conditions, and district headquarters. All other institutions were to intensify their recruitment of permanent labor or modify their programs to suit their existing labor forces. He also suggested that certain labor-saving procedures be followed, such as giving up the use of thatch, which was very expensive in labor because it required periodic renewal, in new buildings.[50]

The desired result of this new labor policy was that there would be less interference with the cultivation of food and cash crops. But a heavy demand for labor continued—for road improvement, building new schools, construction at Nzara, and afforestation, in addition to normal work for the administration and other departments. Wages were gradually raised to 90 piastres ($2.60) a month for permanent labor. By April 1950 enough permanent laborers were living at Nzara to satisfy the need there, but other establishments were still trying to form adequate permanent labor establishments. Casual labor continued to be difficult to obtain up to the end of the construction period. For example, as the district office tried to implement its restrictions on conscription in 1951, 243 volunteer laborers were obtained for an urgent afforestation project by exempting them from cotton growing for the season.[51]

The construction period was a busy one for the Azande because, in addition to moving their homes, cultivating their normal food crops and large quantities of cotton, and collecting unprecedented amounts of honey, beeswax, and chilli peppers, almost every man was required to work for the government at least a month each year.

SALES OF MANUFACTURED PRODUCTS

In May 1952 the cloth being manufactured at Nzara was put on sale. It was an unbleached calico, referred to as "grays" in the cloth trade, which resembled many other unbleached fabrics available in Zande District, imported from various countries, particularly India, Japan, and Germany. This type of cloth was generally the cheapest obtainable and had many uses. The Nzara cloth was immediately appraised as exceptionally strong, but it was also more expensive than the imported goods of this type. It retailed for 12 piastres a yard at a time when imported grays sold for nine to 10. Other difficulties were immediately obvious: The material was retailed only at the EPB trading division shops located at Yambio, Nzara, Li Rangu, and Sakure. The trading division allowed only a 5 per cent wholesale discount to local traders and would supply the cloth only in full bales of 600 yards. The effect was to prevent most merchants, both large and small, from dealing in it.

The high price and lack of general distribution combined to limit seriously the sales of the cloth. Initial sales had been delayed in order to accumulate a goodly stock at the factory, but by October 1952 the general manager at Nzara was worried about the amount piling up in the stores at the mill. Some 120,000 yards were on hand, and the cost of insurance alone was becoming a considerable item of expense. A year after the cloth was put on sale, the price was lowered by two piastres a yard, the discount to traders was increased to 10 per cent, and the minimum wholesale quantity was decreased from 600 to 300 yards to local traders. The new retail price was still slightly higher than that for other cloth of the same type but was justified by the Equatoria Projects Board on the grounds of the relatively higher quality of the Nzara cloth.

Sales continued to be slow and did not begin to absorb the output of the mill, which was producing almost 40,000 yards a week. The management at Nzara became convinced that the output of the factory could be sold only to governmental agencies and other large organizations. After attempts were made to sell at wholesale in various parts of the Sudan and East Africa, a commercial agent was appointed to sell the cloth in Khartoum, where it found a ready market and was judged to be better than the best imported qualities. Its sale was enhanced by a temporary ban on imports, designed to unload stocks of cloth held by the Sudan government, and by a 10 per cent import duty. A policy "not to starve the northern market" was adopted so that the reputation of Nzara cloth would be well established there by the time selling conditions would become more difficult.[52]

The general policy was to set the price to conform with the market at the various places of sale. Therefore Nzara cloth was sold more cheaply in Khartoum than in Nzara because competing imported cloth was cheaper in Khartoum.[53] This meant that cloth selling for 10 piastres in Nzara retailed for about eight in Khartoum. Furthermore, it could not be purchased at wholesale by organizations or traders anywhere in the south for less than nine piastres.

When I first heard this story I discounted it as one of the false rumors that were constantly circulating in Zande District about the EPB's activities, for its insistence on keeping its commercial operations private gave rise to all sorts of tales. The ordinary Azande knew little more than that cloth was being made at Nzara, but educated persons were keenly interested in finding out what was going on, and the high price of Nzara cloth puzzled and irritated them. Upon checking into the story about the cloth's being cheaper in Khartoum, I found it to be true. The general manager at Nzara himself explained to me that the southern market had been given up as hopeless and that sales in the north were being pressed, because this was regarded as a more stable market. He restated the reasons usually given by the EPB staff for the poor sales of cloth in Zande District: that the Azande and other southerners were not appreciative of the quality of the cloth and that they preferred patterned and colored cloth. When I suggested that much more could be sold at a lower price, he expressed doubts, explaining that the policy was to make as much profit as possible on local sales, which represented only a small proportion of the total production.

Inquiries into the real reasons for the poor local sales of Nzara cloth seemed in order. The explanation that its superior quality

52. Finance Department, Khartoum, file No. 42.2.15, 1 December 1953.
53. Department of Economics and Trade, file No. CR/80.1./3F., Khartoum, 7 May 1953.

was not appreciated locally soon proved untrue. All the traders I talked with, whether Zande, northern Sudanese, or Greek, praised the superior quality of Nzara cloth. The larger merchants bought other cloth simply because they could get it more cheaply. Their general attitude was voiced by a Greek merchant who said to me, "Cloth is cloth, and the cheapest is good enough for the Zandes." The issue was more obscure in the case of local Zande traders, for in the more remote regions I often found alternatives to Nzara cloth that were inferior, yet more expensive. This anomalous situation was explained to me by a Zande trader north of Li Yubu: "We know about Nzara cloth and we know it is good, but we must buy what we can get. None of the general merchants here buy cloth from Nzara. They buy cloth in Wau, and we have to buy from them." Zande traders often had to buy goods at, or slightly under, the retail prices. The Azande were quite capable of discerning the superior strength of Nzara cloth, but many times I have observed them admiring it and then buying imported cloth of the same type. The reason given was invariably the price, which was undoubtedly the most important factor in the Zande selection of cloth.

All traders questioned agreed that the Azande definitely preferred colored and patterned cloth to white or unbleached cloth. Colored piece goods certainly formed the largest category of imports into Zande District, as for much of Africa. But the traders were careful to point out that unbleached cloth, such as Nzara cloth, comprised the next most important category of all items sold in their shops. It could be put to many uses: for funerary purposes (it had largely replaced bark cloth in wrapping corpses for burial), for bedding and towels, for all types of undergarments, and for the cheapest line of clothes made at the shops. It was, in short, the cloth used when colored fabrics were unsuitable or too expensive. That there was an enormous unsupplied demand among the Azande for just the sort of cloth being manufactured at Nzara from the cotton they cultivated became abundantly clear in the course of my inquiries. Only a few individuals had enough money to buy even the basic clothes and bedding they desired. If the Nzara cloth had been cheap, it undoubtedly would have been bought in great quantity. If it had sold at the same basic price in Zande District, minus the cost of transport to Khartoum, the

Azande would have been able to buy it at a price more favorable than that of any imported cloth.

Cost was not the only factor, however, for distribution would also have had to be improved. The remoter parts of Zande District were very poorly supplied in general and in some of those regions bark cloth had not yet been completely superseded by woven cloth. I met a number of Azande who were cultivating cotton but had not seen any Nzara cloth in the third year of its manufacture. Transport, which was entirely in the hands of the large merchants, was a major bottleneck in the commerce of Zande District. As an experiment, I transported 300 yards of Nzara cloth from Yambio to Li Yubu, where it was not available at the time, for one of the more enterprising local traders. In a month's time he had sold it all and wanted 450 yards more. He preferred the Nzara cloth to other unbleached cloth, because it was strong enough to make the cheap shorts that were a large item of trade in his shop. In time he worked out an arrangement to get more Nzara cloth.

The general manager of the production division at Nzara was informed late in 1953 of a brisk demand for Nzara cloth in Juba. He was also told of the comment of a Juba merchant that Nzara cloth could be bought in Khartoum and sent back to Juba, and still undercut the trading division wholesale price.[54] The general manager replied that the prices in Khartoum would have to be raised, now that the price differential had been discovered, but that a sufficient quantity of Nzara cloth should be available in Khartoum to keep the jobber and his customers supplied and eager for more.[55] The Khartoum price was not raised, but the situation came to a head when a missionary organization succeeded in buying a quantity of Nzara cloth in Juba for less than the trading division wholesale price. This cloth had been shipped to Khartoum at the expense of the EPB, sold through commercial channels, and then shipped back to Juba! In September 1954 the Yambio area manager for the trading division sent a strongly phrased letter to his superior in Juba, in which he explained the local dilemma. He wrote that the selling price for Nzara cloth was considered to be "absurd" and that no amount of explanation on the part of the salesmen could hope to shake the general belief

54. Letter, Trading Division, Equatoria Projects Board, Juba, 7 October 1953.
55. Equatoria Projects Board, Nzara, file No. 50-1.

that the EPB was "profiteering." He pointed out that Yambio merchants were buying competing cloth at five piastres a yard,[56] when Nzara cloth cost them nine. The reaction of the general manager's office in Nzara was to reduce the local retail price to eight and one-half piastres a yard and the wholesale price to eight piastres. One year after the sale of cloth to Khartoum had been started, the office acknowledged that quantities of Nzara cloth were being bought in the north, transported to the south, and retailed below the selling price in the trading division shops.[57]

This change hardly made the situation easier in Zande District, for in Nzara itself Indian and Japanese unbleached muslin was still cheaper than the cloth manufactured there. The reduction of the prices after all this time, when wages and the purchase price of cotton had actually gone up, simply served to confirm the suspicions of everyone that the EPB was either profiteering or grossly ineffective. The damage done to the administration's relations with the Azande was incalculable. The ordinary people could not understand why cloth made locally should cost more than imported goods; the educated Azande were bitter about the high cost of cloth made, as they put it, with cheap labor and cheap cotton; while others, such as European missionaries and officials not in the EPB, were puzzled by the sale of Nzara cloth 1,500 miles away at about 80 per cent of the local price. A Zande worker in the Nzara spinning and weaving mill called my attention to his ragged shirt, which was made of Nzara cloth. He wanted to know why he could not earn enough to keep himself properly clothed wearing the cloth he was helping to make. Others in the factory wanted to know where all the cloth was being sold and why it cost more than imported cloth.

As the effectiveness of the oil press at Nzara increased, the production of edible oil rose until between 100 and 200 tons were produced per year, depending on the size of the cotton crop. This oil was of excellent quality and in good demand wherever it could be obtained in Zande District—which proved, as with the Nzara cloth, to be only at the four EPB retail shops. Even there the

56. Trading Division, Yambio Area Headquarters Office, file No. Y.2.A., 24 September 1954.
57. Letter, Equatoria Projects Board, Nzara, file No. 50–1, 20 October 1954.

supply was erratic, while the remoter regions of the district got virtually none. It was relatively expensive and was considered by the large traders to be a safe item of sale only in communities where there were regular wage earners.

In the Li Yubu market in January 1954 I noticed a crowd of people virtually mobbing a vendor who was selling cooking oil. There was an acute shortage of oil, as usual during the dry season, and he was the only person in the market selling it. He had brought his stock from the northern part of the district, where considerable quantities were expressed from the seeds of the shea-butter trees *(Butyrospermum niloticum)* common in the drier regions. This appeared to be the favorite oil, since I observed more of it in use than any other kind. But upon inquiry it turned out to be low in the order of preference, whereas sesame oil and cottonseed oil stood high. The shea oil was commonly used because it was more available and usually cheaper than the other types. The preference for cottonseed oil was surprising, for it was seldom to be seen in Li Yubu, about 130 miles from Nzara, owing to lack of transport and distribution facilities. To test its salability, I transported 12 gallons of Nzara cottonseed oil from Yambio to Li Yubu for two small traders who sold it by the bottle or by using a small tin measure. It was gone within a week. One of the traders wanted 28 gallons more immediately.

After the oil had been expressed from the 1953–54 season's cottonseed at Nzara, a rumor spread that all of it had been sold out of the district. This proved to be true, for the trading division shop in Yambio had insufficient Nzara oil even for the needs of the Nzara-Yambio area. Later, cooking oil had to be imported from Khartoum to supply the needs of the towns in Zande District. In a discussion of this matter, the secretary of the Board at Nzara indicated that he saw it only as a commercial transaction. He stated that it had been more feasible for the EPB to sell all the oil in Juba, for consumption elsewhere in the Sudan, than to try to sell it locally. His only regret was that there had not been more oil to sell, for both the outside demand and the price had been good.

The reader will be aware of the disparity between this action and the basic aim of the Zande Scheme. Whenever that aim was alluded to, the reply given by EPB employees was that the principle of self-sufficiency had been abandoned early in the planning stages of the Scheme. There were frequent allusions to "business principles," and great reliance was placed on the secrecy of the transactions of the EPB.

The EPB had no effective distribution channels within Zande District. The work of the trading division there had been mainly to establish four retail shops in the centers and three traveling vans, all of which were administered from Juba. Many Azande did not know that these sales facilities were in any way different from those of other traders. The trading division and the production division became two separate entities, related only through their headquarters, which were 350 miles apart. The trading division, as a provincial affair, had no more interest in Zande District than in any other district in the province; but the production division was required to sell its produce through the trading division in Juba, and no effective means existed for getting the produce of the Zande Scheme back to the Azande. Most of it was sold more than 1,000 miles away, while similar goods were imported to be sold in Zande District. Although the trading division was founded in order to improve distribution facilities, the fact that Nzara products were sold exclusively through the division constricted rather than broadened distribution facilities within Zande District. The capital of the typical Zande merchant was too small to allow him to purchase even 300 yards of cloth at a time, as required by the trading division. No transport was directly available to him, and the EPB could not furnish transport for local traders, as some of the large merchants did.[58] The plans for assisting Zande traders by the provision of credit and wholesale facilities through the trading division never developed. Credit was extended to some local traders near Yambio, but a number of civil suits quickly ensued. The large merchants had conducted a whispering campaign among the local traders, telling them that they would get into trouble if they dealt with the EPB. The Yambio lawsuits gave quick confirmation to these rumors.

The irritation and suspicion engendered in the people by the sales policies and lack of distribution of Nzara products added to their dissatisfaction with the low prices given the cultivators for

58. Reining, 1962, pp. 543–50, goes into greater detail about activities of local traders.

their cotton, and contributed to the decrease in cotton production, which in turn led to the financial collapse of the Scheme.

COTTON PRODUCTION AND PRICES

As each area was resettled, cotton cultivation was begun in the newly established homestead plots. Each of the 5,000 families re-settled in Yambio Subdistrict during the 1945–46 dry season was expected to cultivate one-half acre of cotton in its new holding as soon as the rains began in March and April 1946.

The first season's cotton harvest was encouraging. Despite difficulties with the germination of the seed of the new variety of cotton and an unusually early end to the rains, the average yield in the resettled portion of Yambio Subdistrict was over 500 pounds an acre, compared with about 350 pounds an acre in Iba Sub-district, where cotton was still being grown in the same manner as it had been prior to the Scheme.[59] The trend in the second season was similar. The resettled portions of Yambio Subdistrict produced 2,900,000 pounds of cotton on 5,400 acres, while Iba Subdistrict yielded only 740,000 pounds from 2,320 acres.[60] Furthermore, 66 per cent of the cotton from the Yambio region was of best quality, while only 35 per cent was so graded in Iba. The crop in the new program surpassed expectations, and no one could doubt either the suitability of the region for the cultivation of cotton or the willingness of the Azande to participate in the new development scheme.

A change in the world cotton market was to have a marked effect upon the policies of the Zande Scheme. As can be seen in Appendix III, by the time Zande Scheme cotton began to be produced, prices for cotton lint had increased three- to fourfold from the level used by Dr. Tothill in his proposals. The favorable world price made the export of Zande cotton much more profitable than could have been imagined at the outset of the Scheme. Early in 1947 the chairman of the Equatoria Projects Board expressed the view that the size of the ultimate cotton crop as planned for in Zande District was too small. He urged that advantage be taken of

59. Minutes of fifth meeting, Equatoria Projects Board, Yambio, April 2–3 1947, Appendix A, p. 1.
60. Appendix II shows cotton yields for the period 1947–55.

the high cotton prices then prevailing and suggested that the original figure of 5,000,000 pounds of cotton for the spinning and weaving mill should be increased as much as possible in order to produce revenue for Zande District while the favorable conditions existed. The fact that the cultivators might be disappointed should prices drop did not seem to him a valid argument against the expansion of cotton production. He also urged that the possibility of increasing cotton production by plantation methods be reexamined, implying that the resettlement program was producing only "scattered" cultivation of cotton on a peasant basis.[61]

The second district commissioner disagreed flatly, stating that the high prices paid for cotton should not produce any deviation from the announced policies, particularly those involving resettlement and the supervision of carefully selected plots. He pointed out that communal fields had been tried for two years in the older cotton-growing areas of Iba Subdistrict and that, although higher yields had been obtained, the government ecologist had condemned the system as pernicious. The commissioner denied that the Zande cotton crop had been restricted by the speed or nature of resettlement or by any other administrative action, maintaining that the acreage had been limited during the first season solely by a shortage of seed, while in the second season there had been a shortage of supervisory staff and again a seed shortage. Finally he recalled the fundamental ideals of the Scheme and asserted that disregarding the principles of self-sufficiency and independence of world market conditions would amount to "backing out of a bargain with the Azande."[62]

Despite the administration's stand, the area in which cotton was cultivated was steadily expanded far beyond the original plans, with a view to exporting cotton while the industrial end of the Scheme was under construction and while the good prices held. The second district commissioner's desire for universal resettlement worked against his desire to keep the aims of the Scheme unchanged. As areas were resettled, the introduction of cash crops was naturally expected by all concerned. Various

61. Letter, Department of Agriculture and Forests file, Khartoum, EPB/12, 10 February 1948.
62. Letter, Zande District, file No. 2.B.3/1, 4 March 1948.

trials of peanuts, sesame, and sorghum as alternate cash crops failed, mainly because of low prices, for in a number of places the people refused to sell their "government" grain at the price stipulated. Cotton seemed a better cash crop, and some of the chiefs whose areas were not designated for cotton asked that their people be allowed to cultivate it, too.[63] Cotton continued to do well in most areas. Its area of cultivation was increased each year, and a peak was reached in 1950 when the total crop was over 8,000,000 pounds and the average yield was over 460 pounds an acre.[64] The original goal of 5,000,000 pounds had been exceeded even before the industrial site was ready to process the cotton, but of course the cotton-growing area had been expanded to far beyond a 50-mile radius from the ginnery and included a much larger fraction of the population than was originally stipulated. Since the price of lint was at a peak in the export market when this large crop was produced, it was sold at a considerable profit to the EPB. The cotton area was expanded farther, even into the more arid northern regions of the district, which had been judged by the ecologists as unsuitable for cotton. The intention was to cultivate cotton in these marginal areas only while the world price stayed above a certain figure.[65]

The 1951 crop was disappointing, for despite a substantial increase in acreage the total yield was a good deal less than in the previous year. As this downward trend continued, cotton was withdrawn from the marginal areas. As a consequence, many resettled families that had been growing cotton for only two years were left without a cash crop. The slump in cotton production was explained by insect damage, faulty rainfall, and apathy toward the crop on the part of the people. The original enthusiasm for cotton cultivation was noted to wane after the first few crops. This tendency could not be satisfactorily accounted for, and the downward trend was to continue, unevenly, until a point was reached in 1955 when not enough cotton was produced to keep the Scheme in operation.

A prime factor was the amount paid for cotton during the first years of the Scheme. The price of cotton as purchased from the

63. Zande District Annual Report, 1950–51, pp. 21–22.

64. See Appendix II for a summary of cotton yields, by years.

65. Minutes of fifteenth meeting, Equatoria Projects Board, Nzara, 28–30 March 1951, minute 27.

Azande by the EPB was set by the Board so that the average price for the three grades was 40 piastres for 100 pounds of seed (unginned) cotton. This average figure was what Dr. Tothill had urged as an absolute minimum. Considerable reluctance to raise prices was evident, in spite of the great increase in the selling price of the exported lint. The amount paid to the Azande was based on the pre-Scheme prices, which had been denounced as pernicious by Dr. Tothill, and was raised only because of comparison with Congo prices. In 1948 the district commissioner found that the Azande were comparing cotton prices with the Azande in the Belgian Congo; he calculated that the Congo price for the highest grade was about 65 piastres, compared with the EPB's 50 piastres. The local notion that one piastre equaled one Congo franc made the Congo price seem even higher to the Azande, since the official rate of exchange was 140 francs to 100 piastres. The commissioner urged that every effort be made to equal the Congo price.[66] The Board decided against his recommendation because it felt that "considerable importance [is] attached to keeping the price stable" and that "present prices are not likely to prove a deterrent to development." Some concern was even expressed that the relatively high quality of cotton purchased during the first season of the Scheme had caused the average, as estimated by the financial secretary's office,[67] to be exceeded. Further pressure must have been brought to bear, however, by unrecorded means. At the following meeting the Board noted the financial secretary's approval of an increase in the purchase price of Zande cotton, in order to bring the Zande Scheme price more in line with that paid in the Congo and thus avert the danger of EPB cotton being sold there.[68]

A comparison with Congo buying prices for cotton from the 1945–46 season through the 1953–54 season is shown in Figure 12. During the first years of the Scheme the Board price followed, but never equaled, the upward trend of the Congo price. In later years the Board price leveled off, while the Congo price, which was tied to the world price, continued to rise. Also, in the Nuba Mountains of the Sudan, the cotton purchase price increased threefold be-

66. Zande District Annual Report, 1948, p. 3.
67. Minutes of fifth meeting, Equatoria Projects Board, Yambio, 2–3 April 1947, p. 2.
68. *Ibid.*, sixth meeting, Khartoum, 14 December 1947, p. 4.

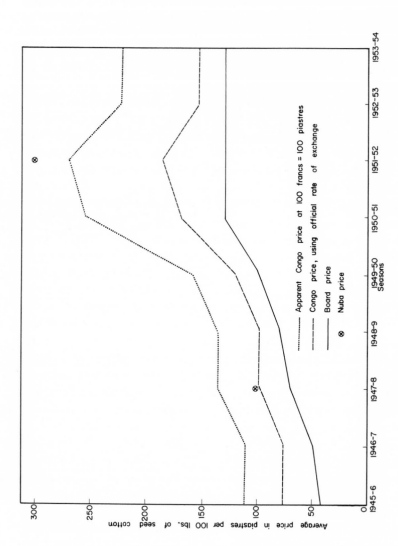

FIGURE 12

COMPARISON OF ZANDE COTTON PRICES WITH THOSE OF THE CONGO,
1945–46 TO 1953–54

tween the 1947–48 and the 1951–52 seasons[69] to a level almost three times that paid to the Azande for quite similar cotton. This Nuba figure was not available to the Azande for ready comparison, as was the Congo price, but serves here to show the trend of policy in the Zande Scheme.

Cotton production, as we have seen, did not keep pace with the expansion of areas under cultivation, but instead started to drop. A crisis began to develop with the cotton crop of 1952–53, which was a disappointment to everyone. The poor yield was attributed to heavy insect damage, a severe drought at planting time, and excessive rainfall late in the season when the cotton should have been ripening. In some areas the crop was almost a complete failure. The average yield for the district dropped from 320 to 145 pounds an acre, while in Tembura Subdistrict some chiefdoms had average yields as low as 60 pounds an acre, which meant that many cultivators received 25 piastres or less for the year's cotton crop. The effect was forcibly to verify the feelings of the people that cotton was an enormous nuisance. The price had been kept at the same level as in the previous year and compared quite unfavorably with the prices in the Belgian Congo. Some cotton may have been smuggled across the border, but this was a risky venture, for the types of cotton were not the same and the Sudan Azande ran the risk of being imprisoned in the Congo.

By 1954, when it became evident that the Scheme was in difficult straits and that its future depended upon expanding the production of cotton, some basic reforms were instituted in the cotton-buying system: The bonus payments were dropped, the grades of cotton were reduced from three to two, and the prices were raised. The price for the clean grade was set at 180 piastres per 100 pounds of seed cotton and that for the dirty grade at 80 piastres—an increase of 50 piastres over Grade I and 30 piastres over Grade III for the respective new grades. Actually these prices were chosen so that, for a crop of 75 per cent clean and 25 per cent dirty cotton, the cost to the EPB would be little higher than it had been under the old prices with the bonus.[70] All three reforms were much needed, since the old system of three grades of cotton had been confusing to the Azande and much trouble for the agricultur-

69. Department of Agriculture and Forests, file EPB/65, 9 February 1952.
70. Zande District Annual Report, 1950–51.

alists, who admitted that consistent grading into three categories was not possible under market conditions. The mill at Nzara used all grades, mixing them at the first stages of spinning. The main purpose of grading had been to provide incentive for the Azande to clean and sort their cotton well, but the effect of the wide difference of price between first and third grades had been mainly to discourage the picking of the poorer quality of cotton. The raising of the minimum price was intended to increase the total yield by making it more worthwhile to pick the poorer cotton.

The rise in prices was approved by the Board in October 1954, but the Azande had little notion of what the price was going to be and therefore reckoned on the amount they had received in the past. Hence the increase did not avert the disastrous crop of 1954–55. The tensions of the political situation added to the dissatisfaction with cotton cultivation and prices. In addition, the district commissioner's office decided that the time had come to end compulsory cultivation of cotton and informed the agricultural section of the EPB that persons who did not grow cotton would no longer be punished. While this change was not uniformly promulgated and unofficial pressure may have been put upon the chiefs to continue their compulsion, an observer could see many fields whitened by the ripe, unpicked cotton falling to the ground. No correspondingly severe drop in cotton yields occurred in the neighboring areas of the Belgian Congo. Also, at the Yambio Experimental Farm the plots used to simulate Zande agricultural practice showed no corresponding reduction in yield.

The attitude of the Azande was not unknown to the administration. In 1953 the agricultural section of the EPB had noted that the dissatisfaction of the Azande with the price of cotton was one reason for the relatively low production of cotton. The EPB realized, therefore, that it was losing a good deal of money in a favorable export market for cotton lint because of the lack of interest of the cultivators. Why, then, was there consistent reluctance to raise the level of prices paid to the cultivators for their cotton? It is possible to account for this enigma by examining the attitudes of both Azande and Europeans toward the rewards offered the Azande in the development scheme. We have already seen that the Azande were disillusioned and discouraged by the course of events. Let us inquire further into the nature of their reactions and then do the same for the Europeans whose policies directed the Scheme.

ZANDE ATTITUDES TOWARD REWARDS

Investigation of the Zande version of the decline in cotton production revealed that the Azande can be put into three categories according to their interpretation of the relationships involved in rendering goods and services to the Europeans: (1) the ordinary cultivators, (2) the ordinary unskilled laborers, and (3) the more worldly wise.

The Cultivators

The planners of the Scheme had hoped that the Azande would absorb the cultivation of cotton into their subsistence economy, but the Azande considered cash cropping to be different from their normal activities. Cotton had to do with the government; its planting and cultivation were compulsory. It had to be brought to special cotton markets, usually apart from shops and ordinary markets, at specified times, in order to be sold at arbitrary prices to the European representatives of an organization designated by the government as the sole buying agency. From the Zande point of view, the cultivation and marketing of cotton was in the same class as taxes or conscript labor for administrative projects.

The cultivators applied their ideas of personal relationships, as based on the traditional patron-client relationship, to their roles in the cash-cropping activities of the Scheme. The compulsory aspects of the cotton program confirmed their view that in growing and selling cotton they were rendering special services to the governmental officials. When the Scheme began, they felt they were entering upon a new relationship. They expected to be repaid for their work, their cooperation, and their respectful attitude. Their rewards would come not just from selling their cotton but from participating in the new relationship. At the time of my observations the cultivators had become disappointed and confused, but they were still attempting to work under the only terms they knew, those of personalized relationships. They said they had been enthusiastic when the development scheme had been proposed because they believed a long-delayed era of economic progress was to begin. They were willing to work hard in the resettlement and the cultivation of cotton because they expected goodly repayment in time. They were even willing to wait longer for what they considered to be the proper returns for their efforts than would an industrialized population accustomed to a money economy. Aside from rather vague, and often inaccurate, estimates of the price paid for cotton in the Belgian Congo, they were at a loss to give suitable amounts for rewards. But the Azande were not devoid of a "money sense," as Europeans often assume, for they had a precise knowledge of the prices of goods in the shops, even though, as has been shown in Chapter IV, they considered money as separate from ordinary life. But to them a money reward not only had a distinct value in terms of what it would buy in the shops, but also served to indicate the generosity of a patron. The poor payment for the work required of them by the administration showed poor regard for them as individuals. So the cultivators were virtually unanimous in their resentment against the administration because of its insufficient rewards for growing cotton. That they did not regard cash-crop activities as commercial transactions was shown by the frequency with which rewards were assessed in terms of needs rather than production. The most frequent complaint about the returns for cash crops was that the administration was not "taking care" of its people properly, as behooved a good and infinitely powerful patron.

The personal element in the administration had been represented for many years by the district commissioner. He was looked upon as a sort of paramount chief, but with the advent of the development scheme he became more distant and it was less and less easy to identify him with a patron. The British inspector of agriculture of the locality, who was responsible for the cultivation of cash crops, was often the only European seen by the cultivators. He visited cotton cultivations from time to time and was present at all cotton buying. He therefore served to give some degree of personality to the administration of the Scheme.

The noticeable drop in enthusiasm that occurred after the second sale of cotton in each of the regions was explained by the Azande. After the first crop they were disappointed but thought that an adjustment would be made later. After the second poor payment they began to suspect that there might never be greater rewards. (They would, of course, have reacted immediately had they received no money for their cotton at a market.) Their final reaction to what they considered inadequate rewards was delayed because they believed the British to be good patrons who would, in time, make amends. The British, despite their unprogressive ways, were the best liked of the three kinds of European administrators because of their personal attitudes. Therefore, assumed the Azande, they would be the most generous in their rewards for cultivating cotton.

The fact that the European planners did not understand the time lag in the Zande reaction to unsuitable rewards led to serious miscalculations. The time lag was not unknown to the officials. They had noted that the people were most enthusiastic in the first years of cotton cultivation, and often mentioned the danger of their losing interest in any project after an initial period. In assuming that the good cotton production of the first years of the Scheme was due "largely to the childish delight of the Azande in the novelty of these new 'games' "[71] the administrators failed to comprehend the Zande view of the situation or the motivations that created the original enthusiasm. The assumption seems to have been that enthusiasm was a normal state among the Azande and that they themselves were responsible for maintaining it. The Europeans knew that they were not paying the Azande one one hundredth as much as they themselves would have required to maintain interest in the cultivation, but the fact that the Azande had been willing to start working hard supported the belief that the dual standard was sound. Lack of effective communication deprived the Azande of the personal relationships to which they were accustomed. And their feeling of disappointment was heightened because they had worked so hard and waited so long for the proper returns.

Out of the stabilization fund for cultivators, the Board decided to award in 1951 a bonus of 75 piastres to each cultivator who had followed instructions concerning cultivation and the cleaning up and burning of the cotton stalks after the harvest. The purpose of this payment, which was voted in lieu of a price increase, was to encourage good cultivation and stimulate cotton production. Apparently it had rather the reverse effect. The bonus payments were particularly confusing and irritating to the Azande. They considered them to be gifts from the government officials for the trouble of growing cotton—gifts in the manner of patronage. As

71. McCall and Lea-Wilson, 1954, p. 3.

one young chief put it: "The money at the market is for the cotton, but the bonus is for their [the people's] tiredness." As it happened, this notion was not too much at variance with the administration's description of the bonus as an "appreciation payment." A separate payment was taken by some Azande as an admission by the administration that the proper price had not been paid for the cotton, and the bonus was offered as something of a bribe to keep them quiet. The dissatisfaction of those who did not receive a bonus or who received less than others far exceeded the satisfaction of those who received the full amount. As the bonus system was altered, in an attempt to use it as a medium for punishing laggards, the negative effects became stronger. Alterations and reductions in the amount of the bonus produced hard feelings, which reached a culmination in 1953, when Azande in some parts of Tembura Subdistrict angrily handed back the bonus to the inspector of agriculture. The latest change in the bonus system had penalized many people in that region, which is unfavorable for cotton growing. They explained afterward that they had been incensed at the pittance, about 20 to 40 piastres, given them as a bonus. They believed they had been shabbily treated; and not only had they been consistently underpaid for their cotton, but they had also been consistently offended by the smallness of the bonus "gifts." The bonus payments, in adding to the confusion, probably helped to delay the final reaction of the cultivators, which led to serious consequences for the Scheme.

The cultivators I observed were virtually unanimous in their resentment against the British for not giving them sufficient rewards. Rarely did I find anyone at cotton markets who was satisfied with the amount he had received for his cotton. There were open emotional outbursts. One man furiously proclaimed that if the British required him to plant cotton again he would tell them "to shoot me instead." Another went about the market shouting indignantly that he had been cheated and showing everyone the coins he had just received, until he was subdued by the threat of a caning by a chief's policeman. A much more common reaction, however, was apathy and resignation. Many persons pleaded with me to tell the British to give more reasonable prices for cotton.

In Zande homes one of the most frequent topics of discussion was the price of cotton, with expressions of frustration and resentment. Often the Azande asked how they could become civilized (*ngara*) if they did not receive more money for their work. A man remarked that the Azande could be forced to cultivate cotton but that they could not be forced to sell. it. The wisdom of his comment was often demonstrated by fields in which cotton had fallen to the ground from the ripened pods, unpicked. Cotton, as has been mentioned, was considered to be an enormous nuisance. Very common were statements that the Azande had been better off before the Scheme because they could then raise more food crops, both for use in the homestead and for sale. After the Scheme started, they described themselves as always being "run after" by supervisors who told them to cultivate cotton, clear residence lines, or work on the roads.

A frequent allegation was that the British were cheating (*ka nanga*) the Azande in cotton sales. When asked who specifically was cheating them, my informants maintained that the persons buying the cotton, the agriculturalists and in particular the British inspectors, were taking enormous amounts of money that belonged to the Azande. When I tried to explain how difficult the embezzlement of funds would be, my informants replied that, although I was being deceived, they were certain about this matter. One group, unconvinced by my explanations, gave as evidence the fact that the local British inspector of agriculture had just purchased a new, expensive American pickup truck. They were certain how he had acquired the money for it. Where else could their money be going? Attempts to explain the routine expenses of the supervisory and technical staff and the industrial equipment at Nzara always elicited indignant responses, such as "The British should pay the people who do the work."

It must not be thought, however, that money was the only aspect of the relationship that interested the ordinary Azande. The fairness and the face-to-face attitudes of the officials were also important. A young British assistant district commissioner was praised by a number of people because he judged cases so well, particularly those that involved Greek or northern Sudanese merchants versus Azande. They felt that he judged such mixed cases with due regard for their own rights. Instances to the contrary were cited when I asked them to elaborate upon their dislike of the northern Sudanese, who were replacing the British officials in the southern Sudan in 1954 and 1955. Their specific objections concerned court cases involving northern Sudanese and Azande, in which the Sudanese district commissioner was considered by the Azande to have given judgments preferential to the northerners. The Azande said, furthermore, that the northerners "look at us as though we are trees, not people," an attitude that gave credence, they stated, to the stories their fathers and grandfathers had told them about the slave-raiding days.

The Laborers

Unskilled laborers, by and large, worked for reasons other than to earn a living, as was the case with cultivators of cash crops. Most people in both categories tended to regard money wages as evidence of the personal esteem in which they were held. Laborers, in my experience, had even more difficulty than the cultivators in identifying specific patrons. Nonetheless they still attempted to apply criteria based on personal relationships in their roles as employees of the administration or other agencies. The vagueness of the relationships and the obviously great power and wealth of the administration produced confused and often fantastic appraisals of appropriate rewards for services rendered. Laborers did not have a clear-cut standard of comparison in judging the fairness of rewards, as the cultivators had in the Congo cotton price, for laborers' wages in other places were seldom cited. When pressed to give bases for the desired wages, the Zande laborers most often cited the high prices in the shops. Some of them felt they should earn at least enough to buy adequate clothing and bedding for themselves and their families and have a little in reserve for meat and other special foods; this they could not do on their wages. Their tendency to base rewards on needs rather than on performance was similar to the reasoning of the cultivators.

Laborers were particularly unrealistic in their ideas of what amounts would constitute desirable rewards. The enormous social distance between Europeans and Azande left the latter with little basis for comparison, and their lack of knowledge about the administration led to fantastic notions about the wealth of their patrons—the representatives of that all-powerful, nebulous entity, the British government. Laborers, at a time when they were earning about one pound a month, suggested that they should be earning from three to 60 or even 100 pounds. Most of them gave figures of 15 to 25 pounds a month for the work they were doing. When they were asked where the vast sums of additional money would come from, their answers were extremely vague, usually indicating a belief in the infinite ability of the government to coin money. When it was pointed out to them that additional funds for road-workers' wages, for example, would have to be raised locally, mainly from personal taxes, they said they would gladly pay higher taxes if they could get higher wages. They could not appreciate their difficult position in the world economy, a position that had inspired the Scheme and that justified, to the Europeans, their low wages. When one laborer stated a particularly large sum as his idea of a fair wage, I asked him how much he thought I earned each month, since the amount he had cited was considerably more than my pay. He waved at the three large circular areas of peanuts spread to dry in his courtyard and stated that the pounds that I must be earning each month were as numerous as those peanuts. Because there were thousands of them, I could not help laughing; but he was hurt that I should be amused, for he had been quite serious.

The pay for volunteer labor had been raised, during the Scheme, from one and one-half piastres a day (about $1.25 a month) to five piastres a day ($5.50 a month). But the laborers were still dissatisfied with their wages and felt that they were being ruthlessly exploited. The Europeans justified the low wages paid to laborers and clerks on the same basis as they justified the cotton prices: that the wages had been increased several times over since the beginning of the Scheme. But the Azande rejected this reasoning. They said that in the days when they were paid one piastre a day for conscripted labor they had not had the option of refusing to work, nor had they had any control over the rates of pay. The continuation of pre-Scheme standards also served to confirm the notion of the Azande that they were participating in a special kind of relationship different from commercial relationships. At the same time, laborers were in general more cynical than cultivators about monetary rewards. Some of them, particularly at Nzara, appeared to be beginning to react against patronage, as will be seen later, along with the educated and other worldly-wise Azande.

The Worldly Wise

The more widely traveled and experienced Azande had quite definite bases for the wages they wanted and accordingly gave less fantastic figures for ideal wages than did the laborers. Clerks and artisans, earning between three and 10 pounds a month, considered fair wages to be from two to five times their present pay. They arrived at such figures by comparing their wages with those of the northern Sudanese at Nzara and with those paid in Uganda and the Belgian Congo. They gave estimates of how much money they required for food, clothing, bedding, and other necessities, which coincided fairly well with their desired wages. Like the cultivators and unskilled workers, they consistently pointed out how little they could buy at the shops for the money they earned, but they focused upon the inadequacy of wages, as compared with prices, rather than upon needs that should be taken care of by powerful patrons.

The low level of wages was frequently discussed by clerks and other educated Azande. They placed the blame for the particularly low pay scale in Zande District squarely on the second district commissioner, who, they claimed, had informed the central government that "the Azande had plenty of food and did not need much money." His influence had been great, stated my informants, on all the new European staff members who came to the district with the advent of the Scheme, since they modeled themselves on him. The educated people without exception stated that the Zande Scheme had been much "admired" in its early stages but that the difficulties brought on by resettlement, low wages, and low prices for cotton had quenched everyone's enthusiasm. Also they complained frequently that those who had come to teach them civilized techniques had not taught them well. The northern Sudanese technicians and supervisors especially were considered to be "haughty" and lacking in any desire to educate the Azande. By 1954 the mood of the educated Azande was bitter. Some of them said that the "whole EPB is bad," that they had been "tricked" into doing things that did not lead anywhere. A complete change of personnel was suggested by some, while others wanted to get rid of the Scheme altogether, "to be free again," as one of them said. Just prior to the riot in the factory in Nzara in July, which preceded the general uprising against the northerners in August 1955, some Zande employees of the Board at Nzara told me that they were considering drawing up a petition which would request the withdrawal of the Scheme from Zande District, for they believed it had brought nothing but trouble to the people.

The main desire of educated persons was for an expansion of the basic educational system, many indicating a need for government schools free of mission influences. They also wanted higher education, so that there could be "real educated" persons— recognizing that many people were only partially trained for the positions available. They wanted equal pay for equal work and wished that the Azande could be given a chance to occupy some of the higher positions. They felt they had been discriminated against; that they should be "second-class citizens" in their own country and that "strangers and foreigners" should have all the best positions was a bitter subject. Another wish was that wages and prices be brought closer together, for they felt helpless in the industrialized situation that did not permit them to cultivate crops and made them dependent upon purchased food. Also, they often lamented having been trained to want things, particularly imported things, that they were not able to buy.

While most of the ordinary Azande were still applying features of the patron-client alignment to their relationship with the government, the more experienced ones were growing cynical. This attitude came out most clearly at Nzara, where there were many persons who were tired of living and working under the chiefs and who had had some experience of other places. They realized more clearly than did the cultivators that protection of kin or patron was no longer vitally important, and based their hopes on the regular, small increases in pay that they had been promised. They were most apprehensive of any practice that might take the place of these increases in pay, and had become very suspicious of any form of patronage that might be used to keep them from getting their just dues.

In 1953 a canteen was started to provide one free meal daily for the workers at Nzara, modeled on a canteen in a large ginnery in the northern Sudan. At first the project was a success, because those workers who had difficulty in finding prepared food were able to get one large meal each day. The cost of the food was a good deal higher than had been anticipated, but the expense appeared worthwhile to the management because of a noticeable improvement in efficiency, particularly in the latter hours of the working day. Then, after some weeks of operation, the canteen was suddenly boycotted and no one dared go near it. A deputation received by the management had no complaints about the food, asking only that the workers be allowed the option of receiving money instead of food. That was not possible, decided the management, and so the boycott continued. Men who wanted to eat at the canteen were kept away by threats from the others. As in the case of the bonus payments rejected by the cultivators, the workers were willing to do without something desirable in order to show their disapproval.

Later the Azande explained that the trouble had started with the married men, who did not gain as much from the free meals as did the unmarried men. The married men preferred to eat at home, and wanted to have the money instead so that their families could also benefit. Then, too, the workers feared that the free meals might result in the loss of future increases in pay. The management had promised that the cost of the food would not be taken from their pay, either present or future, but the men were afraid that the canteen would place them at a disadvantage and they chose to forgo food that some of them undoubtedly appreciated and needed.

In a discussion with the secretary of the Board, who was at this time acting manager of the works at Nzara, I learned that the men's fears had been justified. The meals had turned out to cost nearly three times as much as the original estimate of one piastre a meal, despite the exclusive use of local products and meat from the EPB's own beef herds. The original intention had been to absorb the expenses of the canteen in the budget of the EPB, but the high cost of food made this impracticable. Faced with the possibility of a general pay raise, the management had started to consider changing or withdrawing the bonus for good attendance to compensate for the cost of canteen meals. The secretary of the Board told me that the money originally allotted for the canteen could not be given to the men because they would not use it for food, but would spend it on "women and beer."

The fear of patronage in lieu of pay came out most clearly when, in June 1955, the new Sudanese general manager at Nzara, who had just replaced the British general manager, called an open meeting to discuss setting up a social center. The workers were generally hostile to the idea and asked where the money would come from for the building and equipment. When they were told that the EPB would pay for it, they asked that they be given the money, as individuals, instead. The general manager explained that a prorated amount to every worker in Nzara would be very small. He used the example of the radio, which was to be the first piece of equipment, saying that if the £45 it would cost were to be divided up among the 1,500 workers, each would get about three piastres (about 10 cents). A man replied that he would rather have this amount, with which to buy cigarettes, than have a share in a radio. He voiced the general sentiment of the members of the crowd; they did not want free services for fear of prejudicing their future wages. They said they were tired of being fobbed off with paltry gifts instead of the money for which they had worked.

Here we can see the beginnings of an awareness of different standards in a small part of the population and an accompanying disillusionment with promises implied on the basis of a vague patron-client relationship. While the cultivators were withdrawing their services from an unfavorable relationship, the more sophisticated persons were trying to avoid becoming involved again in this sort of relationship.

Why was the obvious dissatisfaction of the people with the Scheme ignored year after year? The misinterpretation of Zande standards of rewards, the lack of effective communication between the Europeans and the Azande, and impersonalized commercial standards are factors bearing on this question.

ATTITUDES OF EUROPEANS
TOWARD REWARDS FOR THE AZANDE

Comparing the attitudes of Europeans with those of the Azande about the rewards involved in the Scheme is a useful approach, because wage and cotton purchase price levels were more or less deliberate matters of policy. The general policy of European officials on monetary rewards in the Scheme was based on three assumptions: (1) that the scale of wages and cotton prices was favorable in relation to pre-Scheme standards; (2) that the people had to be protected against too rapid changes leading to industrialization and urbanization; and (3) that the Azande did not understand what was best for themselves.

A favorite point made by the officials was that wages and cotton prices had risen two, three, or more times since the beginning of the Scheme. The Azande denied the validity of the wage scale prior to the Scheme, because it was arbitrarily set for conscript labor. The fact that wages in this district were higher in 1911[72] than in 1940 shows the good sense in the Zande argument. Dr. Tothill had argued strongly against low cotton prices in the province prior to the Scheme, yet these were used as a basis for prices during the Scheme. Although the Azande were not always realistic in their expectations, they were more so in this instance than were the Europeans. The Azande used the prices paid in the Congo, which were tied to world market prices by a complex formula, and the cost of goods in the shops as guides to what appropriate returns should be. The cost-of-living index in the Sudan had gone up threefold between 1938 and 1952, while the general cost of cloth, the most important item of import to the Azande, had increased sevenfold in the same period.[73] Wages for most kinds of work available to the Azande had been based on the arbitrary figure used for conscript labor for government work. The figure had been held at about the same level during most of the colonial period, while the prices of goods had increased several times over.

Money was needed and wanted by the people; the Europeans in charge agreed that they should have some. But how much money would be sufficient, and how much more would be deleterious? This became the tacit problem. While the Azande universally lamented the small rewards, most Europeans believed, implicitly if not explicitly, that a low monetary income was really desirable for the Azande. Money was a potential source of harm, particularly if the Azande got too much too quickly. The benefits of restricting wages and prices paid for produce were continually stressed. The general manager in Nzara stated in conversation, in 1953, that the relatively low scale of wages at Nzara was a good thing because it prevented the formation of a "landless class of

72. *Bahr el Ghazal Handbook*, 1911, p. 73.
73. Sudan Foreign Trade Report, Department of Statistics, Khartoum, 1952.

workers" whose "ties with the land" might be severed if they were paid more. He also pointed out that higher wages for factory workers might make the cultivators unhappy with their lot. An example of official reasoning can be found in the advice given by an agricultural officer, before the start of the Scheme, that an estimated annual income of £1.400 ($4.00) a family was too much, when added to the proposed monthly wage and the produce of its cultivations. He suggested that all or part of the money received for cotton at the market be compulsorily banked for the Azande.[74] When we consider that the wage of which he wrote was 15 piastres (43 cents), to be advanced monthly on the sale of cotton, we can get an idea of how little was considered to be sufficient for the monetary requirements of the Azande.

Another view of the dangers of increased money income was expressed by a missionary in Yambio in 1949. Writing about the effects of resettlement and the cash crop on the educational program in the district, he asserted that widespread unrest among the mission teachers was being caused by the display of financial resources on the part of the administration in the execution of the Zande Scheme. This invited "invidious comparison with the necessarily meagre resources" of a missionary society. He went on to say that the fundamental cause of the unrest seemed to be "an infection with the spirit of secular materialism, which appears always as an uncomfortable and highly dangerous companion of rapid economic development."[75]

While most of the official and technical European staff would probably have considered the above statements to be extreme, they would no doubt have agreed with the sentiments expressed by the senior research officer of the Yambio Experimental Farm. Having pointed out the danger that a cash crop might upset the balance of the subsistence economy in a way which would not be compensated for by the money received, he concluded that a warning should be observed in the "misery of the man in a white shirt, a hat, and with a pack of cigarettes compared to the happy wearer of bark cloth."[76] This comment illustrates a sincere concern to protect the natives against the hardships and disruption

74. Ministry of Agriculture, Meridi, file No. 9.X.41, 4 April 1941.
75. Zande District, file No. 2.B.3/1, p. 68.
76. *Ibid.*, pp. 52–53.

that change has brought to parts of Africa as well as the dilemma that persists despite the best of intentions—for the problem of how to change African societies without some unpleasant consequences has not yet been solved. It also reveals the tendency of the European to choose the features of his culture that he believes should be adopted by the African undergoing a transition to a different way of life. Finally, it demonstrates a common failing on the part of the European: to evaluate the misery and happiness of the African on a basis neither recognized nor accepted by the African himself.

The reasons given by the inspector of agriculture who opposed a rise in prices in 1953, when greater cotton production was desperately needed, illuminate the manner in which arbitrary and inconsistent standards were applied to the requirements of the Azande. He had officially stated that an increase in price or a change in the bonus system was not necessary to increase the cotton production. The current crop looked good in the fields, and he believed that "the cultivators have every prospect of obtaining a return for this crop which will satisfy them, at the present state of our Zande economy."[77] His opinion was crucial in the Board's decision not to raise the prices at that time, when pressure was strong to do so. When I asked him how he could take such a stand, in view of what he knew to be the feelings of the Azande, he replied, in effect, that what the Azande thought was not important because they would have to do as they were told. The virtual boycott on cotton production in the following season showed that he was wrong in his judgment of the power of punishments to override the continued effects of a low level of rewards and that his version of paternalism was not productive in the long run. Within five months he was forced to reevaluate his stand and recommended an increase in price and an end to the bonus system.

Throughout the Scheme fear was expressed by Europeans that high prices to the cultivators would result in loss of interest if prices had to be lowered again. Thus a low level of return was maintained in order to avoid a setback. This reasoning implied that the Azande were incapable of adapting to, or understanding, fluctuations in prices received for cash crops; it ignored the fact that while chilli pepper prices had fluctuated wildly in the years

77. Equatoria Projects Board, Agricultural Office, Ezo, file Z.EPB., 7 November 1953.

past, the Azande had continued to collect peppers for marketing. Also ignored was the phenomenon well enough known to economists to be labeled the "perverse response of peasant producers," in which production rises when prices fall, in order to maintain the same level of income. In the early days of cultivating cotton as a cash crop in Uganda production had risen when cotton prices fell at the beginning of the depression of the 1930's.[78]

The fact of the matter is that the Europeans in the Zande Scheme were not dealing with specifics, such as Uganda or the Azande, but with vague impressions about "primitives" in certain "stages of development." As will be shown in the next section, they actually had little specific knowledge about the situation of the Azande.

An allied belief held by many of the British administration and technical staff was that the Azande, in common with other primitive people, had first to be taught to want money and then to learn its "proper value." As late as 1955 a member of the Board stated in informal conversation that he believed the basic purpose of the Scheme was "to teach the Azande the value of money." This argument has been repeated throughout the history of the European administration but has never been explained further. When questioned on this point, the Europeans would make vague assertions that primitive people do not know how to deal with money. The Azande, they said, bought foolish things with their money—which meant that they did not buy what the Europeans thought they should buy. Often the reasons given simply amounted to resentment that the Azande were not eager to work for money, with no realization of how unattractive the available wages were. The Azande, it is true, were not aware of all the changes money could bring about, particularly in making possible impersonalized relationships in marketing goods and services. But the Europeans in charge did not fully understand these possibilities either. Or if they had such insight, they did not apply it. Even though the Zande concept of money had some special characteristics, these did not interfere with their desire for it or their acuteness in gauging the significance of amounts of money—which seems to be what the Europeans meant when they spoke of "money sense." Again, they usually referred, in generalizations, to "primitive"

78. Wrigley, 1959, p. 60.

peoples rather than to the Azande specifically. The point of view of the Azande was unknown or ignored, as was the fact that they were not earning money for the same purposes as do Europeans.

The argument that the Azande were at a "state of development" in which they did not have a proper "sense of money values" carried a broader implication—that they did not have the ability to make proper decisions for themselves and hence had to be protected from their own erroneous desires. The European officials' tendency was to disregard whatever the Azande said, rather as a matter of principle, assuming that they were not capable of making valid decisions. The Azande were often likened to children, unable to reason adequately and behaving in strange ways. The notion of the Zande as the "happy-go-lucky child of nature" was a prevalent one, whereas the Azande of course considered themselves to be fully capable adults. Within this European attitude toward the Azande lay much of the justification—if any was needed—for the lack of inquiry into Zande desires and for the lack of any effective attempt to have the people participate in the formulation of policies. While the Azande were losing interest in the growing of cotton and in their work, owing to the feeling that they were being deceived, the officials continued following a policy that they believed would ultimately benefit the Azande. But that policy set standards for the Azande that neither the Azande nor the Europeans would apply to themselves.

THE LACK OF EFFECTIVE COMMUNICATION

Through close and prolonged contact with the Azande an outsider could come to appreciate their attitudes, but the Europeans generally avoided such contact, preferring to deal with the chiefs and the educated staff. They spoke English with the educated Azande and, more usually, Arabic with the others, chiefs and commoners. The Arabic used by the Azande was a pidgin trade language very limited in scope. The few Europeans who learned to speak the Zande language were not able to communicate effectively because they dealt with the people mainly through administrative channels. Even when they spoke directly with ordinary Azande, their condescending attitude often stood in the way of mutual understanding.

The great difference in the way of life of Europeans and Azande also tended to keep them apart. The average European official or technician received as much pay as about 100 Zande laborers, and the house of a European employee cost the government from 500 to 1,000 times as much as the mud and thatch house occupied by a laborer. This difference in the scale of living was accompanied by differences in standards of values and interpretations. Furthermore, there were enough Europeans employed under the Scheme to be able to form their own communities away from the Azande, thus contributing to the great social gap between the two peoples.

The European officials and their families lived in the commercial and administrative centers, with concentrations of about 15 households in Yambio and about 20 in Nzara during the early 1950's and as few as one or two in places like Li Yubu, Li Rangu, and Ezo. There was a rough social alignment corresponding to the idealist and the commercial factions already discussed, for the administrative officials and the EPB staff members were drawn from different classes and locales in Britain. The administration tended to recruit its members from the graduates of Oxford and Cambridge, with a heavy representation from "county" gentry, as in the British Colonial Service; the professional and technical people were usually from other universities or without university training. The administration was without question the senior service, and subtle deference—often with equally subtle resentment— was paid to the district commissioner and his British staff by the other British personnel. Next in line were the university-trained professional persons, such as the physicians and the agricultural and forestry officers. Then came the commercially oriented administrators of the EPB. At the bottom of this vaguely formulated social structure were the technicians, such as the spinning and weaving masters of the Nzara factories. These alignments were by no means hard and fast, and individual preferences made for exceptions, but the pattern of social interaction was nonetheless discernible. Spatial arrangements also made a difference, so that the social alignments of the British staff at Nzara and Yambio were made more distinct by the 14 miles between the centers, despite readily available motor transport to the British communities. Some of the EPB officers stationed in Yambio had more contact with the administrators and agriculturalists there than with their associates at Nzara. On the whole, contact was relatively slight between the British in the two towns.

The administrative and technical officials were all British, except for one family of Belgian nationality, and their social contacts were confined almost entirely to others of their kind. Some social interaction occurred with the British missionaries of the Church Missionary Society, much less with the Italian Verona Fathers, and hardly any with the Greek and northern Sudanese merchants or the northern Sudanese technicians at the factory in Nzara. Many of the British were bachelors, and they often seemed to prefer each other's company, living a somewhat different life than the married officials.

Social activity, although almost exclusively with other Europeans, was intense. Since office hours started very early, before breakfast, and ended early in the afternoon, before lunch, there was a good deal of time to meet socially—for lunch, tea, tennis, pre-dinner drinks, and on into the evening, with dinner served late. It was a close-knit, "compound" type of existence with intensive communication and interaction and with a relatively limited range of activities. Conversation was the primary activity, and the favorite topic was the British community, including not only the local group but extending to Juba and even Khartoum. So small and tight was the expatriate group that distance was not an obstacle to the flow of information. Moreover, because there were no hotels or other public accommodations in the district, except for unfurnished rest shelters, European travelers were almost always given meals and lodging by other Europeans. The fewer the number of European families in a center, the more often they would have guests and through their hospitality were kept fully informed of the activities of their compatriots.

One factor stood out extremely clearly: the lack of informal social interaction between the Azande and the British. Virtually their only contacts were in formal working situations and during office hours. The sole exceptions were Zande servants in European households, although even there the relationship was hardly "social" in the popular sense. Furthermore, the British often preferred non-Zande servants, regarding the Azande as inefficient. (This view was again partly due to inadequate communication.

Most Azande were not proficient in pidgin Arabic, which served as the lingua franca in Zande District.) Servants from the northern Sudan were considered to be the most desirable. Nevertheless a fair number of servants in European households were Azande. They had, despite their restricted relationships with their employers, an extraordinary opportunity to observe Europeans from a vantage point normally not accessible to the Azande. Undoubtedly they served as sources of much information about the European way of life. The significance of the role of servants from the local community in situations of culture contact has not been well studied.

The life of the Europeans in Zande District was as luxurious as circumstances permitted. Their houses were spacious, and their lawns and flower gardens often encompassed several acres. The implicit effort was to come as close as possible to the British country estate, with the second district commissioner's large, thatch-covered brick house, set in expansive grounds, as the immediate model. Heavier and bulkier furnishings were made in the Sudan, but many imported items were in evidence, especially linens, china, glassware, silver, and the like. Also imported were alcoholic beverages and many items of food. Most Europeans managed to get some local supplies of meat, milk, and vegetables. The dairy herds and government vegetable gardens in the larger centers had been established for the European community. The urban markets also provided locally produced food, but individual tastes varied as to the acceptability of foods foreign to the British palate, such as cassava, various leafy vegetables, peanuts, maize, and sweet potatoes. Because of the poorly developed marketing and distribution system and because the district was at the end of a long line of transport from the outside world, nothing local or imported could be relied upon. It seemed that some vital item was always unavailable. Even local fruit was in erratic supply, although plentiful compared with other staples like meat, eggs, and butter. Some European households kept their own flocks of domestic fowl to supplement commercial supplies.

Services and utilities were most primitive. Only in Nzara was piped water available to the European homes, permitting the luxury of water-borne sewage. Elsewhere water was carried in from springs and streams in gasoline tins on the heads of porters, and sanitation was in the form either of pit latrines or the bucket system of sewage disposal common in towns of the northern Sudan. There was electricity in Nzara, though only during working hours at the factory. Everywhere else kerosene lamps, usually the highly effective pressure types, were utilized for lighting. Wood was the only fuel for cooking and heating water, thus necessitating isolated kitchens, often in buildings separate from the houses. The lack of utilities was countered by hiring numbers of servants—an unsatisfactory substitution, judging from the frequent irritations evident on both sides of the employer-servant relationship.

The British official community lived as well as possible in a difficult situation, but there were plenty of shortcomings to offset any advantages: the hot climate, the threat of disease and parasites, poor food, constant shortages of essential supplies, isolation, the lack of formal entertainment facilities, the monotony of the social life, the inefficiency of servants, and so on. It was, in short, colonial living in an exceptionally remote place, to which individual personalities adapted in widely varying degrees. The Europeans devoted a great deal of time, energy, and emphasis to the material aspects of life, and more was done in the interests of an expatriate community in the tropics than in terms of the Azande or the Zande Scheme.

Because of difficulties in communication, the Azande could exert very little influence on the officials who made and implemented the policies that regulated Zande life. No Zande, chief or commoner, ever sat upon a policy-making body or was even consulted about policy. The cultivators' consultative committees, which were organized in the latter days of the Scheme as coordinating bodies, one for each subdistrict, might be considered an exception. But these committees included no cultivators, being composed of chiefs, subchiefs, agricultural assistants, teachers, and European officials. So far as the records indicate, each of the committees met only twice and covered only general topics. Very few Azande knew about them, and those who did assured me that they were powerless bodies.

The people's lack of control over policy formation in the Scheme was enhanced by the lack of monetary sanctions upon the EPB officials. They were hired on contract and were paid regu-

lar salaries, so that the success or failure of a crop had no effect
upon their incomes. The senior research officer at the Yambio Experimental Farm contrasted for me the detached attitudes of the
Scheme officials with those of the directors of commercial agricultural enterprises whom he had known in the Belgian Congo.
He maintained that a different atmosphere would have prevailed
had the pay of the officials in the Zande Scheme depended upon
its financial returns.

A striking illustration of how little the Europeans knew about
the Azande, owing to lack of communication, was afforded by the
Zande District Local Advisory Committee, which had been set up
late in 1949 in response to the district commissioner's insistence
upon a local coordinating body. The committee consisted of the
district commissioner, the EPB senior inspector of agriculture, the
district conservator of forests, the district inspector of education,
the district medical inspector, the manager of the EPB production
division, and the senior officer of the Yambio Experimental Farm.
They were all highly enthusiastic at first, and a profusion of
documentary material is available—in the minutes of the meetings
and in correspondence—to show the problems they discussed.
Among the major ones were the infertility of the Azande, control
of cultivation in small urban plots, nutritional matters, need for
sociological studies, crop-rotation schemes, extension of cotton-
growing areas, policies of the trading division, road-building
programs, and forest reserves. In May 1951 the district commissioner called attention to the large amount of work involved in
keeping the minutes and to the repetitious nature of the discus-
sions. The meetings during the second year were devoted largely
to further discussion of the main topics of the previous year.
Time and again action on the most basic issues was halted by a
lack of information about the people. For example, there was the
question of how the introduction of cotton had affected the diet of
the people. The committee could find no answer, not even indications one way or the other. It could only instruct the senior inspector of agriculture to try to determine in the following season,
when the yields of all crops could be studied, whether there had
been any changes in Zande diet. This study was never made, and
no data would have been available for comparison if it had been
made. Again, when considering the adequacy of the food supply to

the towns, the committee believed that serious shortages existed and that perhaps on certain designated lines food should be grown for the towns instead of cotton.[79] At the next meeting the position was reversed because of the pronouncement that the situation had improved during the year and that a satisfactory amount of food was coming into the centers. The committee then found it unnecessary to direct any section of the population to provide food for laborers and resolved that an annual check on the supply of food to the towns would suffice. In the event of emergency, the head of an institution was to inform the district commissioner of any shortage of food. The commissioner could then close small surrounding markets until the situation improved.[80] Nothing more came of this discussion although I observed that the markets in the centers were often short of food. Urban plots were often overcultivated because the laborers' women tended to cultivate food on the small plots for sale in the local market as well as for their own families. The Azande assured me that the food situation had always been difficult in the stations. Evidently, therefore, the committee's decision was based on the merest of impressions.

Since no one on the committee was able to speak from the point of view of the Azande, European standards prevailed. In dealing with the problem of controlling the cultivation of small urban plots, for instance, the majority of the committee was concerned with the possibility of overcultivation. Elaborate crop-rotation schemes were drawn up for half-acre, four-acre, and 12-acre plots, leading toward the ultimate use of the land for trees and other permanent crops. There was considerable discussion of how much land was needed by a laborer and his family, with the members of the committee at complete variance on basic issues, such as whether laborers should buy most of their food or grow most of it.[81] When the committee recommended to the governor that agricultural demonstrators be trained for the supervision of the rotation schemes for the laborers' plots, he questioned the need and desirability for assigning plots as large as four acres to the laborers at Nzara and requested that four-acre plots currently in use be observed to see how much acreage was actually culti-

79. Minutes of seventh meeting, Zande District Local Advisory Committee, 28 April 1951, minutes 194–96.
80. *Ibid.*, minutes of eighth meeting, 27 May 1950, minute 299.
81. *Ibid.*, minutes of seventh meeting, 28 April 1951, minutes 194–96.

vated.[82] The idea of devising experimental plots to test the rotational schemes did not work out. Despite considerable evidence that some of the four-acre plots in actual use were being cultivated completely, the rotational schemes, which would have required a large and vigilant staff, were never attempted. As most of the plots had been allotted by this time, the people cultivated much as they pleased on the small plots. In my experience with the Nzara lines, I found frequent violations of both conservation regulations and normal Zande practice.

The need for sociological investigations among the Azande, a major topic of discussion in the committee meetings, was not prompted by the members' awareness of their need for more information; rather their motivation appears to have been to improve the program of social development for the Azande. Keenly aware of deficiencies in that program, they decided that the stalemate had occurred because there were no specialists "to guide the social adjustment" needed for social development—in contrast to the full complement of technical specialists engaged in the economic side of development. Some of the more optimistic published predictions for the possible applications of anthropology had been interpreted by committee members to mean that anthropology had, in the words of one member, "established laws of social behavior and evolution."[83] The committee and the governor therefore agreed that a way out of the social-development impasse lay in engaging the services of a social expert to "study the natural evolutionary trends of the Zande people and to advise on the lines which social development should follow."[84] Their decision led to the hiring of the writer of this report.

Some members used the meetings to push favorite personal schemes, notably the hedge-strip system of cultivation. It was, briefly stated, a crop-rotation scheme that involved laying out a certain number of plots—ideally in strips across the holdings of the Azande in the lines—with hedges of various useful trees between the strips. The plots were to be designated by types of hedges and were to be cultivated in a definite sequence, as announced by the agricultural supervisory staff. The sponsor of this

82. Letter, Equatoria Province, file No. 20B.1, 7 February 1951.
83. Zande District, file No. 1.C.9/3, pp. 420–28.
84. Letter, Equatoria Province Headquarters, 2.R.2/3, 18 January 1951.

plan, the senior officer of the Yambio Experimental Farm, saw in it a way to simplify pest control and agricultural supervision, without, he claimed, any radical change in the traditional methods of agriculture.[85] Despite the serious doubts of other members about the availability of supervisory staff and the difficulty of imposing more changes upon the Azande, the sponsor of the plan continued to bring it up. He also took it upon himself to write letters to the members of the committee and to the missions in Yambio, suggesting that statistics be compiled for churches, schools, rest houses, chiefs' courts, bush shops, dispensaries, and cotton markets in preparation for a forthcoming committee discussion on "village centers" as related to his broader plans for hedge-strip farming. At that point the district commissioner was obliged to inform all concerned that this action had not been authorized by his office and that the topic was not on the agenda of the committee.[86]

At that point, too, the district commissioner wrote to the governor suggesting that the Local Advisory Committee be abolished, giving these reasons: (1) "The tempo of development involving violent changes in the lives of the local inhabitants has slackened." (2) The earlier situation, in which nearly all knowledge of the district was possessed by one man, had changed; most subjects of importance had been discussed by the committee. (3) The functions of the committee had been repeatedly misunderstood by some members, who in one case had regarded it as an appellate authority against a decision of the governor and in other cases as an executive body with overriding powers. He believed that future affairs of the district could be better handled by normal methods of discussion or correspondence and that other committees already existed, such as the Road Board, the Agricultural Research Committee, and the Educational Council, to provide group discussion, if needed. He recommended the formation of more committees of a new type, to fill other needs: A District Board of Public Health and an embryo General Purposes Committee of Subdistrict Chiefs' Meetings, as forerunners to local government, along with a Social Development Committee to recommend

85. Minutes of eleventh meeting, Zande District Local Advisory Committee, 30 January 1951, minutes 379–406.
86. Letter, Zande District file No. 1.C.9/3, 5 January 1952.

risen during the war and continued to rise fabulously afterward,[91] despite fears that a crash in the cotton markets was inevitable. This high price level had led to an unexpected feature of the Zande Scheme—the fact that cotton lint was actually exported to the United Kingdom at a goodly profit. If Dr. Tothill's figures are used as an index, the minimum price paid to the Azande in 1952 should have been about 380 piastres for 100 pounds of seed cotton, since the lint was sold for 49 pence a pound.[92] The Nuba in Kordofan Province of the Sudan received in 1951 an average price of about 300 piastres per 100 pounds for the same type of cotton,[93] selling at 51 pence a pound. But in that year the average price to Azande was 113 piastres, with a minimum of 50 piastres for 100 pounds of the lowest grade.

In February 1952 the member from Moru District in the Legislative Assembly at Khartoum asked how the price paid for cotton to the cultivators in the Zande Scheme was determined and how it compared with prices paid in the Nuba Mountains. He asked further if the administration was aware that the Azande were "extremely dissatisfied with what they were receiving for their cotton."[94] In his reply, the governor of Equatoria Province, as chairman of the Board, explained that the Board, in determining the price to be paid to the Azande for their cotton, took into consideration the following factors: (1) the price expected to be paid for cotton lint in world markets; (2) the selling price of cloth made at Nzara; (3) the comparative value of food crops and other cash crops in the area; and (4) the need to build up reserves for social development, for the bonus, and for general purposes. He did not compare the figures with those of Nuba cotton, but gave these reasons for the low price of cotton in Zande country: Zande cotton was of poorer quality than Nuba cotton, although of the same type. Transport costs of Zande cotton to Port Sudan were "much higher" than those for Nuba cotton. Within the Zande Scheme responsibility for manufacturing processes was wider than in the Nuba Mountains, where ginning and marketing were functions of the government agency. He also pointed out that a

91. See Appendix III for world prices of cotton lint from 1937 to 1955.
92. Equatoria Projects Board, Nzara, file No. 138.A., 20 January 1953.
93. Department of Agriculture and Forests, Khartoum, file EPB/65, 9 February 1952.
94. Equatoria Projects Board, file No. 133-2, p. 8.

bonus was to be paid to cultivators in the next season and that at the beginning of the Scheme it had not been expected that lint could be exported from Zande District at a price which would give the cultivator "an economic return for his labours." It would, he believed, be folly not to take advantage of the current windfall created by world prices to set up healthy reserves for the future benefit of the region. He concluded that, despite some grumbling about cotton prices, he had been informed that the cultivators were, in fact, well satisfied with the price paid, which had been trebled during the past five years.[95]

The omission of comparative figures is significant, for in the season in question the difference in the selling price of Nuba and Zande lint was only about 4 per cent, while the purchase price for Nuba cotton was about 300 per cent greater than that for Zande cotton. The selling price for Nuba cotton was made public, while that for Zande lint was kept secret. (Only inadvertently was the price for one year made available in the open files.) When the secretary of the Board advised the governor that transport costs were much higher for Zande than for Nuba cotton,[96] he had evidently not made any calculations, since the additional cost of shipping over an average of 100 road miles and 700 miles by river and rail would amount only to about one penny a pound of lint. As for the reserve funds, the point seemed to be that the Zande Scheme, being new, needed to put aside more reserves than did the older Nuba Mountains project. However, the Nuba Mountains industry was at the same time also putting aside large reserves, comparable to those of the EPB. The reserves set aside by the EPB amounted to about 20 per cent of the gross income from the sale of lint for the year of the greatest reserves, and to well under 10 per cent over the entire period from 1946 to 1954.

The total effect of the first two reasons cited by the governor is negligible compared with other variables in cotton marketing and cannot begin to account for the threefold difference in price between Nuba and Zande cotton. The third reason was the crucial one—the much greater expenses of the EPB because of its variety of activities and responsibilities, as contrasted with the simple ginning and marketing functions of the governmental agency in

95. Equatoria Province file No. 2.R.2, 13 February 1952.
96. Department of Agriculture and Forests, file EPB/65, 9 February 1952.

the Nuba Mountains. The Nuba Mountains cotton project did not need the personnel and equipment that created large expenses in the Zande Scheme. In the annual budgets of the EPB the largest items charged against profits were various operating losses, wages, and allowances for expatriate employees and depreciation of buildings and equipment.

Accounting policies had changed markedly as the Scheme had progressed. When the budget for 1948 was being drawn up, the question of starting a reserve or "cotton equalization fund" had been raised. The Board at that time felt that it was most unlikely that any profits would be available upon which to draw for such a fund. The chairman pointed out that "the amount shown as profit after each season's crop was not in reality a true figure, as not only the direct cost of production and transport must be charged against it but also that for supervision." He also observed that a crop yielding 2,500,000 pounds of cotton, as the next one was esti- mated to do, "could not possibly be expected to support, in the years before processing started, the wide staff involved in its pro- duction but intended for its processing in due course." Despite its pessimism concerning any possible profits for Zande cotton, the Board instructed the chief accountant to analyze the costs of pro- duction and to inform the Board of any profit shown at the end of the season.[97]

With the increase in Zande cotton production and the sharp rise in world cotton prices, the Board's early pessimism proved to be unjustified. Sales of lint from the 1949–50 and 1950–51 seasons were so favorable that the EPB had a surplus of £200,000, after accounting for not only the supervision, production, ginning, and transport costs of the cotton exported but also the expenses and losses of all EPB activities. These included depreciation on plant and equipment for the industrial and trading functions[98] as well as full export duty on the cotton exported. That duty amounted to £67,000 on the 1950–51 crop alone,[99] which was approximately what the Azande were paid for their cotton.

About £40,000 were deducted from the surplus for "items re- lating to previous years" and "the adverse balance on the profit

97. Minutes of sixth meeting, Equatoria Projects Board, Khartoum, 14 December 1947.
98. Equatoria Projects Board Annual Report, 1951, pp. 11–12.
99. Letter, Equatoria Projects Board, Nzara, file No. 102–8, 20 May 1952.

and loss account at the beginning of the period." Of the remainder, £80,000 went to a reserve fund for stabilization and bonus to cultivators, £50,000 to general reserve, and £10,000 to a social development reserve, leaving more than £17,000 as a credit item in the profit-and-loss account.[100]

The feeling of the Board, as expressed in a report to the executive council in Khartoum, was one of satisfaction:

> . . . Not only has the Board operated at a net profit while exercising its function in training the Azande in agricultural and industrial production, but it has also made a contribution to the general revenue of the country by way of export duties, quay duties, and river and rail freight on the products it has exported.[101]

The trend continued in the following season, and, despite a drop in the average yield and quality of the cotton, there was a considerable financial surplus after the lint had been sold at the high prices obtainable in the world market. The operating profit on the cotton lint for the season was given as £214,000. After deducting all expenses and losses, including £15,000 for the operation of the trading division, a net surplus of £104,000 remained. This was distributed among the social development, stabilization and bonus, and general reserves, while the credit in the profit-and-loss account was increased by £30,000.[102]

With this profit came a different view of the financial accounting for the Scheme. In contrast to the fear in 1948 that there would not be enough profits even to establish an equalization reserve fund, we find that by 1951 the Board had a firmly established policy to account for losses in all operations against profits, under the head "Exploration and Development," and to establish large reserves. Furthermore, the financial secretary decided that, while the Board was not to pay a fixed rate of interest on the capital advanced by the government, the directors of the Board were to determine when it would be possible to pay dividends, from time to time, with a maximum of 4 per cent.[103] A great deal of the capi-

---

100. Equatoria Projects Board Annual Report, 1951, pp. 2–3.

101. Letter, Finance Department, Khartoum, file No. 42.2.12, 25 January 1953.

102. Equatoria Projects Board Annual Report, 1951–52, Appendices, Balance Sheet, and Profit-and-Loss Statement.

103. Minutes of fifteenth meeting, Equatoria Projects Board, 28–30 March 1951, Nzara, minute 13.

tal grant was held in reserve funds, and even future cash needs were taken out of profits. This meant that a large amount of money for the purchase of cotton, which could have been raised annually on short-term loans (as it was later when the financial situation grew more difficult), was held inactive and not utilized in the development of the Scheme. The total capital grant was not fully exploited until 1953, by which time the Scheme was in financial jeopardy and profits were no longer available.

One of the major expenses contributing to losses was the relatively large cost of the European officials and technicians employed by the Board. The exact figures are not known, but the average annual salary of a European employee of the Board was about £1,200, and his direct cost per year would probably not exceed £2,000. Thus the European employees of the Board cost at least £40,000 a year. Added to this were indirect costs, such as the relatively large expense of houses and other amenities for expatriates. And the expenditures for all departments of the Board were, in the end, taken from the export cotton profits. Not that too many Europeans were employed by the Board; under the given mode of operation more Europeans would have been beneficial to the Scheme, if the cost of maintaining them could have been accounted for in a different manner.

One of the largest items charged against the profits from export cotton was the annual depreciation of buildings and equipment. This amount was on the order of £50,000 a year—a figure approximating the annual cash payment to the Azande for their cotton. The windfall in the profits received for the cotton exported had given rise to the view that all items should be depreciated heavily. In later years when difficulty was encountered in balancing the budget, the annual depreciation charged against staff housing, stores, and offices was reduced from 6 to 4 per cent and, still later, suspended altogether. An official report stated that "as the rate has been so high in the past, a suspension would be justified for some years."[104]

The items being depreciated were mostly those concerned with the aspects of the Scheme other than the export of cotton; this latter activity required only the agricultural section, the ginnery, and transport. The factory accounted for most of the depreciation.

104. Ministry of Finance, Khartoum, MF 42.2.6, 10 October 1954.

Had separate profit-and-loss accounts been kept for the exported cotton, so that the losses in the other accounts would not have been deducted from the profits on exported cotton, the result would have been a very different view of the Scheme.

In all sincerity and magnanimity, an enormous white elephant had been presented to the Azande. The industrial aspects of the Scheme had been preserved by the great efforts of the idealists among the planners, in order to prevent the Azande from being subjected to a cotton-exporting program. The idealists did not realize, of course, that costs would be accounted for as they were. The factory, of subeconomic size and in a very disadvantageous location, had never been intended to operate at a profit on the world market. It was never made clear, in the planning stages, how the inevitable losses and heavy expenses of the industrial project were to be met. In effect, the industrial portion of the Scheme had been left without means of maintenance. If it had not been for the tacit assumption that the Azande could bear the cost, from the unexpected profits on their cotton, some arrangement would have been necessary to provide for losses out of the capital grant or by subsidies or concessions from the central government.

In spite of all the handicaps arising out of the scope of the Scheme, it had been given no concessions by the government other than the capital grant and the abatement of interest on it. Full export and import duties were paid on all commodities. A form of tax abatement would have been feasible in order to make up for some of the special expenses of developing an elaborate scheme in a remote region. As it was, the Board had, by 1954, paid nearly £500,000 in export duties on cotton and in import duties on machinery, stores, and goods for sale.[105] Full freight rates were paid on government-operated railway and steamer services; and evidently no further inquiry was made, after that of the district commissioner in 1945, about getting the same preferential rates for Zande cotton as those for Belgian Congo cotton shipped from Juba to Port Sudan. The steamer services benefited from the additional traffic from the Zande Scheme because the steamers from Juba to the north were often not fully loaded, owing to the low level of exports from Equatoria Province.

105. *Ibid.*

It is natural to assume that the operation of the Equatoria Projects Board would be similar to that of other organizations directing agricultural projects in the Sudan, such as the Nuba Mountains, Gezira, and Gash Delta cotton projects. But the EPB followed very different policies, even in matters comparable to other cotton projects. The Nuba Mountains undertaking most closely resembled the Zande Scheme, for the same type of cotton was grown in similar situations, as to both environment and population. The policies relative to public relations and purchase price for cotton, however, could hardly have been more different.

The Nuba Mountains undertaking followed a stated policy of dividing the net proceeds from the sale of cotton, after deducting all expenses, at 80 per cent to the cultivators and 20 per cent to the government. In times of high prices the full 80 per cent was not paid to the cultivators, some of it being held in a reserve and equalization fund. The reasons given for doing so were (1) the anti-inflationary measure of keeping too much money from going to the people in times of high prices and (2) the need to supplement payments to cultivators when prices fell. When a higher profit was made than anticipated in 1950–51 and 1951–52, the equalization and reserve fund was expanded well beyond its original scope. Later a system of two payments was instituted to allow for a second "appreciation payment." Despite the relatively good prices paid to the Nuba, there was considerable concern that the government was taking too much of their money.[106] (This information was taken from articles in a Khartoum newspaper, based on press releases written in the financial secretary's office.) Had the EPB been able to issue some similar type of explanatory publicity, which would include a statement of the selling prices for cotton lint, the effect upon its relations with the Azande would have been salutary. Instead the EPB relied on secrecy, ignoring the reactions of all concerned with the Scheme. The general manager at Nzara, in an interview with a journalist, refused to give certain figures on production and income. To a resulting unfavorable article in a Khartoum Arabic newspaper he replied that he had the information relating to selling prices and production of cotton and oil but considered these to be "commercial matters" and "secrets of production," that "costs such as that are not nec-

106. *Sudan Star*, Khartoum, May 22 and 26, 1952.

essarily for the press."[107] This attitude was applied locally as well and contributed heavily to the general suspicion and distrust of the EPB and the Scheme.

Reasons for the differences in policy among these various organizations were not available to me, and it is not my purpose to go deeper into the matter than is necessary in presenting the position of the Azande in the development scheme. Obviously, there were reasons for the differences in policy of similar supervisory agencies, on a number of which the same individuals sat at times. That the Azande were given a much lower rate of monetary return than other peoples in the Sudan must have stemmed from notions of the relative needs of the Azande and their tractability. We know that the Azande were selected, among other reasons, because of their "amenability." A further clue is found in the insistence of the educated Azande that the second district commissioner had influenced official views of Zande needs. They consistently averred that he had told the central government, "The Azande do not need much money because they have plenty of food and other things to live on." Often there was considerable truth in the assertions of these educated individuals—a group that included the clerical workers who typed the letters and maintained the files of the administrative offices.

It is ironical to consider that one reason for setting up a controlling Board was to avoid commercial exploitation. In the Nuba and Gash projects, commercial companies were ruled out, in favor of direct governmental supervision in the first case and a board of government officials in the second.[108] These projects had served as prototypes for the Zande Scheme and its Equatoria Projects Board. But commercial principles entered into the EPB's policies to such an extent that to the people the Zande Scheme came to mean gross exploitation.

A further irony is found in another reason for forming the EPB: to ensure cooperation among the various governmental agencies involved in so complex an operation as the Zande

107. Equatoria Projects Board, Nzara, file No. 138-A, 23 January 1953.
108. Henderson, 1953, pp. 492–94, gives an insight into the thinking on the matter of commercial *vs.* government supervision in the Nuba cotton scheme in the words of Sir Douglas Newbold, who was governor of Kordofan Province when Nuba cotton growing was expanded there and civil secretary in Khartoum when the Zande Scheme was first broached.

Scheme.[109] The division of opinion between the local administration and the EPB, plus the use of commercial standards, led
the EPB into a position where it could render only superficial
cooperation and managed to be more rigid and autonomous
than any private company could probably have been in the
circumstances.

In an effort to clarify the operation of the EPB, certain business principles had been instituted that led to the primacy of sol-
vency. We can see, in retrospect, that the Azande bore these costs
out of the money they could have received for their cotton. The
EPB's consistent reluctance to raise the prices it paid for cotton
stemmed from the need to balance its accounts. When the Azande
eventually grew disillusioned with the low level of rewards, cotton
production declined seriously, as has been shown. Thus the financial structure of the Scheme, which depended upon production of
a large amount of cotton to be sold at high prices, was upset. The
drop in production forced a new view of the financial arrangements, and by 1954 the Scheme was in dire financial straits. It had
lost money in the previous season, and an operating loss was predicted for the current season unless cotton production could be
increased—and there was no assurance of that. The minister of
finance reported to the Council of Ministers in Khartoum that the
previous years had been extraordinary in allowing large profits
on the cotton exported and that governmental subsidies would be
necessary in order to keep the Zande Scheme operating in the future, even after all possible economies. His report attacked the
problem by separating the Scheme into four parts: cotton production, cloth production, other manufactured products, and agricultural development. The success of the cotton-growing portion
of the Scheme depended upon the price paid to the Azande, the
world price, and the size of the crop. The report stressed the importance of holding the yield at about 7,000,000 pounds. If that
amount could be attained and if the price paid to the Azande was
not increased again, cotton growing could just about pay its own
way—after many economies and dropping much of the supervision program.

109. *Ibid.*, p. 493, shows Newbold's concern to provide cooperation among government agencies involved in Nuba cotton growing, in view of the absence of a Board on the
Gash model.

Cloth production, however, would be unlikely to pay its way; previous losses had been paid for out of the profits on cotton exported as lint. On separating the two aspects of the Scheme, the Ministry of Finance predicted a deficit of approximately £35,000 a year for the cloth made at Nzara. The report pointed out that a projected mill in the northern Sudan was to be subsidized from the start. All costs at Nzara, except for unskilled labor, were higher than they would be at the new mill; yet there had been no subsidies at Nzara. Other manufactured products, mainly soap and cooking oil, would be making an annual profit of about £7,500, which could be applied to general operating expenses.

In recent years the EPB had received £20,000 a year from the government, for use in general agricultural development. This amount was not considered to be enough to cover the costs, and the report suggested either that the entire program be taken over by the government or that the grant be increased. Otherwise the new program to introduce cultivation of coffee, oil palms, and citrus to Zande families would have to be dropped.

Deliberations were also held about the fate of the trading division, whose consistent losses had been paid out of profits on export cotton. The minister of finance commented at the time that the Scheme had not been started as a commercial undertaking for the making of profits but as a social experiment, and that the possibility of profits from high cotton prices had perhaps concealed its real purpose. He also indicated that nearly half of the government's investment of £1,000,000 in the Scheme's activities had been recovered through export duties on cotton and import duties on machinery, stores, and goods for sale.[110]

After an excursion of several years into the realm of commercial independence and business principles, the EPB was brought back to the original purposes of the Zande Scheme. When profits were no longer available, the social theme was brought up again and the position of a small industry in a difficult location was recognized. But the ignoring of Zande reactions up to that point was to make the situation still worse. The nature of the following crop showed conclusively the temper of the Azande; it was a catastrophically small one, yielding less than half the minimum amount needed to keep the Scheme going at the proposed level of

110. Letter, Ministry of Finance, Khartoum, MF 42.2.6., 10 October 1954.

subsidies. As shown in the section on cotton production and prices, a number of factors had combined to produce the poor crop, but most important, without doubt, was the Azande's dissatisfaction with the prices they had been paid. Poor communication had meant that most of the people were unaware of the new price and grading policy until the cotton selling took place. In the meantime much cotton had been neglected, and, as already noted, unpicked.

The Scheme entered the 1955–56 season with considerable uncertainty. To its financial and production problems was added the confusion caused by major changes in the national political scene. The replacement of British officials by Sudanese had been accomplished in a much shorter time than anybody had foreseen. By the middle of 1955 all administrative police and military officials were Sudanese, the majority from the north. Most of the agricultural and research staff had also been replaced by Sudanese; only a few British engineers and other technicians remained in Nzara. The British senior inspector of agriculture, who also remained, announced a new concentration of effort to produce more cotton—which meant, from the Azande's point of view, stronger compulsion to cultivate cotton. A new spark of positive interest was likewise observed, owing to the handsome amounts of money received by some lucky people who had sold large amounts of clean cotton under the new price and grading system of the previous year. The new cotton plots looked good, but the confusions and tensions so often alluded to in this report were to have a tragic climax that put an end to my observations and disrupted the operation of the Zande Scheme.

On July 26, 1955, a riot started when the new Sudanese general manager at Nzara attempted to remove from the factory a Zande worker who had allegedly insulted one of the northern Sudanese staff earlier in the day. Shortly before, he had dismissed about 300 workers, many of whom had not left town but had added their dissatisfactions to the general tensions already created. The direct action of the general manager toward the accused factory worker set his fellow workers to throwing objects at the general manager. They then left the factory building, moved through the compound and on to the marketplace, shouting for the northern Sudanese to go home and throwing bricks and other objects in a disorganized fashion. Individuals from the populace joined in, and their aggression toward the northern Sudanese in the shopping area was met by gunfire. Troops were rushed in from Yambio, and a number of persons were injured, some fatally, by gunshot wounds. Others were drowned crossing a stream to escape the shooting. The aggression was directed entirely toward the northern Sudanese, who were by then completely in charge of the mill, except for a few British technical supervisors. I happened to be in the factory compound when the rioting started, and some of the workers asked me to leave, lest I be hurt by accident.[111]

A grim period followed, during which martial law was imposed on the area and additional troops were brought in. After three weeks of curtailed communications and supplies and great uneasiness, a general uprising took place in the three southern provinces. It was sparked by the mutiny of the southern troops in Torit, some 500 miles east of Zande District, against the northern Sudanese who had recently replaced the British officers. The Nzara incident had helped to set the stage for the uprising, having made the southern troops apprehensive about the possibility of being forced to fire on their own people. But the situation was complicated by many other factors, including some political incidents not discussed here.[112] The Zande region was then caught up in a spontaneous uprising that spread across the southern tip of the country within 36 hours. The local garrisons of soldiers and police mutinied, and in the tragic chaos that ensued the only theme was to kill all possible northern Sudanese.

My wife and son and I were within a week of our scheduled final departure. When Europeans were asked to leave, we also left the Sudan by way of the Belgian Congo, along with a small party of British technical supervisors from the factory. The uprising died out in a few days, and after about six weeks northern troops occupied the area. Information has been difficult to obtain since then, but, according to verbal reports, the Scheme was resumed after some months. A relatively large amount of cotton was purchased later in the 1955 season from the Azande, the factory was

111. For very good background material relative to the incident and to the ensuing general uprising, see "Sudan, Republic of the," 1956, in the Bibliography.

112. *Ibid.*, pp. 91–97.

restarted, and cloth was again produced. In 1963, however, unconfirmed information was received that the Nzara factories were being moved to another location.

Very few of the Azande had seen the Zande Scheme as an isolated phenomenon; they viewed the activities that resulted from it as representing long-delayed progress toward civilization. For our purposes also it may be best to combine further reviewing of the effects of the Scheme on the people with the following summary of data presented in the previous chapters.

VII

RETROSPECT

The period of colonial administration of Zande District can be divided into two parts, characterized by contrasting aims in policy. After a preliminary military administration, the government in the period from about 1915 to 1940 was concerned with protecting the population, along with the entire southern Sudan, from disturbing changes. The period following 1940 was dominated by the development scheme, with its deliberate changes put forth as a pilot program to fit the people of remote parts of Africa into the world economy. Our analysis of the social situation shows, however, that the two periods cannot be divided so distinctly. Most major social changes had already started in the earlier period. The very fact of European administration, with its introduction of wages and commerce, had brought indirect changes, while certain deliberate changes had been instituted in the earlier period.

Although the original proposals for the development scheme were intended to introduce new thinking into administration and to overcome the old standards of caution and economy, the direction of the Zande Scheme took most of its principles, largely unwritten and even unspoken, from the previous administrative policy. Concerned almost entirely with maintaining order, with a

218

bare minimum of facilities, this policy had undertaken to protect the people by prohibiting much and encouraging little. Sir Douglas Newbold, when he was civil secretary in Khartoum, said that the former "southern policy" had contained too many "don'ts" and not enough "do's." This general attitude continued to prevail throughout the Zande Scheme. The knowledge that what they were doing was for the ultimate benefit of the Azande allowed the officials to rely upon negative incentives, and the means they used were justified by well-intentioned, if not very clear, ends. The colonial administrators throughout retained control over the policy-making processes, since nothing came of the suggestions for "partnership" with the Azande in the conduct of the Scheme. The suggested establishment of an industrial complex that was to be as self-sufficient as possible can be seen as an extension, economically, of the isolation of the previous protectionist policy. And the dispersion of the population under the resettlement project again led toward greater isolation.

A salient feature of the situation in Zande District was the presence of several types of social background, of which the British and the Zande were the most prominent. Representatives of the two societies acted in terms of what they knew best. It should be noted, however, that the behavior of British individuals in Zande District was not always consistent with their behavior at home. The implicit belief of some of the officials in extensive governmental supervision of Zande life, for example, contrasted strikingly with their intense dislike of governmental intervention on the British scene. Also, the Europeans were not always typical of the outside culture they represented—as often happens in situations of culture contact. A good illustration was the seemingly fanatic distaste for urban life shown by the second district commissioner, which led him to introduce changes in settlement that imposed avoidable social costs on the Azande; at the same time he was valiantly attempting to counter the introduction of commercial procedures that were to impose different kinds of avoidable social costs.

The Europeans had brought to the Zande District certain valuable ingredients for development: stable administration, contact with the world economy, benevolent ideas, technical knowledge, and capital investment. The Azande possessed equally valuable ingredients: interest in their own development, the productive potential of their labor, and detailed knowledge of their environment. They had worked out an adaptation to their setting that was difficult to improve upon, given their technical resources. They liked their country and their way of life, despite an awareness of certain shortcomings. The Europeans in Zande District had limited experience of Zande life and also limited motivation to take the Zande point of view into consideration. They were therefore unable not only to design policies adequate for the development of the Azande but to forecast the ramifications of the changes they introduced. The Azande, on the other hand, could not become Europeans simply because of their desire to progress, and they, too, did not understand the ramifications of the changes introduced into their lives. On the whole, the Azande were amenable to change and eager to accept new ideas, but the educational processes offered them failed to give the average Zande an understanding of the innovations that he really wanted to accept. Certainly the standards of values behind these innovations were not comprehended. In fact, a principal reason for the confusion among the Azande was that so many changes were made on the basis of values external to Zande culture. Although generalizations about social change are risky to make, it is safe to say that changes arising from within a society, or modified by its culture, are likely to cause less disturbance than changes imposed from the outside. In Zande District the tenuous relationship between the European officials and the people, along with the official control of policies regulating the life of the Azande, made it possible for two different standards of values to operate concurrently.

Although the Azande had little part in the making of administrative policy, many areas of decision making were still available to them, even if hedged about with confusing restrictions. This was particularly true of the domestic and subsistence spheres, and in these areas they held some clearly conceived principles to which they often adhered tenaciously, as in marriage practices. In other areas, such as cash cropping, they had no clear principles or goals and could understand only vaguely what the administration was trying to accomplish. The Azande I observed were in a state of transition from one way of life to something quite different, but were advancing unevenly. In some respects their manner of living had been so little changed that they could easily return to the traditional practices, especially in agricultural and other subsistence activities. In other respects, however, the changes had been so great that reversion to the old ways was not likely, as illustrated by the modern Zande preference for life along the roads. Yet on the whole, much confusion existed in the minds of the people. They were trying to play new roles in a new way of life—roles in which they did not know the cues. They were working with remnants of their old ideas and values, combined with an imperfect understanding of innovations brought, directly and indirectly, from the culture represented by their conquerors and administrators.

The formerly independent Zande chiefdoms had lost their distinctive qualities and had been coalesced under European administration. In most cases the descendants of the former chiefs were still in power. They were still the wealthiest men, for in their new position, between the administration and the people, they were able to retain some of the means for acquiring the subsistence commodities that were still a source of power and prestige. But the chiefs had lost their decisive position in the Zande political structure because they had been deprived of their military and commercial power and had become the agents of an authority other than their own. As a result there was less need for an alliance of commoners and chiefs. Since the changes in the powers of the chiefs were not well understood, both chiefs and people tried to operate in the new and largely inexplicable setting with their old ideas—while exploiting new features to personal advantage whenever possible.

At the time of this study, the household made up of one man and his dependents still occupied a crucial position in Zande society. Although the household activities and the appearance of the homestead had been altered relatively little, important structural changes had taken place, not only within each household but in the groups made up of several households. The need for households to agglomerate into these larger groups had diminished, and some of the forces that kept individuals in the household had been weakened. Contributing to such structural changes were the early administrative regulations concerning marriage and divorce procedures. These regulations, designed to alleviate hardships and to improve the status of women, had aided in altering both the capacity of the household to hold the persons within it and the alliances of households. Some aspects of marriage and divorce procedure had been changed arbitrarily, without the introduction of corresponding changes in the concepts involved. The Azande still regarded the husband's relationship with the bride's kin as the all-important one, but many spoke of the difficulties encountered nowadays in properly maintaining this relationship. When European standards stressing the husband-wife relationship were imposed on the Azande, these proved inadequate for the maintenance of stability in marriage.

Among influences that helped to alter the significance of the Zande household were the introduction of money and wages and the freedom of movement brought about by the period of peace during colonial administration. The resulting increase in the range and ease of interpersonal relationships carried with it a corresponding increase in individual responsibility and a decrease in significance of kin relationships—in contrast with former days when it was necessary for a person to work with his kin in most matters outside the household. Not that all persons were coping for themselves, for the head of the household was still the crucial figure in most of the relationships between the members of his household and persons or groups outside it. But now young people could break away from their parents much more easily and safely than before, and there was a pronounced tendency for new households to be formed by persons who were younger than in previous generations. Moreover, related households tended to disperse, spatially and socially. The need for mutual protection had formerly led toward loose agglomerations of households. The removal of this external unifying force revealed a weakness in Zande social structure—the lack of an explicit formulation for the grouping of households into large social units.

This point was most evident during the resettlement project, which had as its purpose the stabilization of the population in relation to the land. The administration dealt with the households as independent units in arbitrarily assigning them to plots of land. The rigidity thus introduced to provide stability of location prevented either the re-formation of the original groups or the formation of new ones. Yet the universal reaction of the people showed that the need to form aggregates of households was still important, despite fragmenting influences.

Underlying the administration's plan to stabilize the population on the land was a concern to cultivate that land wisely and profitably. Shifting cultivation was considered inappropriate for the development of cash crops, and an effort was made to allocate enough land to each family so that it could be cultivated indefinitely, under rotation. Not all the administrators agreed on this issue, which was never clearly expressed. However, their general approach was very different from that of the Azande, who had no notions of land as property and who were concerned primarily with their rights in the use of land rather than with enduring tenure. Since no shortage of land existed and since the shifting of cultivation did not produce nearly as many shifts in residence as the administration supposed, the hoped-for absorption of the cash crop into the subsistence routines was probably more hampered than aided by the assignment of families to fixed pieces of land.

The resettlement project demonstrated not only that arbitrary assignment of people to definite plots does not produce stability on the land but also that regularity or rigidity of settlement pattern has little to do with such stability. In fact it pointed up the Azande's need for flexibility and mobility of homestead units in order to achieve optimum stability. The project proved to be the most profoundly disturbing feature of modern times in Zande District. An untenable form of settlement, it gave rise to tensions that were deleterious to the working of the development scheme, which it had been intended to advance.

The resettlement project, then, was contrary to the specific aims of the Zande Scheme and contrary to the usual trend to concentrate populations being developed. Moreover, it also violated basic considerations for any program of directed change: It was not necessary, it did not take account of the people subjected to it, and their participation was obtained only when they were ordered to execute it. Finally, the resettlement idea violated one of the most sensitive of all areas of human life; for to move a population is to change it in so many ways that serious difficulties are bound to result. Since earliest times it has been a military principle that the resistance of conquered people is best overcome by changing their settlement patterns, thereby breaking up the social units in which resistance might take root. If the purpose should be to break up social units and to form them into something different, then a change of residential pattern is a most effective method, but a clear idea of the development aims must be held throughout. Since the reshaping of social groups is rarely an accepted part of modern development projects, care must be taken not to introduce uncontrolled change by tampering with settlement patterns.

Only a small fraction of the Zande economy had to do with money transactions at the time of this study, since a household produced most of the subsistence goods it consumed. The amount of money income in the average Zande household was small, in comparison with other places in Africa and in relation to the potential value of goods consumed. For the Azande, money was a special commodity in the complex of imported goods, although it provided, in some respects, a general scale of values. In this latter role, not yet fully developed, it had already affected some of the formerly specialized spheres of exchange in the realm of social relationships—for example, altering the social significance of the marriage payment, in which money had been substituted for spears. The Azande expressed a desire for money in terms of the imported goods they could obtain with it; yet as incomes increased a greater use of money to meet social obligations could be observed. If this trend had continued, the pattern of unspecialized subsistence production in each household would probably have changed in the direction of a more specialized productive economy, accompanied by greater internal trade. This would have led to a change in the manner in which wealth was converted from the subsistence sphere of exchange to the social sphere of exchange. The separation of these spheres would probably have been eliminated if the full validity of money as a medium of exchange had taken effect.

The transition toward a more specialized economy did not take place in the course of the Zande Scheme, partly because of the officials' fear lest disturbances occur with the increase in cash incomes. The restrictive policy of preventing social disturbances by keeping the monetary returns small was largely self-defeating. The Azande were dissatisfied with the rate of returns and, therefore, finally lost interest in cultivating cotton, which was the basis of the Scheme. Different notions of appropriate returns to the

Azande were held by the officials and by the Azande. Neither side could communicate its views to the other, and what the Azande considered reprehensible behavior the officials considered to be the conduct most beneficial to the Scheme. The difference, however, lay in complex and not necessarily consistent standards held by the respective cultural elements of the Scheme, not merely in a linguistic or some other mechanical aspect of communication.

But difficulties existed in the mechanics of communication as well. The structure of the social complex created by the Zande Scheme was imperfect and unbalanced. The governing Board created a new hierarchy of agriculture staff for the purpose of communicating agricultural instructions to the Azande, utilizing the chiefs, whose power had been modified by the previous administration, largely to mete out punishment for noncompliance with those instructions. The flow of information from the officials to the people was so poor that none of the fundamental principles behind the Scheme were ever conveyed to the people. The flow of information in the other direction was even poorer, so that the people had no influence over the officials, other than by the withdrawal of services. The long period of time—long by European standards— that elapsed before the decisive reaction of the Azande gave the officials a false sense of security and led them to regard the initial performance of the people as normal.

The divergence of ideas on these matters should not give the impression that there was no common ground between the Europeans and the Azande, for they shared some basic views, although not for the same reasons. We should not overlook the fact that they all believed in the objective of the Scheme: the development of the Azande. Neither side knew the precise methods of achieving this objective, but each in its own way wanted to improve the life of the Azande. The Europeans wanted to give the Azande better standards of education, agriculture, and public health and the chance to earn a little more money. The Azande wanted better opportunities for converting subsistence commodities into imported goods of the money complex and to become more civilized.

Here is revealed another point of agreement: No one expected cotton, or any other cash crop, to change significantly the basic economy. Such apparent agreement was based on differing reasons, however. The Azande had little information to indicate that radical changes in their way of life should or could result from the addition of a cash crop. They were interested in the prospect, promised by the Scheme, of increasing their cash income. While they wanted more money, they preferred to earn it through the sale of fortuitous surpluses of food crops or of handicrafts, which were largely regarded as leisure-time activities. They considered cotton cultivation to be a special activity that had its difficulties, but was worth trying since it might provide a greater and more reliable income than collecting forest products. In other words, the Azande wanted to stay with their way of life, while earning more money. The expectations of the European planners that cotton would be absorbed into the subsistence routine of the Azande rested on the assumption that subsistence agriculture would continue to be the dominant factor in their economy and their lives. Implicit in all the plans was the belief that the Azande would continue to feed and house themselves by traditional means, while obtaining "a modest cash income for reasonable imported amenities."

On the other point, then, both elements agreed: They assumed that development would be expressed in the form of money. Somewhat greater and more uniform income for the Zande population was a basic aim of the economic side of the development scheme, according to the Europeans. The Azande had long felt themselves to be frustrated in their desire for the "things of the white man," which could be obtained only with money at the shops. Money, despite its varied and vague meanings, was for both sides the tangible expression of personal relationships within the Scheme. The difference in interpretation, however, contributed heavily to the failure of the Scheme. The presence of a common valued objective did not create common understanding of that objective, or anything else. The officials tried to deal with Zande labor as a commodity, while the Azande considered their work to be an expression or a part of a personal relationship. The efforts of the officials to put the relationship on a strictly cash basis were enormously handicapped by poor payment for cotton.

The Zande Scheme introduced more money, but still not enough to affect the basic life of the people. It introduced more Europeans and imposed their standards of values upon the Azande much more than before, but not in such a manner as to coordinate them with Zande standards. The Zande cultivators, with little specific information about the workings of the Scheme, tended to impute to it promises for the future that sometimes bordered on the fantastic. The persistently low level of rewards led to disappointment and resentment, after an enthusiastic beginning. Lacking means of communication and of control over the situation, the Azande sold less and less cotton, despite all devices used to encourage them. The resulting serious decline in cotton production wiped out the profits of the EPB. A reversion to the original aims of the Scheme proved to be too late.

The Azande had wanted the development scheme because they felt that they had been held back too long from the benefits of education and economic development. The Scheme was thus seen as long overdue but part of the normal course of events. They wanted, of course, to have the development occur on their own terms; that is, they wanted to be able to convert subsistence activities into money more readily, without changing their way of life. They did not understand why this could not be done. As it turned out, the development scheme brought them only inconvenience and distress.

The planners, too, wanted to improve the Zande way of life without altering it drastically, for they were aware of some of the hazards involved in development. A theoretical solution was attempted in the isolation of development from all other motivations, but they knew of no specific ways of carrying out the broad intentions of the Scheme. When European business principles were applied, they proved inadequate, since some aspects of the Scheme, particularly the industrial experiment, could not be operated economically on the basis of these principles. Because of a lack of information about the Azande and a lack of understanding of their values, they relied on a series of ad hoc impressions in developing an arbitrary formulation of Zande needs. This proved to be only a temporary expedient, because the Azande did not accept the standards on which it was based. The Europeans, by and large, overlooked the local situation and used ideas derived from European experience. Even when attempts were made to describe Zande culture, the concepts used were usually very general and vague. Consequently, more changes were introduced than were necessary and all too often rested on bases foreign to the

Zande situation. In the directing of social change, as in development schemes, all possible precautions should be taken to effect no changes that are not absolutely essential to the end desired. Everything should be done in terms of the society and the ideas contained within its culture, and as far as possible the people should be allowed to decide how the necessary changes are to be enacted. These considerations apply to the most minute and superficial-seeming features of the way of life of any people, since it is extremely difficult to predict what the ramifications of change will be.[1]

Instances in which changes were kept to a minimum are found in the successful cotton-growing projects of the Nuba Mountains of the Sudan and in Uganda—projects that have furnished most of the comparisons used in this study. In Uganda, cotton was introduced as a cash crop in the early 1900's by the simple expedient of issuing seed to certain Ganda chiefs. Cotton was entirely a native affair for the first few years. Compulsion was used by some chiefs at first, but within a system understood and accepted by the cultivators, who soon began to cultivate cotton of their own will. Despite certain governmental restrictions, which had to be imposed later to protect the overall quality of the cotton, the crop gained so rapidly in popularity that often not enough seed was available to satisfy the demand.[2] In the Nuba case, the crop was introduced, in a tentative manner with a minimum of supervision, in 1924. It was readily accepted as a source of cash, and production rose steadily. In 1929 certain plans were formulated to improve husbandry in order to "increase the general standard of living." When very little interest was shown in the demonstration plots, a decision was made not to force European methods of agriculture. By 1938 the policy was established to build upon existing methods rather than to introduce systems from the outside, however sound they might seem. The cotton growing has been very simply directed. Government-issued seed must be used, and the agricultural staff gives advice to growers, where possible, and takes action to combat pests.[3] Uganda cotton production has

1. See Mead, 1955, pp. 271, 285, 287, 289, for statements about the lack of predictability in technological change. Not much has transpired since the publication of this work to alter the situation.
2. Wrigley, 1959, pp. 16–19.
3. March, 1948, pp. 844–45.

been an outstanding example of a successful peasant-grown cash crop, and the Nuba Mountains cotton has steadily maintained a high yield and good quality.

Every possible effort should be made in situations of directed change to get the people themselves to understand the implications of the changes to be introduced and all foreseeable repercussions.[4] The extent to which such understanding can be achieved will vary greatly, depending upon the level of education of the people, the nature of the channels of communication, and the understanding of the potentialities of the development plans by those persons attempting to explain them to the people. As shown in the Zande case, a people's apparent agreement to the introduction of change does not mean that they understand the nature of the change or the reasons for its introduction. Least likely to occur is a realistic appraisal of the results of change. All too often even the outside persons directing it have an imperfect grasp of its aims, as illustrated, again, by the Zande Scheme. Something more than passive understanding is needed, because successful change requires a true involvement of the people. If that cannot be achieved, it would be wiser to abandon the attempt. The Zande Scheme illustrates a breach of this injunction, because of its reliance upon compulsion and faulty channels of communication rather than upon the understanding and involvement of the people.

The Zande Scheme, through a series of ad hoc decisions and gradual shifts, had been changed from a unique and bold altruistic venture to test possibilities for the social and economic advancement of the remote populations of Africa to what seemed to the people to be gross exploitation. The original plans, while appropriate to the environment in many respects, were unusual in the economic theories utilized. The combination of industrialization with isolation was a novel idea in development schemes, and particularly alien to the usual industrialization measures, which seek to bring about a closer contact with the world economy. The management of the Zande Scheme very early found the self-sufficiency principle to be impractical, thus justifying not only the deletion of this feature but other changes in the original plans, as well as the ultimate adoption of commercial principles that con-

4. Walinsky, 1963, elaborates upon this point.

trasted sharply with the intent of the original plans. The division of opinion about the orientation of the Scheme permitted its directors to disengage themselves from the immediate situation and to use non-Zande bases for their decisions.

A further weakness in the plans was the basic difficulty of formulating their philanthropic principles. This resulted in divergent opinions on how to proceed and left the philanthropists among the administrators clutching at straws. Commercial standards were applied because of their familiarity and apparent soundness. The philanthropists insisted on retaining the industrial aspects of the Scheme after the original justifications for its uneconomic location had been voted down. The fortuitous rise in world cotton prices then led to the policy of paying for expensive factories out of profits on exported cotton. In retrospect, we can see that the Azande paid the costs of the extraordinary features of the Scheme out of the money they might have received from the sale of cotton. Because the officials lacked ideas of how to control economic change, however, they tended to restrict the amount of money the Azande were allowed to earn. The policy of paying low prices for cotton, which was exported at large profit, was justified by the intention behind the Scheme: to help the Azande improve their lot. An extraordinary chance to attract the interest of the people by the positive incentive of good returns for their cotton was thus lost. It is unfortunate that the philanthropic aims of the Scheme could not have been expressed in the form of worthy rewards. That the frankly imperialistic cotton projects of the Belgian Congo should have seemed to the Azande to be more generous must be viewed as high irony.

One can only speculate about the effect better payment for their cotton would have had on the Azande, but in all probability higher prices would have improved their attitude toward cotton growing. As we have seen, they frequently compared their small returns with the large amounts of money some Congo Zande families received for a season's cotton. If the Congo price could have been matched or exceeded, some Zande District families would probably have put forth special efforts with their cotton cultivation which could have brought relatively impressive sums in payment. And if the Nuba prices could have been matched when world prices were at their peak, memorable amounts could have been received by some Azande. This would probably have done a good deal to improve morale, especially in view of the personalized esteem represented, in Zande eyes, by payment for cotton. The policy of holding prices down to avoid setbacks did a disservice to Zande mental abilities. Moreover, it failed to recognize the principle that peasant producers do not respond to current trends in prices but to those of three to five years previously, as has been demonstrated in the case of the growers of cotton in Uganda.[5] Really good prices would have given the Azande something to shoot for, even if fluctuations had occurred, and would have demonstrated to them the good intentions of the administrators.

The Zande Scheme proved that it is possible to establish an industrial community in the center of Africa, if cost is no object, and that the Azande could adjust to industrial procedures with aplomb and could produce large amounts of cotton when interested in doing so. But the Zande Scheme also proved that many things cannot be done. Some of its weaknesses—especially those in ecology, social organization, and communication—will be found, in one form or another, in other widespread attempts at economic aid and community development.

Development is in the spirit of our time and is desired by both the "backward" peoples and their technological "superiors." The Zande Scheme has shown us how extraordinarily difficult it is to direct development. Yet there can be little technological development of the type that is most desired without creating relationships between social elements of different cultural backgrounds. An effort has been made in this book to add to the body of data concerning changes resulting from European conquest, administration, and technological development and also to indicate methods by which the administrators and technicians can be included in the study of a society undergoing change. I suggest that technological officials and experts be as much a part of the research as are the people being developed. In other words, the totality of the development project should be studied, rather than just the people being developed. Then all influences from the various cultures involved can be taken into account, and confusion can be detected at all levels before it becomes part of the accepted

5. Wrigley, 1959, pp. 60–61.

pattern. The developers must expect, ideally, an examination of their own motivations, procedures, and aims, and if cross-cultural development is to succeed, they must be willing to compromise and change their points of view as the project progresses. If analyses of motivations and goals can be defined early in the planning phases of a development scheme and if the scheme can be adapted to keep up with changes—in a manner similar to what has been suggested here in retrospect—a good deal of unnecessary cost and failure can be avoided.

APPENDIX I

PRICES PAID TO THE AZANDE FOR THEIR COTTON, 1939–55, IN PIASTRES

(100 piastres = 1 pound Egyptian or £1.6ₛ.)

Season	Average total paid per cotton plot	By grade, per 100 lbs.			Average paid at market per 100 lbs.	Average, with bonus, per 100 lbs.
		I	II	III		
1939–40	‡	28		25	‡	No bonus
1940–41	‡	28		25	‡	No bonus
1941–42	‡	32		25	‡	No bonus
1942–43	‡	32		25	‡	No bonus
1943–44	‡	32	25	18	‡	No bonus
1944–45	‡	37.5	27.5	20	‡	No bonus
1945–46	‡	45	35	25	‡	No bonus
1946–47	‡	50	40	25	‡	No bonus
1947–48	114	70	55	35	‡	No bonus
1948–49	117	80	60	40	64	No bonus
1949–50	159	100	70	50	86	No bonus
1950–51	285	130	100	50	113	No bonus
1951–52	188	130	100	50	105	136
1952–53	82	130	100	50	86	147
1953–54	208	130	100	50	111	140
1954–55	80*	180		80	93†	No bonus

From Zande District annual reports and the annual reports of the Agricultural Section, Equatoria Projects Board

*Estimate.
†Approximate, for Yambio Subdistrict only.
‡Not available.

APPENDIX II
SUMMARY OF COTTON AREA AND YIELDS FOR THE ZANDE SCHEME,
1947–48 TO 1954–55*

Season	Total acreage	Total yield in pounds	Average yield in pounds per acre
1947–48	8,850	4,000,000	450
1948–49	9,585	3,520,000	370
1949–50	12,650	4,760,000	380
1950–51	16,943	8,130,000	480
1951–52	22,649	7,910,000	350
1952–53	22,697	4,130,000	182
1953–54	17,500	6,370,000	370
1954–55	16,500†	2,700,000†	165†

From Zande District annual reports and the annual reports of the Agricultural Section, Equatoria Projects Board, Yambio, 1947 to 1955

*These figures are for the entire area under the Equatoria Projects Board and include a portion of Moru District, in addition to Zande District.
†Estimated.

APPENDIX III
SPOT PRICES FOR AMERICAN MIDDLING 15/16-INCH COTTON LINT
IN THE UNITED KINGDOM, 1937–55*

		Pence per lb.
Average for	1937.	6.37
Average for	1938.	5.12
31 March	1939.	5.10
31 March	1940.	7.80
31 March	1941.	9.39
16 March	1942.	8.95
1 February	1943.	7.95
17 April	1944.	12.45
24 September	1945.	12.45
27 May	1946.	13.45
Average for	1947.	20.47
Average for	1948.	22.81
Average for	1949.	24.92
Average for	1950.	35.81
Average for	1951.	46.49
Average for	1952.	39.27
Average for	1953.	31.82
Average for	1954.	32.96
Average for	1955.	31.78

Figures obtained from *Industrial Fibres*, Commonwealth Economic Committee, HMSO, London, 1939 to 1956

*Figures for Zande cotton lint were not available; it sold at a somewhat higher level.

235

BIBLIOGRAPHY

Bahr el Ghazal Handbook, 1911. Anglo-Egyptian Handbook Series, His Majesty's Stationery Office, London.

Baldwin, K. D. S., 1957. *The Niger Agricultural Project: An Experiment in African Development*. Basil Blackwell, Oxford.

Baxter, P. T. W., and Butt, Audrey, 1953. *The Azande and Related Peoples*. International African Institute, London, 1953. Part IX, East Central Africa, Ethnographic Survey of Africa.

Beals, R., 1953. "Acculturation," in Kroeber, A. L. (editor), *Anthropology Today*. University of Chicago Press, Chicago.

Beaton, A. C., 1949. *Equatoria Province Handbook, 1936–1948*. Sudan Government, Khartoum.

Bohannan, P. J., 1955. "Some Principles of Exchange and Investment among the Tiv," *American Anthropologist*, Vol. 57, No. 1, pp. 60–70.

Catford, J. R., 1953. "The Introduction of Cotton as a Cash Crop in the Maridi Area of Equatoria," *Sudan Notes and Records*, Vol. XXXIV, pp. 153–71.

Culwick, G. M., 1950.

A Dietary Survey among the Zande of the Southwestern Sudan. Ministry of Agriculture, Khartoum.

De Graer, A. M., 1929.

"L'Art de Cuérir Chez les Azande," *Congo*, Vol. I, pp. 220–51 and 361–408.

De Schlippe, P., 1956.

Shifting Cultivation in Africa. Routledge and Kegan Paul, London.

Evans-Pritchard, E. E., 1928.

"The Dance," *Africa*, Vol. I., pp. 446–82.

————, 1934.

"Zande Therapeutics," in *Essays Presented to C. G. Seligman*, various editors. Kegan Paul, Trench, Trubner, London.

————, 1934(a).

"Social Character of Bridewealth, with Special Reference to the Azande," *Man*, Vol. XXXIV, pp. 172–73.

————, 1937.

Witchcraft, Oracles and Magic among the Azande. Clarendon Press, Oxford.

————, 1956(a).

"A History of the Kingdom of Gbudwe," *Zaire*, Vol. X, pp. 451–91, 675–710, 815–60.

————, 1956(b).

"Zande Clan Names," *Man*, Vol. LVI, p. 62.

————, 1956(c).

"Zande Totems," *Man*, Vol. LVI, p. 110.

————, 1957(a).

"Zande Warfare," *Anthropos*, Vol. 52, pp. 322–43.

————, 1957(b).

"Zande Border Raids," *Africa*, Vol. XXVII, No. 3, pp. 217–31.

————, 1957(c).

"Zande Kings and Princes," *Anthropological Quarterly*, Vol. 30, pp. 618–90.

————, 1957(d).

"The Origin of the Ruling Clan of the Azande," *Southwestern Journal of Anthropology*, Vol. 13, pp. 322–43.

————, 1957(e).

"The Zande Royal Court," *Zaire*, Vol. XI, pp. 361–89, 493–511, 687–713.

————, 1958(a).

"The Ethnic Composition of the Azande of Central Africa," *Anthropological Quarterly*, Vol. 31, pp. 95–118.

————, 1958(b).

"An Historical Introduction to a Study of Zande Society," *African Studies*, Vol. 17, pp. 1–15.

——————, 1959.   "The Distribution of Zande Clans in the Sudan," *Man*, Vol. LIX, p. 24.

——————, 1960(a).   "A Contribution to the Study of Zande Culture," *Africa*, Vol. 30, pp. 309–24.

——————, 1960(b).   "Zande Clans and Settlements," *Man*, Vol. LIX, p. 24.

——————, 1960(c).   "The Organization of a Zande Kingdom," *Cahiers d'Etudes Africaines*, Vol. 4, pp. 5–37.

——————, 1960(d).   "The Ethnic Origin of Zande Officeholders," *Man*, Vol. LX, p. 141.

——————, 1961.   "Zande Clans and Totems," *Man*, Vol. LXI, p. 147.

Ferguson, H., 1949.   "The Zande Scheme," *Empire Cotton Growers Review*, Vol. XXVI, No. 2, pp. 109–21.

——————, 1954.   "The Zande Scheme," Bulletin No. 14, Ministry of Agriculture, Sudan Government, Khartoum.

Goodenough, Ward H., 1963.   *Cooperation in Change*. Russell Sage Foundation, New York.

Henderson, K. D. D., C. M. B., 1953.   *The Making of the Modern Sudan*. Faber and Faber, London.

Herskovits, M. J., 1958.   "Some Thoughts on American Research in Africa," *African Studies Bulletin*, Vol. 1, No. 2, pp. 1–11.

Lagae, C.-R., 1926.   *Les Azande ou Niam-Niam*. Bibliothèque-Congo, Bruxelles.

Larkin, G. M., 1923.   "Zande Notes," *Sudan Notes and Records*, Vol. VI.

——————, 1926.   "An Account of the Azande," *Sudan Notes and Records*, Vol. IX.

——————, 1927.   "Impressions of the Azande," *Sudan Notes and Records*, Vol. XIII.

——————, 1930.   "Impressions of the Azande," *Sudan Notes and Records*, Vol. XIII.

——————, 1955.   "Notes on the Azande of Tembura and Yambio, 1911–1930," in Leitch, T.A.T. (editor), *Zande Background*. Mimeographed. Equatoria Projects Board, Nzara.

Library of Congress, 1963.   *Agricultural Development Schemes in Sub-Saharan Africa: A Bibliography.* U. S. Government Printing Office, Washington.

McCall, A. G., 1950.   *A Note on the Agriculture of the Azande.* Bulletin No. 2. Ministry of Agriculture, Sudan Government, Khartoum.

McCall, A. G., and Lea-Wilson, K. L., 1954.   *Some Notes on Zandeland.* Memoirs of Field Division, No. 6, Ministry of Agriculture, Khartoum.

March, G. F., 1948.   "Kordofan Province," in Tothill, J. D., *Agriculture in the Sudan.* Oxford University Press, London.

Maurice, G. L., 1930.   "The History of Sleeping Sickness in the Sudan," *Sudan Notes and Records,* Vol. XIII, pp. 211–45.

——————, [n.d.].   "Sleeping Sickness." Typescript, Li Yubu Hospital files.

Mead, M. (editor), 1955.   *Cultural Patterns and Technical Changes.* New American Library, New York.

Phillips, J. E. T., [n.d.].   "Development of Indirect Administration in the Southern Sudan." Typescript, Balfour Library, Pitt-Rivers Museum, Oxford.

Reining, C. C., 1959.   "The History of Policy in the Zande Scheme," *The Proceedings of the Minnesota Academy of Science,* Vol. 27, pp. 6–13.

——————, 1962.   "The Role of Money in the Zande Economy," *American Anthropologist,* Vol. 64, No. 2, Part 1, pp. 39–43.

——————, 1963.   "Zande Markets and Commerce," in Bohannan, P. J., and Dalton, G., *Markets in Africa.* Northwestern University Press, Evanston.

Rose, M. F., 1951.   "The Nuba Mountains Cotton Crop," *Empire Cotton Growing Review,* Vol. XXVII, p. 103 ff.

Schapera, I., 1935.   "Field Methods in the Study of Modern Culture Contacts," *Africa,* Vol. VIII, No. 3.

Schweinfurth, C., 1878.   *The Heart of Africa*, translated from the German by Frewer, Ellen E. Third edition. Sampson Low, Marston, Searle and Rivington, London.

Seligman, C. G. and B. Z., 1932.   *Pagan Tribes of the Nilotic Sudan*. Routledge, London.

Steiner, F., 1954.   "Notes on Comparative Economics," *The British Journal of Sociology*, Vol. V, No. 2, pp. 118–29.

Sudan Foreign Trade Report, 1952.   Department of Statistics, Khartoum.

Sudan Government Files:
   (a) Zande District Headquarters, Yambio.
   (b) Tembura Subdistrict Headquarters, Ezo.
   (c) Agricultural Section, Equatoria Projects Board, Yambio.
   (d) Production Division, Equatoria Projects Board, Nzara.
   (e) Ministry of Agriculture, Khartoum.
   (f) Finance Department, Khartoum.
   (g) Equatoria Province Headquarters, Juba.

Sudan, Republic of the, 1956.   Report of the Commission of Inquiry into the Disturbances in the Southern Sudan during August 1955. Khartoum.

Tothill, J. D., 1943.   "An Experiment in the Social Emergence of Indigenous Races in Remote Places," Memorandum in Ministry of Agriculture, Khartoum, File 2–1, Vol. 1.

—————, (editor), 1948.   *Agriculture in the Sudan*. Oxford University Press, London.

Walinsky, Louis J., 1963.   *The Planning and Execution of Economic Development*. McGraw-Hill, New York.

Wright, J. W., [n.d.].   *The Zande Scheme from the Survey Point of View*. Survey Department, Sudan Government, Khartoum.

Wrigley, C. C., 1959.   *Crops and Wealth in Uganda*. East African Studies No. 12, East African Institute of Social Research, Kampala, Uganda.

Wyld, J. W. G., 1949.   "The Zande Scheme," *Sudan Notes and Records*, Vol. XXX, Part 1, pp. 37–57.

————————, 1951.　　　"Background to the Development of a Central African Tribe." Text of a lecture given at the Institute of Rural Life at Home and Overseas, London, 7 February, 1951. Typescript in Equatoria Projects File No. 133, Nzara.

————————, 1953.　　　*A Flora of Zande District*, mimeographed. Equatoria Projects Board, Nzara.

Zande District Handbook, 1936 and 1954.　　　Unpublished reports in the Zande District files.

INDEX

Abino, 70
Acres, conversion to *feddan,* 144*n*
Ad hoc planning committee, 147–48
Administration, colonial, 1, 8, 17, 18, 181
   change in southern policy, 141
   influence on Scheme, 218–19
   lack of partnership in, 219
   Newbold on southern policy, 219
   see also Cotton; Development; Equatoria Projects Board; First district commissioner; Scheme, Zande; Second district commissioner; Standards
Adok, proposed as Nile port, 148
Adultery
   cases heard, 49
   punishments for 54, 65
   and Women's Charter, 53, 64
   see also Promiscuity
Agricultural Research Committee, 202
Agriculture. *See* Cultivation
Agume, 40
"Aide Memoire," by second district commissioner, 155–56

Altitude, 2
Animals; 2, 72, 74, 75, 116–17
Anthropology, officials' views about, 201. *See also* Changes; Fieldwork, anthropological
Appeal system, extent of use by people, 23
Approved village schools, 9. *See also* Education
Arabic, as lingua franca, 196–97
Area, Zande, 1–2
Artisans, 160–61
Assimilation, of other tribes, 7. *See also* Conquest
Ati, 70
Avungara, 13, 14, marriage with, 100. *See also* Chiefs

Ba, 45
Baboons, 72
Bachelors, British, 196
   as factor in marriage stability, 60–61
Bananas, 2, 71
Barkcloth, 77, 79
   production and uses, 80

Basketry, 78
Bedding, 84, 184
Beer, 79
Beeswax, 164
  demand for, 89-90
  trade in, 77
Betrothal
  responsibilities in, 55
  Zande ideas about, 62
  see also Infant betrothal
Bicycles
  desire for, 84-85
  Tothill on parts production, 146
Birth rate, lowness blamed on venereal
  disease, 64
Blankets, importance of, 84, 184
Board. *See* Equatoria Projects Board
Boldness. *See* Scheme, Zande
Bonus
  for good attendance at Nzara, 188
  Zande views on cotton bonus,
  181-82
Bricks
  Tothill on making, 145
  use in building, 150
Bride wealth. *See* Marriage; Spears
British
  accused of cheating on cotton,
  182-83
  bachelors, 196
  communication among, 195-96
  compared to other colonials, 181
  contributions for development, 219
  cost of employing, 209
  hospitality to compatriots, 196
  ideas in common with Azande,
  225-26
  inconsistency of individual behavior, 219
  life of, 195-98
  relationship to missionaries and
  traders, 196
  replaced by northern Sudanese, 215
  standards for Azande, 194
  views of Zande intellect, 192-194
  see also Administration, colonial;
  Equatoria Projects Board; First
  district commissioner; Scheme,
  Zande; Second district commissioner

Brutality
  administration's desire to eliminate,
  67
  differing concepts about, 37-38
Buildings
  innovations, 70
  types and construction, 70
Bulrush millet, 71
Burlap sacks
  industry never discussed, 149
  Tothill's proposal for, 145
Bush schools
  start of system, 9
  see also Education
Bush shops. *See* Shops
Butyrospermum niloticum, 78, 170

Cambridge, administrators from, 195
Canteen, at Nzara, 187-88
Capital investment
  amounts, 155
  expenditure of, 208-209
  furnished by government, 151
  Tothill's recommendations, 146,
  147
  see also Scheme, Zande
Capsicum minimum. See Peppers
Carpentry. *See* Woodworking
Carving, 178
  of utensils, 83-84
  see also Woodworking
Cash crops, 174. *See also* Cotton;
  Peppers
Cassava, 4, 71
  as indicator of stability, 72-73
  processing, 72
  reserve crop, 78
Caterpillars
  as food, 76
Cement
  building uses, 150
Census. *See* Population
Changes
  avoidance of unnecessary, 227-28
  Azande in transition, 220-21
  difficulty of prediction, 220, 228
  lack of ideas about, 230
  need for understanding of implications, 229
  study of, xv, xvii

in terms of people affected, 228
Charcoal, 78
  not used in vehicles, 150
  Tothill on production, 145
  use in power station, 150
Chickens, 2, 74
  use in oracles, 73
Chiefs, 221
  acceptance of gifts, 36–37
  affected by money, 36
  authority weakened 1953, 33
  Avungara, 13, 14, 100
  confusion over cotton cultivation, 31
  effects of humanitarianism, 34
  functions, of, 13–14
  identity of chiefdoms with, 13
  increase in number, 20
  as obstacle to communications, 36
  pledged support of new administra-
    tion 1955, 34
  in pre-European ivory trade, 14
  "reinstatement" in 1920's, 19–20
  and their people, 14, 16, 27–30
  views about resettlement, 117–18
"Child marriage." *See* Infant betrothal
Chillies. *See* Peppers
Church Missionary Society. *See* Mis-
    sionaries
Cigarettes, 86
Citrus, 71
  as family crop, 214
Civil administration. *See* Administra-
    tion, colonial
Clans
  Avungara, 13, 14
  features of, 100
Clients. *See* Patron-client relationship
Climate, 2–3, 5
Cloth
  attitudes about quality of, 166–67
  Nzara production and sales, 165–69
  price used as standard, 83
  production at Nzara resumed 1956,
    216
  production uneconomic, 214
  Tothill's proposal for making, 145
  uses for, 167
  see also Clothing
Clothing, 86
  needs for, 81–82, 184
  traditional styles, 81

see also Cloth
Coffee, 104
  as family crop, 214
  as plantation crop, 149
  Tothill's proposals for, 144–45
Colds, epidemics of, 7
Colonial administration. *See* Adminis-
    tration, colonial
Commerce. *See* Trade
Commercialism. *See* Scheme, Zande;
    Standards
Common ideas
  Zande-European, 225–26
Communal fields
  disapproved, 102
  see also Cultivation
Communication
  poverty of, 9–10
  Zande-European, 184, 194–95, 196–
    97, 198, 199, 215, 220, 224–25
Community centers
  lacking in resettlement, 137
Community forms, 102
Condominium, 7–8
Congo
  attitude of official compared, 199
  comparison with humanitarianism,
    34
  comparison of marriage stability,
    57–58, 67
  cotton prices compared, 175–77,
    190, 230
  more generous in Zande view, 230
  preferential rates for cotton ship-
    ment, 210
  stability of homesteads, 122–23
  wages compared, 186
  Zande chiefs' position, 35
Conquest
  by Azande of Sudan area, 15
  by Europeans, 7–8
Conservation
  forest, 101, 104–105
  game, 20, 74–75
  soil, 102, 149
Conscript labor. *See* Labor
Construction
  in Scheme, 159–64
Cooperation, among governmental
    agencies, 213*n*
Cosmetics, 78

Cost-of-living index
  increase 1938 to 1950, 190
Costume. *See* Clothing
Cotton
  bachelors' inefficiency in growing, 47
  compared with peppers, 76
  compulsion in cultivation, 30, 31–32
  disease, concern about, 102
  effect on chiefs' roles, 30–32
  entire stock spoiled 1948, 160
  expansion held up in 1948, 156
  export duties, 207, 210, 214
  exporting schemes disapproved, 154
  fear of price fluctuations, 192
  ginnery, 150, 160
  grading of, 177–78, 215
  introduction in Congo, 1920's, 10
  introduction in Sudan, 1930's, 11, 141
  introduction for Scheme, 102–104
  prices to Azande, 174, 203–204, 215, 230–31
  prices compared to Congo, 175–77
  production of, 172–74, 178, 213, 214–15
  purchases after uprising, 216–17
  sales of lint, 207, 208
  as a source of cash, 90
  stopping of cultivation around Tembura, 32
  and subsistence economy, 225–26
  supervision of, 102–104, 120–21
  Tothill on prices, 142, 150, 175, 204–205
  Tothill's proposals for, 144–45
  unchallenged as primary crop, 149
  unpopularity in 1930's, 141
  world prices, 172–74
  Zande views about, 174–78, 225–26
  Zande views of prices, 182–83
Courts
  adultery and divorce cases, 49
  chiefs' courts established, 22–23
  by early British administrators, 18–19
  pre-European chiefs', 14–15
  unofficially at chiefs' homes, 22–23
  and unregistered marriages, 64, 66
  womens' favored position in, 54
Courtyards. *See* Homesteads

Crafts, 77–81
Crops, 4, 71, 72–73, 78, 93, 120, 149.
  See also Cotton; Cultivation
Cucurbits, 71
Cultivation, 221
  agricultural development program, 214
  apparent lack of system in, 73
  de Schlippe's systematization of, 73n
  failure of rotation plans, 120, 129
  field locations, 70–71
  hopes for rotation, 128
  kitchen gardens, 70–71
  land overuse in lines, 128–29
  pre-resettlement extent of, 126
  prohibited near streams, 101, 104–105
  relationship of shifting cultivation to residence, 127–28
  in urban plots, 200
  see also Cotton; Crops
Cultivators consultative committees, 198
Culwick, G. M.
  on marriage stability, 50
  on position of women, 63
Currency. *See* Money

Dairy herds, for European community, 197
Depreciation, in EPB accounting, 207, 208–10
Descent groups, 13, 14, 100
Development
  difficulty in direction of, 231
  lack of predictability on both sides, 227
  study of, 231–32
  Zande and British contributions toward, 219–20
  see also Scheme, Zande; Social Development
Discipline, domestic
  restrictions on, 53, 55
  Zande ideas about, 62
Discipline, tribal, chiefs as keepers of, 26–27
Diseases
  cotton, 102
  human, 6–7, 64, 101

Distribution, lack of facilities, 168, 171
District commissioner. *See* First district commissioner; Second district commissioner
Disturbances. *See* Uprisings
Dividends, out of EPB profits, 208–209
Divorce
  cases heard, 49
  new regulations 1951, 64–66
  by a woman via prison, 54–55
  see also Marriage
Dogs, 2, 74
Domestic organization. *See* Discipline, domestic; Homesteads
Dry season, effects of, 5

East Africa, as possible market for Nzara cloth, 165. *See also* Uganda
Ecological survey, of Equatoria Province, 141
Economic development, as opposed to social, 153–54, 157, 158, 159. *See also* Development; Equatoria Projects Board; Scheme, Zande
Educated persons
  competition with chiefs, 29
  power passing to, 34
  views about resettlement, 118–19
  views on second district commissioner, 212
Education
  elementary level only, 10
  of girls, 10
  history of, 9
  rebuilding of schools, 164
  Tothill's ideas abandoned, 151
  Tothill on universal education, 144, 146
  types of schools, 9
  universal education discussed, 150–51
  Zande desire for more, 187
Educational Council, 202
Egypt, Azande working in, 86
Elections, 29
Electricity at Nzara, 161, 198
Elementary vernacular schools, 9. *See also* Education
Elephants, 72
Eleusine, 2, 71
  importance of, 72

misunderstanding of instructions about, 120
  processing of, 72
English, as school subject, 9. *See also* British
Equatoria Projects Board
  agricultural supervision by, 30–31
  attitudes of officials compared with Congo, 199
  autonomy of, 156–57, 158–59
  charter of, 153
  distinction "EPB" and "Board," 151
  economic aspects emphasized, 153–54, 157, 158, 159
  established, 151
  original purposes restored, 214
  origins of officials, 195
  policies compared with other Boards, 211
  policies of, 165–72, 204, 205–207, 211–12, 213
  relations with administration, 213
  Trading Division, 152–53, 165–72, 214
  Zande bitterness toward, 186–87
  see also Capitol investment; Cotton; Scheme, Zande
Erosion, soil
  concern about, 102
  effects of annual crops, 149
  see also Soil conservation
Europeans. *See* British
Evans-Pritchard, E. E.
  division of Zande history, xiii*n*
  on marriage, 61
  on polygymy, 60
Exchange
  hierarchy of, 93–94
  pre-European, 68
Expatriates. *See* British
Export duties. *See* Cotton
Exports, 77, 89–90, 164. *See also* Cotton, Ivory, Peppers
Ezo, 13
  British in, 195

Factory. *See* Scheme, Zande
Family, defined, 40. *See also* Kin
Feasts, 95–96
Feddan, conversion to acres, 144*n*

Fibers, sources and uses, 77. *See also* Barkcloth; Nets
Ficus. See Barkcloth
Fields. *See* Cultivation
Fieldwork, anthropological
approach, xi–xvi
effected by resettlement, 112
time of, xi
Fig. *See* Barkcloth
Filaria, 6
Fire, use in hunting, 74
Firearms
desire for, 84–85
licenses for chiefs, 24
in pre-European ivory trade, 15
restrictions on, 17, 175
First district commissioner
arrival at Yambio, 27
early relations to chiefs, 18, 27
estimate of 1911 situation, 17
not identified, xvii
retirement, 8
view of women's plight, 52–53, 64
Fishing, 75
Flies, 6
Food
gathering of uncultivated, 78
supply in towns, 199–200
see also Crops; Cultivation
Forced labor. *See* Public service
Forest, types of, 5–6
Forest conservation, cultivation prohibited near streams, 101, 104–105
Freight rates, no concession on, 210
French Equatorial Africa
comparison of cultivation, 126–27
comparison of marriage stability, 57, 67
as source of meat, 95
stability of homesteads, 123, 126
Zande views on witchcraft, 125
Fuel, 86, 146, 198. *See also* Charcoal
Fungi, 78

Game conservation
comparison of laws, 74–75
effects on ivory trade, 20
Gash Board, as Tothill's model, 146
Gasoline
Tothill on restricting imports of, 146

Gathering, food, 78
Gbaria, jargonized, 137–38
Gifts
money as, 95, 96
nature of, 96
Ginning. *See* Cotton
Greek, merchants, 167, 196
Greene, Dr., tree crops recommended by, 149
Guinea worm, not present, 6
Gume, 40
Guns. *See* Firearms

H-plan settlement, 104–106
comparison with straight-line, 136–37
see also Resettlement
Handicrafts, 77–81
Hashish, 37
Hasps, 86
Head of houshold. *See* Household
Hedge-strip system, 201–202
as cause of abolition of Local Advisory Committee, 202
Hinges, 86
Homesteads, 221–22
courtyard analysis, 69
courtyard organization, 40–43
factors affecting stability, 122–23
fate after deaths, 45, 123–24
head's authority, 44–48
head's relations with wives, 40
maintenance, 69
terminology, 39–40, 70. *See also* Residence
Honey, 164
demand for, 89–90
trade in, 77
Household. *See* Homestead
Humanitarianism
comparison with Congo, 34
effects on chiefs, 34
Hunting, 74–75

Iba Subdistrict, unpopularity of cotton in, 135
Idealists. *See* Scheme, Zande; Standards
Imperata cylindrica, as thatching grass, 70
Imports, 81–86, 87, 90–91

cash increase not used for, 95
duties on, 24
used by Europeans, 197
Income. *See* Money
Independence for Sudan, effects of expectation of, 34
Indirect rule, idiom of, 25
Individualization, 46–47
of marriage arrangements, 56–58
Industry. *See* Scheme, Zande
Infant betrothal
confused with child marriage, 56
echo of prohibition, 65
prohibited, 53
request for reinstatement of, 62
responsibilities in, 55
Insects, 6, 69, 75–76, 101
Inspection, medical. *See* Sleeping
sickness
Intermediate   school,   9.   *See   also*
Education
Ironworking, 78, 79, 80, 81, 146, 151
Isolation
caused by resettlement, 114
felt by Europeans, 198
Ivory
changes in trade pattern, 20
early surplus of, 87
pre-European trade, 15

Juba
airport at, 10
as Nile port, 10
Trading division headquarters, 153
Jur River, navigability to Wau, 8
Jute, 144–45, 149

Kenya, Azande working in, 86
Kerosene, 86
Tothill on restricting imports of, 146
Khartoum, 28
Azande working in, 86
as market for Nzara cloth, 166–67
Kin
decreased importance of, 222
definitions, 40
in political organization, 15
in residence, 99–100
Kporo, 39–40

Labor, 184–85
for chiefs, 24
as commodity *vs.* personal relationship, 226
conscript labor as wage base, 185
cost compared, 214
cotton cultivation as public service,
150
in lieu of taxes (1920's), 87
public service, 24
as punishment for cotton defaulting,
31
reasons for working, 27–28, 184
Scheme's demand for, 163–64
sexual division of, 43–44
see also Wages
Lamps, oil, 86
Land. *See* Cultivation; Resettlement
Latitude, 2
Latrines, 118–19, 198
Leather, 80
Levirate. *See* Widow inheritance
Li Rangu, British in, 195
Li Yubu, 28
British in, 195
Lines. *See* Resettlement
Lingasi River, as limit of main road,
162
Lint. *See* Cotton
Local Advisory Committee
composition, 199
established, 157
functions, 158, 199
terminated, 202–203

Mail, paucity of services, 10
Maize, 2, 71
Malaria, 6
Mango, 162
importance of, 71–72
introduction of, 71
March, G. F., on Scheme's trading
functions, 152
Marriage, 221–22
adultery and stability, 48–49
cash expenditures for, 94
conflict with Zande practice, 65
contemporary procedure, 50–52
divorce cases, 49

economic aspects of payments, 58n
effect of money upon stability, 58–59
individualization of arrangements for, 56–58
limited exchangeability of spears, 94
linkages through payments, 58–59
money in payments, 47–48, 94
negotiations, 46
new regulations 1951, 64–66
stability compared with Congo and French Equatorial Africa, 57
stability influenced by age at marriage, 60–61
timing of payments, 51–52
vulnerability of men in, 63
Zande vs. European ideas about, 63–64
see also Betrothal; Infant betrothal; Women
Matches, 86
Meals, free, at Nzara canteen, 187–88
Measles, epidemics of, 7
Meat, sources in game and fish, 74, 95
Medicines, 78
Medium of exchange, 54. See also Money; Spears
Member of parliament
for Moru on cotton prices, 205
for Zande East arrested, 34
Meridi
benefitted from Zande Scheme, 89n
route to, 162
Military administration. See Administration, colonial
Missionaries, and British community, 196
Church Mission Society arrival, 9
exclusive spheres of, 8–9
sizes of missions, 8–9
Verona Father's Mission arrival, 9
Mobility
enhanced under colonial rule, 48
of homesteads, 122–23
reduced by resettlement, 116
Money, 222, 224
Azande unaware of effects, 193
broader medium than spears, 94
conversion of pounds Egyptian, 9n

convertibility to subsistence goods, 93–94, 95–96
European fear of excess, 190–91, 224
income, 89, 93, 226
introduction of, 87
in marriage, 47, 58–59
no money economy, 91–92, 94, 224
role of, 90–96
"sense of," 193–94
social significance of, 93–96
special features of, 94
Zande-European agreement about, 226
see also Capital investment
Monkeys, 72
Monogamy
examples of household, 42
ratio of, 59–60
Mosquitoes, 6
Motor transport, 10, 88. See also Roads
Mutiny. See Uprising
Mupoi, mission and schools, 9
Nails, 86
Nets
in hunting, 74
making of, 78
Newbold, Sir Douglas
on cooperation in Nuba Scheme, 213n
on southern policy, 219
on supervision, 212n
Nile, navigability to Juba, 8
Nile-Congo divide, as boundary marker, 1, 7
Normal school, 9. See also Education
Northerners
as merchants, 196
replaced British in administration, 215
as servants, 197
as technicians, 196
Zande attitude toward, 183–84, 186, 214–16
Nuba Mountains
compared with Zande Scheme, 134, 205–206, 211, 230
cotton introduction, 228–29
Nzara
British in, 195, 196, 197

canteen at, 187–88
construction at, 160–62
factories at, 161, 216, 217
good attendance bonus at, 188
riot at, 215–16
see also Cloth; Oil, cooking; Scheme,
  Zande; Soap

Obligations, eased with money, 95–96
Occupations, 77–81
Oil, cooking
  production and sales, 161, 169–70,
  214
Oil palms, 71, 104
  as family crop, 214
  as plantation crop, 149
  Tothill's proposal for, 144–45
Oilseeds, wild, 78, 170
Oracles
  consulted for marriage, 51
  consulted for moves, 123–24
Out schools, 9. See also Education
Oxford, administrators from, 195

Papaya, 71
Parliament
  elections for, 29
  question about cotton prices, 205
  Zande East member arrested, 34
Partnership
  lack of, 151, 219
  Tothill's recommendations for, 146
Patron-client relationship
  applied to cotton growing, 179–80
  disillusionment with, 187, 188–89
  effects of money upon, 36
  functions on each side, 16
  laborers cynical about, 184, 185
  pre-European significance, 15
Peanuts, 2, 71
  as cash crop, 174
  to designate wages, 185
Peppers, 164
  cultivation of, 76, 92
  date of introduction, 76
  price fluctuations, 192–93
  as source of money, 76, 92
  trade in, 76, 87, 89
Perverse response, of peasant cultivators, 193

Pests
  animals in cultivations, 75, 116–17
Philanthropy. See Scheme, Zande
Phonographs, 86
Piece goods. See Cloth
Pineapple, 71
"Pin-money" economy, 91–92
Plaiting, 78
Planning committee, 147–48
Poisons, 78
Police, 26
  chiefs, 23
  chiefs as corruptible police, 37
Policy. See Administration, colo-
  nial; Equatoria Projects Board;
  Scheme, Zande; Standards
Political organization, pre-European,
  13. See also Chiefs
Polygyny
  decrease in, 59, 60
  examples of households, 40, 42
  as stabilizing factor, 61
Population
  census 1953, 59
  distribution of, 1
  inaccuracy of registers, 119
Pottery, manufacture of, 78, 79, 83
Prices. See Cloth; Cotton; Imports;
  Rewards; Scheme, Zande
Produce, sale to towns, 93
Production. See Cloth; Cotton; Oil,
  cooking; Soap; Sugar
Profits
  on cotton exports, 207–210
  early profits exceptional, 213
  see also Equatoria Projects Board
Promiscuity
  alleged reason for resettlement, 119
  marriage payment raised to discourage, 65
  official view of, 64
  Zande views of, 62, 66
  see also Adultery
Public Health Board, proposed, 202
Public service. See Labor
Pulses, 71
Punishments. See Courts

Radios, 86
Railroads, lack of, 10

Rainfall, 2
Rainy season, 5
Remoteness
  factor in Tothill's plans, 143
  remained without compensations,
    148
Research. *See* Fieldwork, anthropological
Reserve funds
  policy, 207–208
  Zande and Nuba, 206, 211
Resettlement, 222–24
  administrative assumptions about,
    107–108, 121–22
  attitudes toward, 102–103, 112–13,
    116–19, 117–21, 131–32, 134–35
  community facilities lacking, 137
  confusion in 1940, 101–102
  effects of, 109, 112–17, 119, 124,
    128–29, 131, 138–39
  H-Plan, 104–106
  in 1920's, 19, 101
  plot size, 109
  poor planning for, 136
  procedures for, 102–103, 106–107,
    115–16, 132–33
  rigidity *vs.* stability, 116, 223
  as separate from Scheme, 98–99
  straight-line pattern, 105–107
  and urbanization, 135–36, 137
  Zande terms for lines, 138
  see also Residence
Residence
  choice of locale, 129–30
  dual, 125–27
  groupings of homesteads, 129–30
  kinship in, 99–100
  needs misinterpreted, 130–31
  pre-European pattern, 4, 99–101
  preference for roadsides, 130
  relation to cultivation shifts, 127–28
  See also Resettlement
Resources, natural, lack of, 86
Rewards
  different interpretations, 224–25,
    226–27
  justification for lowness of, 230
  self-defeating policy on, 224
  see also Cotton; Labor; Wages
Rice, 71

Rienzi
  chiefly homestead, 14
  son as candidate for parliament, 29
Riots. *See* Uprisings
Road Board, 202
Roads
  development of, 10, 88, 162
  Juba route, 148–49
  preference for life along, 130
Roofing
  restriction on thatch, 164
  shortage of sheets 1948, 160
  Tothill on import restriction, 146
  use of metal sheets, 150
Rotation, crop. *See* Cultivation
Rubber, 77

Salaries. *See* Wages
Salt, 86
  preparation and uses, 78
Sanitation, 118–19, 197–98
Savings, 94–95
Scheme, Zande
  aims disputed, 153–56
  boldness in, 147, 148–49, 155, 203
  capitol investment, 146, 147, 151,
    155, 208–209
  commercial *vs.* governmental super-
    vision, 212n
  commercialism and idealism, 203–
    204, 210, 212, 213, 230
  common Zande-British objectives,
    225–26
  industrial aspects, 154, 210, 227
  influence of previous policy, 218–19
  factories, 161, 216, 217
  lack of Zande influence on policy,
    198
  reversal of policies, 229
  selection of Zande District for,
    143–44
  see also Cotton; Equatoria Projects
    Board; Wages
Schools. *See* Education
Seasons, 5
Second district commissioner
  on Azande, 27, 119, 133
  on close supervision, 133–34
  influenced policies, 186, 212
  not identified, xvii

and resettlement, 107–108, 128
and Scheme, 143–44, 155–56, 173
on shops and capital in 1944, 152
tenure of office, 8
on urbanization, 135–36, 138, 219
Self-sufficiency
  as essence of Scheme, 143
  restrictions on imports, 146
  Tothill's ideas modified, 147–48
Servants, in European homes, 196–97, 198
Sesame, 71, 174
Settlement. See Resettlement; Residence
Shea oil, 78, 170
Shields, prohibition on manufacture, 17
Shifting cultivation. See Cultivation
Shingles, wooden, 146, 150
Shops
  growth of in 1930's, 87
  plentiful in 1944, 152
  see also Cloth; Oil, cooking
Shortages, during Scheme construction phase, 160
Sleeping sickness, 6, 101
Smelting, iron
  technique lost, 81
  Tothill on revival of, 146
  veto of idea, 150
Soap, 86
  production, 161, 214
  Tothill on making, 145
Social center, proposed at Nzara, 188–89
Social development
  Committee, 202
  Fund, 159n, 208
  lack of ideas about, 203–204
  as opposed to economic, 153–54, 157, 158, 159
  see also Development; Equatoria Projects Board; Scheme, Zande
Social obligations. See Obligations
Sociological
  as administrative faction, 155
  investigations desired, 201
Soil conservation, 101, 102, 104–105, 149
Sorghum, 71, 174

Southern policy, 141, 219
Spears
  limited medium of exchange, 94
  as marriage payments, 47–48, 58–59, 94
Spices, 77
Spirits, distilled, 37
Stabilization fund, 181–82
Standards
  applied by Europeans, 189–90, 194
  commercial vs. idealist, 203–204
  Zande vs. European, 220, 225–27
Staple (cotton) length, 142, 150
Sterility, 64
Straight-line plan
  comparison with H-Plan, 136–37
  see also Resettlement
Streams
  conceptual importance, 4
  cultivation prohibited along, 101, 104–105
  move from 1920's, 6
  pre-European residence along, 4
String. See Nets
Subsistence economy
  and cotton, 225–26
  importance of, 91, 92, 97, 224
  and money, 93–94, 95–96, 224
Sudanese, northern. See Northerners
Sugar cane, 104, 145, 149, 161
Supervision
  close supervision recommended, 133–34
  governmental vs. commercial, 212n
  Zande distaste for, 134, 183
Sweet potatoes, 2, 71, 78

Tanganyika, Azande working in, 86
Taro, 71
Taxes
  amounts, 47, 87
  collection by chiefs, 24
  introduction of, 24, 87
Teaching. See Education
Yambio to Nzara, 163
Tembura, 8, 13, 17
Tembura (sub) district, 8
  difficulties with cotton, 32–33, 134–35, 177
  resettled in 1922, 19

Temperature, range of, 5
Tenses used, xvii
Termites
  as destructive factor, 69
  as food, 75–76
Terrakeka
  port expansion considered, 148
Territorial distribution. *See* Residence
Tiernay, J. F.
  opened industrial center, 161
Tikpo. *See* Salt
Time of research, xi
Tins, gasoline, as utensils, 83
Thatch, 70, 164
Tobacco, Tothill on restricting imports of, 146
Tothill, J. D., 134
  appointment and surveys, 141–42
  on cotton prices, 142, 150, 175, 204–205
  proposals, 142–47
  proposals modified, 147–53, 155, 203
Towns, 8, 13, 17, 27, 28, 195, 196, 197, 160–62
  food supply in, 199–200
  see also Urbanization
Trade, 76–77, 89–90, 164
  changes with European conquest, 87
  distribution difficulties, 168, 171
  shops, 87, 152
  see also Cloth; Cotton; Imports; Ivory; Oil, cooking; Peppers; Trading Division
Trade schools, 9. *See also* Education
Trading Division
  credit to Zande traders, 171
  effects of, 152–53, 214
  establishment of, 152
  and Production Division, 171
  sales policies, 165–72
  see also Equatoria Projects Board
Transport
  difficulties, 10
  human porterage, 10
  motor vehicles introduced, 10, 88
Tree crops, recommended over annual crops, 149
Tribal discipline, 26–27

Tsetse fly, 6, 101

Uganda
  cotton introduction, 228–29
  cotton and prices compared, 142
  for higher education, 9
  response to cotton prices, 193, 231
  trading pattern, 152
  wages compared, 186
Uprisings
  Nzara riot July 1955, 34, 214–15
  in southern provinces August 1955, 34, 215, 216n
Urbanization, dislike of, 135–36, 219
Utensils, household, variety and demand for, 83
Utilities. *See* Electricity; Fuel; Sanitation; Water

Values. *See* Standards
Venereal disease, official views about, 64
Vernacular, as medium of instruction, 9
Verona Fathers Mission. *See* Missionaries
Village registers, 25
Villages. *See* Resettlement
Village schools, 9. *See also* Education
Vuru kporo, 40

Wages
  chiefs salaries, 24
  disparity with prices, 186, 187
  European assumptions about, 189–94
  of expatriates, 209
  levels of Zande, 9, 163, 185
  as source of money, 90
  Zande-European differential, 195
  Zande-European ideas compared, 190, 194
  Zande views on, 184–87
  see also Labor, Rewards
Warfare, 7, 15
Watches, 86
Water, domestic supply, 2, 197–98
Wau, 7, 8, 28, 86
Waugh, Evelyn, quote about Groundnut Scheme, xvi
Wax. *See* Beeswax

Wealth, nature of, 68–69
Weaving, 78, 80
Weddings, 51. *See also* Marriage
West Africa, trading pattern assessed, 153
Widow inheritance
  prohibition of, 53
  prohibition rescinded, 54
Wife exchange, prohibition of, 54
Witchcraft
  concern about, 125–26
  French Zande views about, 125
Wives. *See* Women
Women
  ambivalent position as wives, 57
  differing views on position of, 62–63
  facilities in homestead, 40
  favored position in courts, 55
  prohibition on use as payments, 54
  relative economic independence, 44
Womens' Charter, 52–56, 64
Wood
  as cooking fuel, 198

uses of, 78
Woodworking, 80, 81
  carving, 83–84, 178
World War II, activity during, 88–89

Yam, 71
Yambio, 8, 9, 13, 17, 27
  British in, 195, 196, 197
  construction at, 160
Yambio (sub) district, 8
  cotton production, 134
Yaws, not present, 6
Zande district, selection for Scheme, 143–44
Zande District Local Advisory Committee. *See* Local Advisory Committee
Zande-ization, of conquered peoples, 14
Zande Scheme. *See* Scheme, Zande
ZDLAC. *See* Local Advisory Committee